pragmatics

Palgrave Advances in Linguistics

Consulting Editor:
Christopher N. Candlin,
Macquarie University, Australia

Titles include:

Noel Burton-Roberts (*editor*)
PRAGMATICS

Monica Heller (*editor*)
BILINGUALISM: A SOCIAL APPROACH

Martha E. Pennington (*editor*)
PHONOLOGY IN CONTEXT

Ann Weatherall, Bernadette M. Watson and Cindy Gallois (*editors*)
LANGUAGE, DISCOURSE AND SOCIAL PSYCHOLOGY

Forthcoming:

Susan Foster-Cohen (*editor*)
LANGUAGE ACQUISITION

Palgrave Advances
Series Standing Order ISBN 1–4039–3512–2 (Hardback) 1–4039–3513–0 (Paperback)
(*outside North America only*)

You can receive future titles in this series as they are published by placing a standing order.
Please contact your bookseller or, in the case of difficulty, write to us at the address below
with your name and address, the title of the series and the ISBN quoted above.

Customer Services Department, Macmillan Distribution Ltd, Houndmills, Basingstoke,
Hampshire RG21 6XS, England

pragmatics

edited by
noel burton-roberts
university of newcastle upon tyne

First published 2007 by
PALGRAVE MACMILLAN
Houndmills, Basingstoke, Hampshire RG21 6XS and
175 Fifth Avenue, New York, N.Y. 10010
Companies and representatives throughout the world

PALGRAVE MACMILLAN is the global academic imprint of the
Palgrave Macmillan division of St. Martin's Press, LLC and of
Palgrave Macmillan Ltd.
Macmillan® is a registered trademark in the United States,
United Kingdom and other countries. Palgrave is a registered
trademark in the European Union and other countries.

ISBN 978-1-4039-8699-3

A catalogue record for this book is available
from the British Library.

Library of Congress Cataloging-in-Publication Data
Pragmatics / edited by Noel Burton-Roberts.
p. cm.— (Palgrave advances)
Includes bibliographical references and index.

1. Pragmatics. I. Burton-Roberts, Noel, 1948–

B831.5.P68 2007
149'.94—dc22

2006053450

10   9   8   7   6   5   4   3   2   1
16 15 14 13 12 11 10 09 08 07

Transferred to Digital Printing 2011

contents

series preface

christopher n. candlin

This new *Advances in Linguistics Series* is part of an overall publishing programme by Palgrave Macmillan aimed at producing collections of original, commissioned articles under the invited editorship of distinguished scholars.

The books in the Series are not intended as an overall guide to the topic or to provide an exhaustive coverage of its various sub-fields. Rather, they are carefully planned to offer the informed readership a conspectus of perspectives on key themes, authored by major scholars whose work is at the boundaries of current research. What we plan the Series will do, then, is to focus on salience and influence, move fields forward, and help to chart future research development.

The Series is designed for postgraduate and research students, including advanced level undergraduates seeking to pursue research work in Linguistics, or careers engaged with language and communication study more generally, as well as for more experienced researchers and tutors seeking an awareness of what is current and in prospect in adjacent research fields to their own. We hope that some of the intellectual excitement posed by the challenges of Linguistics as a pluralistic discipline will shine through the books!

Editors of books in the Series have been particularly asked to put their own distinctive stamp on their collection, to give it a personal dimension, and to map the territory, as it were, seen through the eyes of their own research experience.

Pragmatics, edited by Noel Burton-Roberts, admirably captures the essence of this new book series in its deliberate exploration of connection among adjacent disciplines, in the scope of the research methodologies espoused by its distinguished authors, and, above all, in the masterly way it maps out the post-Gricean pathways for the exploration and representation of *meaning* in and through language. Each of the constituent papers has been invited to contribute to a landscape historically and currently chiefly marked by the fuzzy and dynamic boundaries between semantics and pragmatics, but here located and focused on key issues of critical debate: implicature, procedural meaning, relevance, indexicality, and the nature and content of concepts.

Christopher N. Candlin
Senior Research Professor
Department of Linguistics
Macquarie University, Sydney

notes on contributors

Jay David Atlas is Peter W. Stanley Professor of Linguistics and Philosophy and Chairman of the Department of Linguistics and Cognitive Science, Pomona College, Claremont, California. He is the author of *Philosophy without Ambiguity* (Oxford 1989) and *Logic, Meaning and Conversation* (Oxford 2005).

Kent Bach, Professor Emeritus of Philosophy at San Francisco State University, was educated at Harvard College and the University of California, Berkeley. He has written extensively in philosophy of language, theory of knowledge, and philosophy of mind. His books include *Thought and Reference* (Oxford 1987, expanded edition 1994) and, with Robert M. Harnish, *Linguistic Communication and Speech Acts* (MIT 1979).

Diane Blakemore is Professor of Linguistics in the European Studies Research Institute at the University of Salford. She is the author of *Semantic Constraints on Relevance* (1987), *Understanding Utterances* (1992), and *Relevance and Linguistic Meaning: The Semantics and Pragmatics of Discourse Markers* (2002). Since 2001 she has been a co-editor of *Lingua*.

Reinhard Blutner is Privatdozent at the Humboldt-University in Berlin. He began his career in theoretical physics and shifted later to artificial intelligence, cognitive psychology and theoretical linguistics. Currently he lectures in artificial intelligence and cognitive philosophy at the University of Amsterdam. He is co-author of *Optimal Communication* (CSLI Publications 2006) and editor of *Optimality Theory and Pragmatics* (Palgrave Macmillan 2005).

Noel Burton-Roberts is Professor of English Language and Linguistics, Newcastle University. His publications include *Analysing Sentences*

(Longman 1986, 1997) and *The Limits to Debate* (Cambridge 1989). He co-edited (with Philip Carr and Gerard Docherty) *Phonological Knowledge* (Oxford 2000). He is the series editor for Palgrave Macmillan's 'Modern Linguistics', and (with Richard Breheny) of 'Palgrave Studies in Pragmatics, Language and Cognition'.

Herman Cappelen is CUF Lecturer and tutorial fellow at the University of Oxford and Professor at the University of Oslo. His publications include *Insensitive Semantics*, co-authored with Ernie Lepore (Blackwell 2004).

Robyn Carston is Professor of Linguistics at University College London. Her main interests are in the semantics/pragmatics distinction, the explicit/implicit distinction in communication and the relation between pragmatics and theory of mind. Among her publications are *Thoughts and Utterances: The Pragmatics of Explicit Communication* (Blackwell 2002) and (edited with Seiji Uchida) *Relevance Theory: Implications and Applications* (John Benjamin 1998).

Marjolein Groefsema is Associate Head of the School of Humanities, University of Hertfordshire and Subject Leader for English Language & Communication.

Laurence R. Horn is Professor of Linguistics and Professor of Philosophy, Yale University. He is the author of *A Natural History of Negation* (University of Chicago Press 1987; reissued with new introduction, Stanford: CSLI 2001) and co-editor (with Yasuhiko Kato) of *Negation and Polarity: Syntactic and Semantic Perspectives* (Oxford 2000) and (with Gregory Ward) of *The Handbook of Pragmatics* (Blackwell 2004).

Ernie Lepore is Professor and Director of the Center for Cognitive Science at Rutgers University. He is the author of numerous articles and books in the philosophy of language, philosophical logic, metaphysics and philosophy of mind, and is co-author, with Jerry Fodor, of *Holism* (Blackwell 1991) and, with Herman Cappelen, of *Insensitive Semantics* (Blackwell 2004). His edited books include *Truth and Interpretation* (Blackwell 1989) and, with Zenon Pylyshyn, *What is Cognitive Science?* (Blackwell 1999). He is general editor of the Blackwell series 'Philosophers and Their Critics'.

Ira A. Noveck is a cognitive scientist based in Lyon, and also works at the Centre National de Recherche Scientifique (CNRS). He is Director of the Laboratoire sur le Langage, la Cognition et le Cerveau. His publications include *Experimental Pragmatics*, co-edited with Dan Sperber (Palgrave Macmillan 2004). He is an Associate Editor of the *Journal of Semantics*.

He has held visiting positions at the Universities of Princeton, Grenoble, Minnesota and Paris.

François Recanati is a directeur de recherche (senior fellow) at CNRS in Paris, and a member of the Institut Jean-Nicod. Among his publications are *Meaning and Force* (Cambridge 1987), *Direct Reference* (Blackwell 1993), *Oratio Obliqua, Oratio Recta* (MIT Press/Bradford Books 2000), *Literal Meaning* (Cambridge 2004), and *Perspectival Thought* (Oxford 2007).

Dan Sperber is a social and cognitive scientist at the Centre National de la Recherche Scientifique (CNRS) in Paris. He is the author of *Rethinking Symbolism* (1975), *On Anthropological Knowledge* (1985) and *Explaining Culture* (1996), and co-author with Deirdre Wilson of *Relevance: Communication and Cognition* (1986, 1995). He co-edited *Experimental Pragmatics* with Ira Noveck (Palgrave Macmillan 2004). He has held visiting positions at the Universities of Cambridge, London (LSE), Princeton and Michigan.

Deirdre Wilson is Professor of Linguistics at University College London. Her books include *Presuppositions and Non-Truth-Conditional Semantics* (Academic Press 1975), *Modern Linguistics: The Results of Chomsky's Revolution* (Penguin 1979, with Neil Smith) and *Relevance: Communication and Cognition* (Blackwell 1986/1995, with Dan Sperber); she recently edited (with Robyn Carston and Sam Guttenplan) a special double issue of *Mind & Language* (2002, 17, 1–2) on Pragmatics and Cognitive Science.

1
introduction
noel burton-roberts

The theoretical field of enquiry now called 'pragmatics' was effectively launched, from within philosophy, by Paul Grice. His work (brought together in Grice 1989) remains an enduring presence in the field even now when pragmatics is seen primarily as an adjunct to linguistics and psychology, and in the context of reservations as to the viability of Grice's precise conception of pragmatics and the semantics/pragmatics distinction.

The chapters that make up this contribution to Palgrave's *Advances* series address a wide range of issues that have arisen in post-Gricean pragmatic theory and present a range of theoretical positions and approaches. The field is currently characterized by lively debate and this is fully reflected here. The volume includes considerations of relevance theory (Sperber and Wilson 1986/1995 and related work), neo-Gricean pragmatics, optimality theoretic pragmatics, experimental work and philosophical considerations. The specific topics covered include scalar implicature, lexical semantics and pragmatics, concepts and concept-adjustment, indexicality, speech acts, procedural meaning and the notion of 'constraint', the explicature-implicature distinction, numerical expressions, the semantics and pragmatics of negation and negative polarity items, and whether successful communication involves 'shared content'.

Rather than attempt to group these chapters by theme – impractical given that each chapter connects up with others in so many different ways – I introduce them in alphabetical order of the first author, the order in which they appear.

Jay Atlas' chapter ('On a Pragmatic Explanation of Negative Polarity Licensing') is a contribution to the discussion of the long-standing and intriguing problems posed by the expressions *only, even, almost* and *not*

1

quite. What is communicated by utterances of sentences in which these occur clearly includes a negative proposition. But it is not clear just what the status of the negative proposition is in the total signification of the sentence uttered. Atlas approaches the problems through an exploration of the licensing of Negative Polarity Items (NPIs) in such sentences and reconsiders a pragmatic proposal of Horn. Horn (2002) proposed to treat assertion (and non-assertion, or 'presupposition') as speech acts pragmatically independent of semantic entailment. Although NPIs would be licensed by the semantics facts, Horn proposed that they are in fact only licensed by falling within the scope of the (independent) pragmatic act of assertion. Atlas explores and critiques this pragmatic proposal, advancing new data and asking *why* the occurrence of NPIs should depend on the pragmatics of assertion and how we are to characterize assertion, non-assertion and entailment in the representation of utterance meanings.

Kent Bach's chapter, 'Regressions in Pragmatics (and Semantics)', is in part a defence of Gricean principles, but with the refinement of *impliciture* (see, for example, Bach 1994). The paper defends the idea that semantics and pragmatics are strictly separate though interacting in communication. Semantics concerns *sentences*. It captures what speakers actually *say* (in the locutionary sense of 'say', rather than the illocutionary sense of 'state' or 'assert'). It determines what is fully explicit in utterances. Pragmatics concerns what is communicated by the *utterance* of sentences, the performance of speech acts. Fully implicit communication – what is not said but conveyed by the saying of what is said (i.e. implicature) – falls within pragmatics. Bach's idea of impliciture is offered as a way of maintaining this picture while qualifying it. Crucially, saying versus implicating is not exhaustive. Impliciture takes up the slack, accounting for aspects of what is communicated that are neither said nor implicated but required by the fact that sentences may need completing (if utterances of them are to express propositions) and expanding (if utterances of them are to express the intended proposition). Impliciture is implied by what is said (i.e. it is implicit in what is said) – in contrast to implicature, which is implied only by the *saying* of what is said (and is not implicit in what is said). Against this background, Bach identifies nine 'suspect ideas' in current pragmatic theory. He calls them 'regressions' because, he argues, they hark back to pre-Gricean 'ordinary language' philosophy influenced by Wittgenstein's injunction: 'Don't look for the meaning, look for the use'. He argues that this mistakenly imports into semantics what pertains to pragmatics. The nine suspect ideas that he identifies commit, in different ways, the error of conflating pragmatics and semantics.

In 'Constraints, Concepts and Procedural Encoding', Diane Blakemore offers an intricate investigation of procedural meaning, its relation to conceptual meaning and to the notion of 'constraint on relevance'. She approaches the issues through a discussion of a range of parentheticals. The parentheticals that concern her – *as*- and *and*- parentheticals – achieve relevance by providing information about how their hosts are to be interpreted (and they can do this in a variety of different ways). In that respect, they might be described as providing constraints on the relevance/interpretation of another expression, the host. The effect of using one of these expressions, then, might seem to be the same as that of using an expression that encodes a procedure. However, she shows that their encoded meaning is clearly conceptual. She argues that, unlike purely procedural elements, the (conceptual) content of the parenthetical does not drop out of the picture once it has served its purpose of constraining the process of interpreting the host. It contributes to the overall conceptual representation and (again unlike procedural elements) is itself subject to all inferential operations – e.g. strengthening – that conceptual representations are subject to. Thus we need to make a distinction between constraints on interpretation/relevance and procedural meaning. In the light of this, she argues that we need to recognize two notions – and loci – of constraints on interpretation: (a) constraints that are encoded as such – this constitutes procedural meaning, arising at the level of linguistically encoded meaning, and (b) constraints that arise at the level of conceptual representation, through the interpretation of the relation between the conceptual content of the parenthetical and that of the host.

Reinhard Blutner, in 'Optimality Theoretic Pragmatics and the Explicature/Implicature Distinction' offers a wide-ranging discussion that centres on relevance theory's explicature/implicature distinction. It begins by noting problems with how that distinction is defined within relevance theory. Blutner speculates that the distinction might be independently derivable within the framework of optimality theoretic (OT) pragmatics (see Blutner and Zeevat 2004) based on neo-Gricean principles and 'global' considerations governing rational communication. The OT framework invites the development of a 'diachronic' perspective. Blutner suggests the manipulation of the different rankings of a given OT system of constraints is a powerful but computationally simple task. This perspective encourages us to see certain on-line (synchronic) inferential processes as having become fossilized and thus automatized. This makes for highly efficient, speedy, on-line processing, consistent with the experimental results reported in the work of Noveck (see also the chapter in this volume by Noveck and Sperber). The automatization and speed of processing of such processes, Blutner suggests, is consistent with relevance theory's treatment of them as explicatures, rather than with regarding them as the processing (the calculation and potential cancellation) of implicatures.

My own contribution (Burton-Roberts 'Varieties of Semantics and Encoding: Negation, Narrowing/Loosening and Numericals') considers relevance theory's distinction between 'linguistic semantics' (the encoded semantics of linguistic expressions) and 'real semantics' (the propositional – truth-theoretic – semantics of thoughts). I suggest that, on several grounds, 'linguistic semantics' is problematic and argue for a single ('real') notion of semantics, located in the Language of Thought. This implies – with Fodor (1998) and the strongest of Recanati's (2004) contextualist positions – that particular languages like English have no semantics. Distinguishing between 'having meaning' and 'having semantics', I allow that – like all signs – utterances in English do 'have meaning', but argue that this is so only in virtue of their being intended and recognized as standing in a relation of conventional *representation* to syntactico-semantically constituted thoughts. As *representational* of conceptual properties, utterable words are not themselves possessed of any conceptual property (either specific or schematic – Carston 2002). In this connection, I compare 'representation' with relevance theory's notion of 'encoding'. The implications of these ideas are explored with reference to negation (where a sharp distinction is drawn between the utterable English word *not* and the logical operator), 'narrowing' and 'loosening' (i.e. 'concept adjustment') and the problems posed by numerical expressions. A representational perspective, I argue, allows us to acknowledge that the differing concepts represented by uses of the word *three* all include the concept EXACTLY THREE while denying that the word itself has a semantic definition (including, and especially, 'exactly three').

The chapter by Herman Cappelen and Ernie Lepore ('Relevance Theory and Shared Content') is a critique of relevance theorists' claim that grasping what the speaker intends to communicate by the utterance of a sentence does not involve or require duplicating the speaker's thought. The relevance-theoretic (RT) claim is that successful communication involves entertaining a thought sufficiently similar to the speaker's thought. Cappelen and Lepore dub this the No Shared Content (NSC) principle: an audience will never grasp p (the intended proposition) but only another proposition q. They claim that RT is committed to the NSC principle because the only 'similarity' relation implied by RT is that two propositions are similar if they are developments of the same logical form and this is too unconstrained to guarantee anything approaching shared content: two propositions can be developments of the same logical form and yet be utterly different. Furthermore, the NSC is implied if the cognitive effects of a particular utterance on an interpreter depend on that interpreter's assumptions, since such assumptions vary from person to person. In short, there is no 'fixed standard of similarity that RT can appeal to'. Cappelen and Lepore argue that, being committed to the NSC principle, relevance theory fails to account for our general practice of reporting what others say, and assessing the truth of what they say. It also fails to account for coordinated planned action. They write: 'A central challenge in pragmatics is to develop a theory of communication that reconciles two fundamental facts: we can share contents across contexts and communicated content is deeply context sensitive.' The authors conclude with a useful summary of their proposed response to this challenge, 'Pluralistic Minimalism' (Cappelen and Lepore 2004).

Marjolein Groefsema's contribution ('Concepts and Word Meaning in Relevance Theory') is a detailed consideration of relevance theory's treatment of word meaning, concepts and their content. She focuses particularly on the proposal that concepts are triples, having three kinds of 'entry': logical, lexical and encyclopaedic. She argues that this treatment is open to several interpretations. She rejects the idea that the content of concepts might include lexical information, since this would make phonological and syntactic information about words part of the content of the concepts that are supposed to be the meaning of those words. She then considers three further accounts: (1) that the content of concepts is constituted by their logical and encyclopaedic entries, (2) that concepts are unanalyzable atomic entities whose entries do not constitute their content, and (3) that their logical entries, but not their encyclopaedic entries, constitutes their content. Finally, Groefsema considers Carston's (2002) recent proposal to distinguish between encoded concepts and 'ad hoc' concepts derived from encoded concepts by 'concept adjustment'. She investigates each of these accounts in turn and argues that they make different predictions about what proposition is expressed by an utterance (the explicature) and what is implicitly communicated (implicature). Ultimately, as with several other chapters in this volume, it is the explicature-implicature distinction that is at issue in this chapter. Groefsema argues that, since relevance is defined in terms of the cognitive effects derived from the interaction of the proposition expressed/explicature with assumptions in the context, it is crucial that we know how to make the explicature-implicature distinction in principle and in practice.

As Laurence Horn's subtitle indicates, his chapter ('Neo-Gricean Pragmatics: A Manichaean Manifesto') is indeed a wide-ranging manifesto for his neo-Gricean pragmatic stance (for example, Horn 1984, 1989), setting it in its historical context and within a range of philosophical, rhetorical, and cultural contexts. It is 'Manichaean' in the sense of being grounded in the idea of two opposing but co-dependent, interacting principles (Good-Evil for Manichaeans, Yin-Yang for Confucians). In the pragmatic context, the co-dependent oppositions include speaker-hearer, economy-sufficiency, brevity-clarity, minimizing-maximizing, effort-effect (the last also found in relevance theory). Horn's neo-Gricean enterprise 'folds' the several maxims proposed by Grice into exactly two such principles, the R Principle ('Don't say too much') and the Q Principle ('Say enough'). The R Principle is speaker-orientated (minimizing effort) and is 'upper-bounding' in its effect, giving rise to strengthening implicatures. The Q Principle is hearer-orientated (guaranteeing sufficiency) and is 'lower bounding', giving rise to typically scalar implicatures (which, Horn argues, are distinct from strengthening implicatures). Horn illustrates the pervasive influence of the principles – and their explanatory character in offering a 'division of pragmatic labour' – across a wide range of linguistic phenomena: lexical, semantic and logical, not only synchronically but also diachronically, in semantic and lexical change. Horn defends this 'dualist' ('Manichaean') picture against the three principles of Levinson (2000) – Q, I (equivalent to Horn's R) and M (for Manner) – and against the 'monist' position of relevance theory, which is grounded in a single Principle of Relevance. He questions whether relevance theory is in fact 'monist' since, as noted, it too stresses the effort-effect opposition.

In 'The Why and How of Experimental Pragmatics: The Case of "Scalar Inferences"', Ira Noveck and Dan Sperber present the case for an experimental methodology (see Noveck and Sperber 2004). This, they argue, is especially necessary in pragmatics, where the exclusive reliance on intuition is particularly problematic. They point up some interesting contrasts between semantic and pragmatic intuitions in this connection. In particular they advocate an experimental approach in choosing between alternative theories that may agree on the content of the interpretations of utterances, but have different implications for the cognitive mechanisms that derive these interpretations. A case in point is what is generally referred to as 'scalar inference' (e.g. the inference from *some* to *not all* and from *possible* to *not necessary/certain*) – and it is this that provides the focus of their chapter. While the treatment of scalar inference in terms of Grice's Generalized Conversational Implicature (GCI) is intuitive enough, they suggest the implications of that treatment for processing are not attractive. Here they focus on Levinson's (2000) approach, in which the rationale for GCIs lies in the optimization of processing – the relevant inferences are automatic, speedy, one-step, default inferences. Noveck and Sperber doubt this claim about processing, doubt that the relevant inference is scalar and doubt that it results in an implicature. As regards processing, the speed of the inference has to be set against the potential processing cost of cancelling the implicature. They argue for an alternative account in terms of relevance theory. Ultimately, they suggest, the choice between these competing approaches needs to be – and can be – tested experimentally, by timing actual on-line comprehension processing (as Levinson himself has suggested). Noveck and Sperber present the results of their experiments, and compare them with results from similar experiments. They argue that these results strongly favour their own RT account over Levinson's GCI account. They suggest that, while this does not exactly falsify Levinson's account, it does present that account with a serious challenge.

François Recanati, in 'Indexicality, Context and Pretence: A Speech Act Theoretic Account', is concerned with context and context shift. He argues that, in the normal way of things, 'context' refers the objective context of utterance, and context shift is impossible. The reference of genuine indexicals – expressions whose dependence on context is determined by semantic rule, e.g. *I, here, now* – cannot be shifted by speakers' intentions. In this they contrast with context-dependent expressions such as *you, we, John's car*, and demonstratives, whose reference can be shifted at will. However, this difference between genuine indexicals and other context- and intention-dependent expressions has to be qualified in the light of pretence. This is the focus of his chapter. Pretence allows for context shift even with indexicals. Here Recanati distinguishes two types of context-shifting pretence. The first occurs in direct speech reports, delayed communication, the historical present, and, in parallel, 'presentifying' uses of *here*. The second type of context-shifting pretence occurs in various sorts of displayed assertion: non-quotational echoes, irony and free indirect speech. Recanati suggests that the distinction between these two types correlates with the distinction between locutionary and illocutionary acts. In the light of this, he suggests speech act theory must allow for a correlative distinction between locutionary contexts and illocutionary contexts, a distinction between the context of utterance and the context of assertion. As a consequence, context cannot be regarded as an objective given, but as constructed intentionally as an aspect of utterance meaning.

Finally, Deirdre Wilson and Robyn Carston's chapter ('A Unitary Approach to Lexical Pragmatics: Relevance, Inference and Ad Hoc Concepts') reports on their recent work in the domain of lexical semantics and pragmatics. They explore how the concepts encoded as word-meanings are adjusted in the context of utterance. The disparity between lexically encoded meaning and what is generally communicated by the use of words, they argue, is generally accounted for by positing a range of different mechanisms. They accept that concept adjustment appears to take different forms, including narrowing (strengthening), loosening (broadening) and metaphorical extension. However, with extensive illustration, Wilson and Carston argue, against a variety of previous accounts which treat these three phenomena as distinct, that there are no well-defined distinctions among these intuitive types of adjustment. Accordingly, their concern is to develop a more constrained, unified account in which a single inferential process, guided by the expectation of (optimal) relevance, is involved in all three – a single process that derives an ad hoc concept. Narrowing, loosening (including approximation, hyperbole, and category extension) and metaphor are simply different outcomes of this single process. They compare their unified inferential account with that of Recanati, which they argue is only partly inferential, and with what they see as the non-inferential account of Lakoff (e.g 1987, 1994). They conclude by asking whether their account can be extended to cover a range of further figurative phenomena: metonymy, synecdoche, blends, puns and meaning transfers.

references

Bach, K. (1994). 'Conversational impliciture'. *Mind and Language* 9: 124–62.
Blutner, R. and H. Zeevat (eds). (2004). *Optimality Theory and Pragmatics*. Basingstoke: Palgrave Macmillan.
Cappelen, H. and E. Lepore (2004). *Insensitive Semantics*. Oxford: Blackwell.
Carston, R. (2002). *Thoughts and Utterances: The Pragmatics of Explicit Communication*. Oxford: Blackwell.
Fodor, J. (1998). *Concepts: Where Cognitive Science Went Wrong*. New York: Oxford University Press.
Grice, H.P. (1989). *Studies in the Way of Words*. Cambridge, Mass.: Harvard University Press.
Horn, L.R. (1984). 'Toward a new taxonomy for pragmatic inference: Q-based and R-based implicature'. In D. Schiffrin (ed.). *Meaning, Form, and Use in Context (GURT 1984)*. Washington, DC: Georgetown University Press. 11–42.
— (1989). *A Natural History of Negation*. Chicago, IL: University of Chicago Press (Reissued: Stanford, CA: CSLI, 2001).
— (2002). 'Assertoric Inertia and NPI Licensing'. *CLS 38* Part 2. Chicago, IL: Chicago Linguistics Society. 55–82.

Lakoff, G. (1987). *Women, Fire and Dangerous Things*. Chicago, IL: University of Chicago Press.

— (1994). Conceptual metaphor home page. Available at <http://cogsci.berkeley.edu/lakoff/MetaphorHome.html>

Levinson, S. (2000). *Presumptive Meanings: The Theory of Generalized Conversational Implicature*. Cambridge, Mass.: MIT Press.

Noveck, I. and D. Sperber (eds). (2004). *Experimental Pragmatics*. Basingstoke: Palgrave.

Recanati, F. (2004). *Literal Meaning*. Cambridge: Cambridge University Press.

Sperber, D. and D. Wilson (1986). (2nd edition 1995). *Relevance: Communication and Cognition*. Oxford: Blackwell.

2

on a pragmatic explanation of negative polarity licensing[1]

jay david atlas

My interest in this chapter is an advance in the use of pragmatics to explain what were considered to be syntactical or semantical phenomena. The case in question is the explanation of the licensing of Negative Polarity Items. The data are not sentence-types but rather utterance-types and utterance-tokens. The explanatory concepts are the distinctions between assertions and non-assertions, between sentence-meanings and speaker's meanings. I shall examine the most ingenious example of such a pragmatic theory that I know and ask whether the arguments that have so far been used in its support are adequate to their task. The doubts that I raise do not show that the pragmatic theory cannot succeed, but they suggest that other theoretical constructions will be necessary for the proper defence of a pragmatic theory.

Horn (2002a, 62), in response to Atlas (1984, 1997, 2005), claims that adverbials like *almost* and *not quite* may both be analyzed into two semantic components; *x almost F's* means *x is close to F and x does not F* and *x does not quite F* also means *x is close to F and x does not F*. However, the first, 'proximal' conjunct and the second, 'polar' conjunct are not pragmatically on all-fours. There is a difference in the pragmatics of *almost* and *not quite* (Sadock 1981, 264; Atlas 1984, 2005). For example, in (1a,b) the speaker's meaning in (1a) is typically (1a'), and in (1b) is typically (1b').

(1) a. It's too bad you almost died in the accident [– now you'll need therapy].
   a'. It's too bad you came close to dying in the accident.
   b. It's too bad you didn't quite die in the accident [– now I'll have to finish you off].
   b'. It's too bad you did not die in the accident.
   c. I {never quite / *almost} made it to *any* of your parties.

10

In the *almost* assertion the speaker's meaning is the 'proximal' conjunct and in the *not quite* assertion the speaker's meaning is the 'polar' conjunct. Furthermore in (1c) *never quite* licenses the Negative Polarity Item (NPI) *any*, but *almost* does not license it. Why, given their equivalence in sense (truth-conditions), according to Horn, should one license a NPI and the other not? The explanation of the difference in speaker meanings and in the licensing of NPIs requires an asymmetry, according to Horn: *not quite* speaker-means *not*, while *almost* speaker-means *close to*. The claim is that NPIs must be licensed by what the speaker asserts, not by the literal meanings of the expressions. Thus NPI licensing is not a grammatical, sentence phenomenon. Instead, Horn (2002a, 62) claims:

> Semantically entailed material that is outside the scope of the asserted, and hence potentially controversial (Stalnaker 1978), aspect of utterance-meaning counts as *assertorically inert* and hence as effectively transparent to NPI-licensing...

What is relevant to NPI licensing is 'downward assertion' rather than downward entailment; in the case of *not quite*, the asserted content is a downward-entailing proposition, but in the case of *almost*, the asserted content is not a downward-entailing proposition. Thus we explain (1c); the pragmatic, assertoric content of *not quite*, not its sense, is negative and so licenses a Negative Polarity Item.

The accounts of the semantics and the pragmatics of *almost* and *not quite* to be found in Atlas (1984, 1997, 2005) differ from Horn's account. Horn puts himself in this theoretical position, in part, by the semantic equivalence that he posits for *almost F* and *not quite F* and by the assumption that downward monotonic items are required to license NPIs. If he cannot get the downward monotonicity from the sense of the expression-type, he will have to get it from the speaker's meaning communicated by the assertoric use of the expression-token.

Another case for distinguishing the pragmatic force of the meaning components of an expression has been made for *only* sentences. Horn's (2002a, 70) long-standing objection to symmetrical conjunction analyses like *Socrates runs and no one other than Socrates runs* for *Only Socrates runs* is that they offer, he believes, no explanation of why the positive component of the *only* sentence (the prejacent) is 'marginally suspendable' while the negative component is not – see (2a,b); why *only*-initial phrases trigger negative inversion – see (3a,b); or why the nuclear scope of *only* should license Negative Polarity Items – see (4).

(2) a. Only Ann will pay her taxes on time, and # (maybe) even she
        won't.
    b. # Only Ann paid her taxes on time, {and/but} maybe someone
        else did.
(3) a. Only in stories does a dropped glass betray agitation. (Graham
        Greene)
    b. Only one new feature did I notice in the landscape, a large white
        villa.
(4)   Only young writers *ever* accept suggestions with *any* sincerity.
        (Klima 1964)

The evidence in (2)–(4) originally suggested an asymmetric analysis
in which the positive component was not entailed but semantically
presupposed, or conventionally implicated, or pragmatically presupposed,
or conversationally implicated. Horn (2002a, 70) remarks:

> Both liberal and radical asymmetricalist approaches fall afoul of Atlas's
> observation (1991, 1993) that simple cancellations of the prejacent in
> contexts like [(5)] are unsalvageably bad:

(5) a. # Only Hillary trusts Bill, and (even) she doesn't.
    b. # I love only you, but I don't love you either.

Horn (2002a, 71) also remarks:

> I agree with Atlas that *only NP* cannot be a classical downward monotonic
> (DE) operator, given the lack of entailment from [a] to [b]:
> [a]   Only Socrates entered the race.
> [b]   Only Socrates entered the race early.
> Indeed Peter of Spain (*Tract. Syncat.* in Mullally 1964, 33) had observed
> eight centuries earlier a similar lack of entailment either way between
> [c] and [d]:
> [c]   Only Aristotle moves.
> [d]   Only Aristotle runs.

Then Horn (2002a, 71) returns to the problem that still concerns us when
he writes that 'an English language symmetricalist has the NPI-licensing
property of *only NP* to explain, or at least explain away, and I find Atlas's
attempts to wave off the polarity facts as unpersuasive as my own theory
of love'.[2] If a semantic theory cannot explain NPI licensing, perhaps a
pragmatic theory can.

So Horn (2002a, 72) proposes a pragmatic theory of NPI licensing: though *only NP* statements *entail* both conjuncts, they *assert* only the negative one. He adapts the scope-diagnostics for 'conventional implicature' (presupposition) to be found in Karttunen and Peters (1979) and uses them as diagnostics for 'non-assertion'. And he most interestingly proposes (Horn 2002a, 73) that:

(a) Karttunen and Peters (1979) diagnostics demonstrate what's outside the scope of assertion, and
(b) NPIs are sensitive to downward assertion, not downward entailment as such.

Horn (2002a, 2005, 2006) has granted that *Only Muriel voted for Hubert* does entail *Muriel voted for Hubert*. That is, he has granted the semantical anomalousness of (6a,b):

(6) a. # Only Hillary trusts Bill, and she doesn't.
    b. # I love only you, but I don't love you either.

He has also granted the failure of (7a) to entail (7b).

(7) a. Only Socrates entered the race.
    b. Only Socrates entered the race early.

Thus, he grants that *Only Socrates* is not downward entailing and so fails to meet the downward monotonicity condition required by Ladusaw (1980) for a generalized quantifier Noun Phrase (NP) to license the grammatical co-occurrence of Negative Polarity Items – as in (8a), with the 'weak' NPI *ever*, and in (8b,c), with 'minimizer' NPIs.

(8) a. Only John *ever* suspected David Alexander. (Atlas 1993, 1996, 285)
    b. Only your wife *gives a hoot* about what happens to you. (McCawley 1981, 83)
    c. Only Phil would *lift a finger* to help Lucy. (McCawley 1988, Atlas 1996, 285)

It is the minimizer data (8b), (8c) and weak NPI datum (8a) that persuade Horn (2002a, 71) that *only NP* must be 'negative'. Since Horn now admits that the affirmative proposition *Muriel voted for Hubert* is ENTAILED by *Only Muriel voted for Hubert*, his dilemma is this: *Only Muriel voted for Hubert* is not downward entailing, but it is still 'negative', since it licenses some NPIs. How do we make a non-downward-entailing generalized quantifier 'negative'?

The characterization of *Muriel voted for Hubert* as a 'presupposition' was, Horn (1979, 1992) once thought, justified by the diagnostics for presupposition by Karttunen and Peters (1979). Karttunen and Peters gave an account of (9a) whereby the truth-conditions of 'what (9a) says' is expressed by (9b) and the further commitments of an asserter of (9a) are to the presuppositions/'conventional implicata' (9c) and (9d), which are not asserted in the asserting of (9a) (Karttunen and Peters 1979, 12).

(9) a. Even Bill likes Mary.
     b. Bill likes Mary.
     c. Other people besides Bill like Mary.
     d. Of the people under consideration, Bill is the least likely to like Mary.

According to Karttunen and Peters (1979, 13) when such a sentence occurs in a complement – as, for example in (10a) – 'what is said or meant' in (10a) is (10b), not (10c) or (10d) or (10e).

(10) a. I just noticed that even Bill likes Mary.
     b. I just noticed that Bill likes Mary.
     c. I just noticed that other people besides Bill like Mary.
     d. I just noticed that of the people under consideration, Bill is the least likely to like Mary.
     e. I just noticed that Bill likes Mary, that other people besides Bill like Mary, and that of the people under consideration, Bill is the least likely to like Mary.

But the presuppositions/'conventional implicata' in (9c) and (9d) are allegedly inherited by (10a), and the assertion of (10a) commits the speaker to the truth of (9c) and (9d) – as much as the assertion of (9a) does.

It is notable that the contrast between 'what is presupposed' in asserting a sentence and 'what is asserted' or 'what is meant' plays a crucial role in the description of Karttunen and Peters' linguistic intuitions. Their claim that (10a) asserts just (10b) – not (10c–e) – is a strong one. Karttunen and Peters take presuppositions/'conventional implicata' to determine felicity conditions on assertion and thus to contribute to the 'pragmatic presuppositions' of the utterance.

Horn's most recent proposal is to take the Karttunen-Peters observations as drawing a distinction between 'what is asserted' and 'what is not asserted'. Thus he asks whether an assertion of (12a) asserts (12b) or (12c).

(11) a. Only Muriel voted for Hubert.
      b. Muriel voted for Hubert.
      c. No one distinct from Muriel voted for Hubert.

(12) a. It's too bad that only Muriel voted for Hubert.
      b. It's too bad that Muriel voted for Hubert.
      c. It's too bad that no one distinct from Muriel voted for Hubert.

Horn has plausibly claimed that an assertion of (12a) just 'means', or asserts (12c). So he believes that the negative content of an *only Proper Name* sentence is assertorically 'foregrounded' and its affirmative content presuppositionally 'back-grounded'. This is admittedly a natural interpretation of an assertion of (12a). Further, consider (13):

(13) a. It's fortunate that only Hillary trusts Bill.
      b. It's fortunate that Hillary trusts Bill.
      c. It's fortunate that no one distinct from Hillary trusts Bill.

Once again Horn's intuition that a natural interpretation of an assertion of (13a) expresses the foregrounded proposition (13c) seems plausible.

Now, for the moment, let us suppose these Karttunen-Peters-Horn claims are unproblematic. How does Horn use these observations to resolve the dilemma created by his admitting that *Only α Fs* entails α *Fs* and that *only* α is non-monotonic? It is not downward entailing, but it licenses some NPIs and so, on Horn's view, something in it must be 'negative'.

Horn (2002a) suggests that, though *Only α Fs* entails α *Fs*, assertoric utterances of the sentence assert *No one distinct from* α *Fs* but do not assert α *Fs*. IF – and that is a large 'if' – the licensing of Negative Polarity Items depends on 'what is asserted' in an utterance, and the asserted utterance-meaning is downward entailing, then the conventional hypothesis of NPI licensing by a downward entailing, and so logically negative, generalized quantifier NP can be preserved from the refutation offered by Atlas' (1991, 1993, 1996, 1997) semantic analysis of *Only α Fs*. In Horn's pragmatic analysis α *Fs*, though admittedly entailed, suffers from 'assertoric inertia', while *No one distinct from* α *Fs* has 'assertoric momentum'. Thus Horn's pragmatic analysis of *Only Muriel voted for Hubert* is as follows:

(14)   A Speaker who asserts
       (M)   *Only Muriel voted for Hubert*
           (a) asserts *No one distinct from Muriel voted for Hubert*;
       and (b) (M) entails, but its asserting does not assert, *Muriel voted for Hubert*.

Horn (2002b, 7) offers two distinct representations of the utterance, exhibiting both asserted and unasserted components, in (15a) and (15b).

(15)   An assertion of 'Only Muriel voted for Hubert', viz.
      |-- *Only Muriel voted for Hubert*,
      is represented by either:
           (a)   { *Muriel voted for Hubert* & |-- *No one distinct from Muriel voted for Hubert* }
     or   (b)   { *Someone voted for Hubert* & |-- *No one distinct from Muriel voted for Hubert.* },
      where '|--' is the assertoric force marker (Searle 1969).

It is, at the least, mildly ironic that Horn, after rejecting the conjunction analysis α *Fs & no one distinct from* α *Fs* for *Only* α *Fs* in Horn (1969, 1979, 1992), should – in Horn (2002b) – adopt a subtle version of a traditional conjunction analysis in (15a) consisting of a 'presupposition' conjoined with an asserted content (truth-conditions). The second representation in (15b) is akin to Horn's (1996) view that when one asserts *Only Muriel voted for Hubert*, *Someone voted for Hubert* is 'accommodated' (Lewis 1979); the accommodated proposition, when combined with the negative truth-conditions of the assertion, entails *Muriel voted for Hubert*. The propositional contents of (15a) and (15b) are logically equivalent.

But, unlike the view of Horn (1996), Horn cannot now take the view that *Someone voted for Hubert* is accommodated. Accommodation introduces in real time, as an assertion is made, an 'unpresupposed' presupposition-like proposition into the common ground in order that the assertion be 'acceptable', or 'felicitous', in the context of utterance. In order to secure the entailment of *Muriel voted for Hubert*, the proposition *Someone voted for Hubert* cannot be the content of a felicity condition, or a pragmatic presupposition, of the assertion of *Only Muriel voted for Hubert*, since the necessity of a semantic entailment from *Only Muriel voted for Hubert* cannot depend on the contingency of a pragmatic feature like the felicity condition of an assertion in a context of utterance. Furthermore, on the analysis of (15b), the claim made by Horn that the entailed *Muriel voted for Hubert* is assertorically inert is a peculiarly trivial claim. *Muriel voted for Hubert* is not a component of the analysis in (15b) of *Only Muriel voted for Hubert*, so it is not even a candidate for assertoric force in the assertion of *Only Muriel voted for Hubert*. So, of course, it is assertorically inert.

I should point out that an assertion of *No one {distinct from, other than, besides} Muriel voted for Hubert* generally conversationally implicates *Muriel voted for Hubert*, so what Grice (1989) called 'the total signification of the utterance', not 'what is said', consists in *Muriel voted for Hubert & no one distinct from Muriel voted for Hubert*, which, of course, is just the traditional conjunctional analysis, which entails *Muriel voted for Hubert*. From Grice's point of view, if in asserting *Only Muriel voted for Hubert* the speaker asserts *No one distinct from Muriel voted for Hubert*, which is now Horn's position, not 'what is asserted' but 'what is totally signified' entails *Muriel voted for Hubert*.

If one adopts the representation in (15a), the claim that *Muriel voted for Hubert* is assertorically inert stands a chance of being non-trivial, but then the arguments of Horn (1969, 1979, 1992) and of Atlas (1991, 1993) against any conjunctional analysis of *Only Muriel voted for Hubert* would seem to come into play. As I have argued (Atlas 1991, 1993), no statement, with usual intonation and stress, of 'Only Muriel voted for Hubert' is about Muriel, but normal statements of 'Muriel voted for Hubert & no one distinct from Muriel voted for Hubert' are about Muriel (the topic of the first conjunct), so the latter statement cannot be the correct analysis of the former statement.

If Horn replies, as he should, that the statement |--*Muriel voted for Hubert & no one distinct from Muriel voted for Hubert* is not the same as the representation {*Muriel voted for Hubert & |-- No one distinct from Muriel voted for Hubert* }, so that the argument that I just offered against the traditional conjunctional analysis is misdirected against his, I would indeed need to reformulate my argument against his conjunctional analysis. What is the statement *Only Muriel voted for Hubert* about? It is about those who voted for Hubert. What is *No one distinct from Muriel voted for Hubert* about? Its logical form, as noted by Horn, is: $\neg \exists y (\neg (y=m)$ & y voted for Hubert), or equivalently: $\forall y$ (y voted for Hubert $\rightarrow$ (y=m)). As I discussed in Atlas and Levinson (1981, 42–3), utilizing ideas of Putnam (1958) and Popper (1959, 122), *No one distinct from Muriel voted for Hubert*, which does not entail *Muriel voted for Hubert*, is about the set of voters for Hubert (Popper) or about the union of the set of voters for Hubert with the set of non-Murielizers (Putnam). If it is true that only Muriel voted for Hubert, Popper's set is {Muriel}, and Putnam's set is the Domain of Quantification – everyone. If it is false, then either Muriel did not vote for Hubert, or someone else did. So the set of voters for Hubert either fails to contain Muriel, or it contains Muriel and at least one other voter for Hubert (Popper). On Putnam's view, the set contains everyone in either case. So whether the sentence is true or false, Putnam would have to say that the sentence is about everyone. Popper would say that the sentence is about Muriel if true, and either fails to be about Muriel or is about Muriel and at least one other if false. Popper's account is clearly preferable to Putnam's. Thus I shall take *No one distinct from Muriel voted for Hubert* to be about the set of voters for Hubert. So there is no lack of identity between the statement-topics of the analysandum and the analysans, as there was in the traditional conjunctional analysis. Horn's representation is not open to my objection against the traditional conjunctional analysis.

The problem for Horn's pragmatic analysis is to explain what the 'conjunction' of an unasserted sentence with an asserted sentence actually means. It is easy to understand the assertion of a full conjunction of individually unasserted sentences: $|\text{-- } (A \& B)$. It is possible to understand the 'conjunction' of two speech acts $(F_1(P_1) \wedge F_2(P_2))$ as the concatenation of two illocutionary acts of assertion, $|\text{-- } A \cap |\text{-- } B$, as a temporal sequence of speech acts. It is less easy to see how to 'conjoin' or concatenate a propositional content with an assertoric act, that is, it is not easy to see what such a heterogeneous 'conjunction' would mean. Thus the representation in (15a) seems to be a way of having the negative proposition as the statement's truth-conditions, and then adding, 'By the way, the statement *Only Muriel voted for Hubert* entails *Muriel voted for Hubert*.'

The essential claim of Horn's pragmatic theory of the licensing of NPIs by *Only α Fs* is now this:

(16) Downward asserting, not downward entailing, operators license NPIs.

For example, *Only α* is downward asserting (but why not also entailing?), since its asserted content is *No one distinct from α*, which Atlas (1996, 304) notes is anti-additive and so semantically negative (see Zwarts 1996, 1998, Atlas 2001).

Thus Horn (2002a, 2005, 2006) tries to have it all. Admitting the entailment and non-monotonicity claims of Atlas (1991, 1993, 1996, 1997), he preserves the downwardness of *Only α* by using the diagnostics of Karttunen and Peters (1979) for the distinction between truth-conditions and presupposition, now understood as a distinction between 'what is said' (asserted) and what is not asserted. What was once pragmatically presupposed (Horn 1979, 1992) is now entailed but not asserted.

As a pragmatic solution to the problem of NPI licensing that Horn sets himself, this is a clever idea. I certainly cannot object to this pragmatic, speech-act emphasis on assertion, since Horn (2002a) notes that in passing I made similar observations in Atlas (1991, 1993), though I did not anticipate Horn's use of the ideas. His new pragmatic analysis returns to the ideas and data of Horn (1992). He returns to Karttunen and Peters' (1979) data and analysis, now couched in terms of assertion and non-assertion.

The data of (12) seemed to support the Horn-Karttunen-Peters analysis of asserted content, that (12a) just means (12c). But consider (17):

(12) a. It's too bad that only Muriel voted for Hubert.
      b. It's too bad that Muriel voted for Hubert.
      c. It's too bad that no one distinct from Muriel voted for Hubert.
(17) a. It's good that only Muriel waited up for Hubert.
      b. It's good that Muriel waited up for Hubert.
      c. It's good that no one distinct from Muriel waited up for Hubert.

It is clear that an assertion of (17a) does not just mean (17c). The data of (13) also seemed to support the Horn-Karttunen-Peters analysis, that (13a) just means (13c), but consider (18a), where, again, an assertion of (18a) does not just mean (18c).

(13) a. It's fortunate that only Hillary trusts Bill.
      b. It's fortunate that Hillary trusts Bill.
      c. It's fortunate that no one distinct from Hillary trusts Bill.
(18) a. I don't care that only Hillary trusts Bill.
      b. I don't care that Hillary trusts Bill.
      c. I don't care that no one distinct from Hillary trusts Bill.

The data of (17) and (18) are counter-examples to the kind of analysis that the data of (12) and (13) suggested to Horn, Karttunen, and Peters.

Another example that Horn (2002a) used to support the Karttunen-Peters analysis of 'what is asserted' is a sentence with *almost VP*, which he believes has a foregrounded component 'close to VP' and a backgrounded component 'not VP'. For example, an assertion of (19a) is plausibly understood by Horn (2002a, 73) to mean (19b) not (19c).

(19) a. I just discovered that my cat almost proved Fermat's Last
         Theorem.
     b. I just discovered that she 'came close to' proving it.
     c. I just discovered that she did not succeed.

But the opposite intuition obtains in example (20a), asserted by a
mathematician whose speciality is algebraic geometry and who has
discovered the subtle error in Wiles' first proposed proof given by him
in a colloquium in Cambridge. In this context an assertion of (20a) does
not just mean (20b).

(20) a. I just discovered that Andrew Wiles almost proved Fermat's Last
         Theorem.
     b. I just discovered that Andrew Wiles 'came close to' proving it.
     c. I just discovered that Andrew Wiles did not succeed.

Horn believes that (21a), when asserted, has the utterance-meaning
(21b) but not (21c). To the contrary, it seems linguistically obvious that an
assertion of (21a) does not have just the utterance-meaning of (21b).

(21) a. I just took a survey of the White House, and I discovered that
         only Hillary trusts Bill.
     b. I just took a survey of the White House, and I discovered that
         no one distinct from Hillary trusts Bill.
     c. I just took a survey of the White House, and I discovered that
         Hillary trusts Bill.

The point is that for every example that seems to support a Karttunen-
Peters diagnostic for an assertion's utterance-meaning being just a
foregrounded component of its sentence-meaning and a component of
its sentence-meaning not being asserted, one can, with a little ingenuity,
construct an example with no such component of sentence-meaning
exhausting the utterance-meaning of the assertion. But Horn has one
further linguistic argument in defence of his pragmatic analysis.

Horn claims that a given speaker cannot felicitously reassert or question
what he or she has just asserted. For example, (22a) and (22b) are illo-
cutionarily odd.

(22) a. # The cat is on the mat, but the cat is on the mat.
     b. # The cat is on the mat, but is the cat on the mat?

Horn finds (23a) acceptable and (23b) unacceptable, which he takes as evidence that *Only Hillary trusts Bill* asserts *No one distinct from Hillary trusts Bill*, just as he interprets the assertion of (24a) to be (24b) and so purports to explain the alleged illocutionary anomaly of (23b) just as he does (22b).

(23) a. I know Hillary trusts Bill, but does ONLY Hillary trust Bill?
    b. #[sic] I know no one distinct from Hillary trusts Bill, but does ONLY Hillary trust Bill?
(24) a. It's too bad that only Hillary trusts Bill.
    b. It's too bad that no one distinct from Hillary trusts Bill.

Horn thinks that the sentence in (23b) is 'totally impossible', but I disagree. One merely has to spend time with the English middle classes, or the denizens of Harvard Yard, to hear (23b) as an arch, indirect, but linguistically acceptable way of asking whether Hillary trusts Bill.

conclusion

The arguments do not seem to support the view that Horn's constraint on acceptable assertion and Karttunen and Peters' use of epistemic or emotive factives show that, when asserted, *Only α Fs* has the negative proposition *No one distinct from α Fs* as its foregrounded utterance-meaning and the affirmative proposition α *Fs* assertorically backgrounded. Horn reformulates his pragmatic account of α *Fs* in *Only α Fs* as an account of a non-assertion, by contrast with the truth-conditions or the asserted utterance-meaning *No one distinct from α Fs*. Horn attempts to resolve the dilemma of how a semantically non-monotonic *Only α* can still be 'negative' in order to license NPIs, while allowing an entailed α *Fs*, by hypothesizing a downward monotonic assertoric content of *Only α Fs*. Unfortunately his pragmatic account crucially relies on Karttunen and Peters' (1979) observations, which, when re-couched as criteria for distinguishing assertions from non-assertions, do not seem, in general, to be correct.

Even were Karttunen and Peters' criteria, so recast, sound, there would still remain (a) the theoretical question why it should be necessary for the grammatical occurrence of NPIs in a sentence that the sentence be asserted and (b) the task of constructing a theory characterizing the unasserted, entailed, and asserted components in the representations of utterance-meanings.

If one cannot rely on Karttunen and Peters' version of an account of the assertoric meaning of 'presuppositional' utterances, and the arguments like Horn's (2002a, 2005, 2006) that essentially rely upon it, the semantic analysis that I had proposed in Atlas (1996) and the treatment of assertoric force that I gave in Atlas (1991) still seem to me to do justice to intuitions about speech acts and to logical intuitions that we have about the entailments of *only NP* sentences. Horn's pragmatic theory of NPI licensing in *only* sentences is the best 'negative' theory there is – it's a genuine pragmatic advance. But it needs another defence than the pragmaticizing of Karttunen and Peters' (1979) criteria for presupposition into criteria for un-assertion.

notes

1. The discussion below of Karttunen and Peters (1979) was first given in a colloquium lecture in the University of Groningen, The Netherlands, 8 May 2002. I am grateful to my audience, including Henny Klein, Jack Hoeksema, and Frans Zwarts for comments and suggestions.
2. Horn (1992, 182) was once committed to the view that (a) *I love only you* did not entail (b) *I love you*, so that (a) was not a declaration of love, though the recipient was – as Horn piquantly put it – 'pragmatically licensed to hope for the best'.

references

Atlas, J.D. (1984). 'Comparative Adjectives and Adverbials of Degree: an Introduction to Radically Radical Pragmatics'. *Linguistics and Philosophy* 7: 347–77.
— (1991). 'Topic/Comment, Presupposition, Logical Form and Focus Stress Implicatures: the Case of Focal Particles *only* and *also*'. *Journal of Semantics* 8: 127–47.
— (1993). 'The Importance of Being "Only": Testing the Neo-Gricean Versus Neo-Entailment Paradigms'. *Journal of Semantics* 10: 301–18.
— (1996). '"Only" Noun Phrases, Pseudo-Negative Generalized Quantifiers, Negative Polarity Items, and Monotonicity'. *Journal of Semantics* 23: 265–332.
— (1997). 'Negative Adverbials, Prototypical Negation, and the DeMorgan Taxonomy'. *Journal of Semantics* 14: 349–68.
— (2001). 'Negative Quantifier Noun Phrases: a Typology and an Acquisition Hypothesis'. In J. Hoeksema, H. Rullman, V. Sanchez-Valencia, and T. van der Wouden (eds). *Perspectives on Negation and Polarity Items*. Amsterdam: John Benjamins. 1–23.
— (2005). *Logic, Meaning, and Conversation: Semantical Underdeterminacy, Implicature, and their Interface*. New York: Oxford University Press.
Atlas, J.D. and S.C. Levinson (1981). '*It*-Clefts, Informativeness, and Logical Form: Radical Pragmatics (Revised Standard Version)'. In P. Cole (ed.). *Radical Pragmatics*. New York: Academic Press. 1–60.

Grice, H.P. (1989). *Studies in the Way of Words*. Cambridge, Mass.: Harvard University Press.

Horn, L.R. (1969). 'A Presuppositional Analysis of *only* and *even*'. *CLS* 5: 97–108.

— (1979). '*Only, even*, and conventional implicature'. LSA Paper, Los Angeles.

— (1992). 'The Said and the Unsaid'. SALT Vol. 2: 163–92.

— (1996). 'Exclusive company: "only" and the dynamics of vertical inference'. *Journal of Semantics* 13: 1–40.

— (2002a). 'Assertoric Inertia and NPI Licensing'. *CLS* 38 Part 2. Chicago, IL: Chicago Linguistics Society. 55–82.

— (2002b). Handout. CLS 38 Lecture 'Assertoric Inertia and NPI Licensing'. April 2002.

— (2005). ONLY Connect: how to unpack an exclusive proposition. JayFest, Pomona College, Claremont, California. 2 April 2005.

— (2006). Only browsing: looking for values on the exclusive shopping network. Swarthmore College Workshop on Negation and Polarity, Swarthmore College, Swarthmore, Pennsylvania. 15 April 2006.

Karttunen, L. and S. Peters (1979). 'Conventional Implicature'. In C-K Oh and D. Dinneen (eds). *Syntax and Semantics 11: Presupposition*. New York: Academic Press. 1–56.

Klima, E. (1964). 'Negation in English'. In J.A. Fodor and J.J. Katz (eds). *The Structure of Language*. Englewood Cliffs, NJ. Prentice Hall. 246–323.

Ladusaw, W. (1980). *Polarity Sensitivity as Inherent Scope Relations*. New York: Garland.

Lewis, D.K. (1979). 'Scorekeeping in a Language Game'. *Journal of Philosophical Logic* 8: 339–59.

McCawley, J. (1981). *Everything that Linguists Have Always Wanted to Know about Logic but were ashamed to ask*. Chicago, IL: University of Chicago Press.

— (1988). *The Syntactic Phenomena of English*. Vol. 2. Chicago, IL: University of Chicago Press.

Mullally, Joseph. (1964). Ed. and trans. *Tractatus Syncategorematum and Selected Anonymous Treatises [by] Peter of Spain*. Milwaukee: Marquette University Press.

Popper, K. (1959). *The Logic of Scientific Discovery*. New York: Basic Books.

Putnam, H. (1958). 'Formalization of the Concept "About"'. *Philosophy of Science* 25: 125–30.

Sadock, J. (1981). 'Almost'. In P. Cole (ed.). *Radical Pragmatics*. New York: Academic Press. 257–71.

Searle, J. (1969). *Speech Acts*. Cambridge: Cambridge University Press.

Stalnaker, R. (1978). 'Assertion'. In P. Cole (ed.). *Syntax and Semantics: Pragmatics*. Vol. 9. New York: Academic Press. 315–32.

Zwarts, F. (1996). 'Negation: a notion in focus'. In H. Wansing (ed.). *Perspektiven der Analytischen Philosophie. Perspectives in Analytical Philosophy*. Vol. 7. Berlin, New York: de Gruyter. 169–94.

— (1998). 'Three Types of Polarity'. In E. Hinrichs and F. Hamm (eds). *Plural Quantification*. Dordrecht: Kluwer. 177–238.

3

regressions in pragmatics (and semantics)

kent bach

Remember the twentieth century? Around the middle of it, so-called ordinary language philosophers made extraordinary claims about various philosophically interesting terms. Evidently they were operating under the influence – of Wittgenstein, that is – and his slogan 'Don't look for the meaning, look for the use'. In ethics, for example, it was (and sometimes still is) supposed that because sentences containing words like *good* and *wrong* are used to express affective attitudes, such as approval or disapproval (or, alternatively, to perform speech acts like commending and condemning), such sentences are not used to make statements, hence that questions of value and morals are not matters of fact. This line of argument is fallacious. As G.E. Moore pointed out, although one expresses approval (or disapproval) by making a value judgement, it is the act of making the judgement, not the content of the judgement, that implies that one approves (Moore 1942, 540–5). Sentences used for moral evaluation, such as 'Gambling is wrong' and 'Greed is good', are no different in form from other declarative sentences, which, whatever the status of their contents, are standardly used to make statements.[1]

The fallacious line of argument exposed by Moore commits what John Searle called the 'speech act fallacy' (Searle 1969, 136–41). Searle gives further examples, each involving a speech act analysis of a philosophically important word. According to such analyses, the terms *true*, *know*, and *probably* do not express properties. Rather, because *true* is used to endorse statements (Strawson), *know* to give guarantees (Austin), and *probably* to qualify commitments (Toulmin), those uses constitute the meaning of these words. In each case the mistake is the same: identifying what the word is typically used to do with its semantic content.

Searle also exposes the 'assertion fallacy' (141–6), which confuses conditions of making an assertion with what is asserted. Here are two examples. You wouldn't assert that you believe something if you were prepared to assert that you know it, so knowing does not entail believing. Similarly, you would not describe a person as trying to do something that involves no effort or difficulty, so trying entails effort or difficulty. Paul Grice (1961) had already identified the same fallacy in a similar argument, due to Austin, about words like *seems*, *appears*, and *looks*. Because you would not say that a table looks old unless you doubted or were even prepared to deny that it is old, the proposition that the table looks old entails that its being old is doubted or denied. This argument is clearly fallacious, since it draws a conclusion about sentence semantics from a premise about conditions on appropriate assertion. You can misleadingly implicate something without its being entailed by what you say.

These claims from ordinary language philosophy were discredited decades ago. So why do I dredge them up now? Because essentially the same mistakes keep getting made. There continues to prevail an illicit mixing of pragmatics with semantics. Yes, people are no longer serving up misguided analyses of philosophically interesting expressions. Now they have a different concern: to reckon with the fact, appreciated only recently, that the meanings of a great many sentences, at least those we are at all likely to use, generally underdetermine what we would normally mean in uttering them. This can happen even if the sentence in question is free of indexicality, ambiguity, and vagueness, and even if the speaker is using all of its constituents literally. In other words, what a speaker means in uttering a sentence, even without speaking figuratively or obliquely, is likely to be an enriched version of what could be predicted from the meaning of the sentence alone. This can be because the sentence expresses a 'minimal' (or 'skeletal') proposition or even because it fails to express a complete proposition at all.

Many theorists who appreciate the fact that sentence meaning underdetermines speaker meaning grant that semantics concerns sentences (and their constituents) and that pragmatics concerns acts of uttering them. But they will then go ahead and conflate them anyway. They just don't seem to appreciate what makes the pragmatic pragmatic and, in some cases, what makes the semantic semantic either. As a result, some theorists have been led to defend some form of 'contextualism' or 'truth-conditional pragmatics' and others to propose inflated conceptions of semantics. I will not attempt to examine specific theories in any detail but will instead identify a series of ideas that are central to one or another of them. Each idea, I will suggest, in one way or another conflates the semantic and the pragmatic. Before taking up these ideas, I will first (section 1) state my view on what makes the pragmatic pragmatic and then (section 2) give a sample of sentences whose use typically does not make fully explicit what one would mean in uttering them. Then (section 3) I will identify nine suspect ideas underlying different ways of trying to account for the fact that such sentences are typically used in enriched ways. I will suggest that each of these ideas needlessly conflates something pragmatic with something semantic.

1. what makes the pragmatic pragmatic?

A speaker can convey a thought without putting it into words. He can say one thing (as determined by sentence meaning, perhaps relative to context) and mean something else (speaker meaning). In order to communicate something to someone, the speaker has to come up with a sentence whose utterance makes evident, even if the sentence itself does not express, what it is that he intends to convey. The hearer's task is to understand the speaker or, more precisely, to recognize the speaker's communicative intention in making the utterance and, in particular, to identify what the speaker means. The meaning of the sentence provides the hearer with only part of his basis for figuring that out. The hearer needs also to take into account the fact that in that situation the speaker uttered that sentence with that meaning.

The very fact that a sentence is uttered gives rise to distinctively pragmatic facts (Bach 1999). As Grice (1961) observed, it is the fact that a speaker utters a sentence with a certain semantic content (or even that sentence rather than another with the same content) that generates what he would later call a conversational implicature. His first example of this was an utterance of 'Jones has beautiful handwriting and his English is grammatical', made as an evaluation of Jones' philosophical ability, to implicate that Jones is no good at philosophy. A different sort of illustration is provided by Moore's paradox (so-called). If you say, 'Snow is white, but I don't believe it', you are denying that you believe something you have just asserted. The contradiction here is pragmatic. That snow is white does not entail your believing it (nor vice versa), and there's no contradiction in my saying, 'Snow is white, but you don't believe it.' The inconsistency arises not from what you are asserting but from the fact that you are asserting it. That's what makes it a pragmatic contradiction.

By way of asking what would we mean in uttering sentences containing such terms as *good, true, try,* and *appears,* ordinary language philosophers came up with pragmatics-laden accounts of their meanings. They tried to supplant sentences' truth-conditions with conditions for their appropriate (especially non-misleading) use and to equate what a speaker does in uttering a sentence with the semantic content of the sentence itself. However, a sentence has its content independently of being uttered.[2] Understanding it is of a piece with hearing it and parsing it. A sentence's semantic content is a projection of its syntactic structure, as a function of the semantic contents of its constituents, and is something a competent hearer grasps by virtue of understanding the language. The speaker's act of uttering that sentence, with that content, provides or invokes additional information the hearer is to use in understanding an utterance of the sentence – there is no intermediate level of meaning between the semantic content of the sentence and the speaker's communicative intention in uttering it (see section 3.4 below).

As illustrated by generalized conversational implicatures (Grice 1975/1989, 37–8), there are regularities of use that, despite being systematic, should not be confused with linguistic meanings. Such pragmatic regularities can be explained by combining facts about the semantic contents of sentences people utter with generalizations about people's acts of uttering them. To explain these regularities we do not have to resort to fanciful stories about the meanings of expressions based on observations about the conditions for their typical or appropriate use. Instead, we can apply what Robert Stalnaker has aptly described as 'the classic Gricean strategy: to try to use simple truisms about conversation or discourse to explain regularities that seem complex and unmotivated when they are assumed to be facts about the semantics of the relevant expressions' (Stalnaker 1999, 8).

Executing this strategy requires taking into account three key elements of communication. First, there is the distinctive nature of a communicative intention. As Grice discovered, such an intention is 'reflexive': the speaker intends his utterance 'to produce some effect in an audience by means of the recognition of this intention' (Grice 1957/1989, 220). Specifically, although Grice did not identify it as such, this effect is recognition of the attitude the speaker is expressing (whether or not he actually has that attitude is another matter). So, an act of communication succeeds by way of recognition of the very intention with which it is performed. Compare this with, for example, the act of getting an audience to laugh, say by telling a joke. They can recognize your intention to get them to laugh without actually laughing. Normally that would require that they find your joke funny (of course, they could find it funny that you are trying to get them to laugh, but that's not what you intend them to laugh at). In contrast, all it takes for an act of communication to succeed is for the audience to recognize the speaker's intention in performing it. In other words, a communicative intention has this distinctive property: its fulfilment consists in its recognition (by the audience). A communicative intention includes, as part of its content, that the audience recognize this very intention by taking into account the fact that they are intended to recognize it. Correlatively, in figuring out what the speaker's communicative intention is, the hearer takes into account, at least implicitly, *that* he is intended to it figure out.[3] To understand an utterance is to recognize the intention with which it is made.

Second, there is the fact that the speaker said what he said rather than something else. Perhaps he could have said something more informative, more relevant, or more appropriate. So the fact that he said what he said contributes to the explanation of why he said it, hence to the recognition of the intention with which he said it. Perhaps he doesn't know more, perhaps he doesn't want you to know more, perhaps it's obvious what he could have added. Also, the fact that he said what he said in the way he said it, using those words and with that intonation, rather than in some other way, may contribute further to the explanation, as with Grice's manner implicatures (1975/1989, 35–7).

Third, although what the speaker says, the semantic content of the words he utters, provides the primary input to the audience's inference, the audience also takes into account what is loosely called 'context'. This is the mutually salient contextual information that the audience is intended to use to ascertain the speaker's communicative intention, partly on the basis that they are intended to do so. Here, it must be stressed, context does not literally determine, in the sense of constituting, what the speaker means. Rather, at least when communication succeeds, it provides the audience with the basis for determining, in the sense of ascertaining, what the speaker means. What the speaker does mean is a matter of his communicative intention, not context, although what he could reasonably mean depends on what information is mutually salient.

Taking such information into account goes beyond semantics, for what a speaker means need not be the same as what the uttered sentence means. It is generally though not universally acknowledged that explaining how a speaker can say one thing and manage to convey something else requires something like Grice's theory of conversational implicature, according to which the hearer relies on certain maxims, or presumptions (Bach and Harnish 1979, 62–5), to figure out what the speaker means. However, it is commonly overlooked that these maxims or presumptions are operative even when the speaker means exactly what he says. They don't kick in just when something is implicated.[4] After all, it is not part of the meaning of a sentence that it must be used literally, strictly in accordance with its semantic content. Accordingly, it is a mistake to suppose that 'pragmatic content is what the speaker communicates over and above the semantic content of the sentence' (King and Stanley 2005, 117). Pragmatics doesn't just fill the gap between semantic and conveyed content. It operates even when there is no gap. So it is misleading to speak of the border or, the so-called 'interface' between semantics and pragmatics. This mistakenly suggests that pragmatics somehow takes over when semantics leaves off. It is one thing for a sentence to have the content that it has and another thing for a speech act of uttering the sentence to have the content it has. Even when the content of the speech act is the same as that of the sentence, that is a pragmatic fact, something that the speaker has to intend and the hearer has to figure out.

There are various ways in which what a speaker means can go beyond or otherwise be distinct from the semantic content of the sentence he utters. One familiar case is speaking in a nonliteral way, by using metaphor, irony, metonymy, or some other figure of speech, whereby one says one thing and means something else. For example, 'You are the ribbon around my life' and 'That was the cleverest metaphor I've ever heard' are sentences likely used to convey something different from what their semantics predicts. In the other familiar case, of conversational implicature (or indirection generally), the speaker typically means not only what he says but also something else, as in Grice's example, 'Jones has beautiful handwriting and his English is grammatical'.

Less familiar but no less common is what I call conversational 'impliciture' (Bach 1994), where what the speaker means is not made fully explicit and is an enrichment of what he says. This can occur either because the sentence he utters expresses a 'minimal' proposition or because it is semantically incomplete, expressing no proposition at all, even relative to the context. This phenomenon is widely thought to undermine any dichotomous conception of the semantic/pragmatic distinction or at least to pose special challenges in accounting for the relationship between what a speaker says and what he means in saying it. Such worries are illustrated by the nine different strategies to be discussed later for treating cases of impliciture. In my view, however, these doubts are unwarranted, and the strategies they have inspired actually confuse meaning and use. After giving (section 2) an assortment of examples of impliciture, I will explain (section 3) why I regard these nine strategies as regressions in pragmatics.

2. examples

It is generally recognized that most sentences people utter in everyday life have semantic contents that are either too variable or too skimpy to comprise what people mean in uttering them, even when all of their constituents are used literally. Indexicals whose semantic content are a function of context are the source of variable semantic contents, but here I'll focus on sentences whose semantic contents are too skimpy. The semantic content of a sentence can be too skimpy, relative to a speaker's likely communicative purposes in uttering it, either because the proposition it expresses lacks elements that are part of what the speaker means or because what it expresses, its semantic content, falls short of comprising a proposition (presumably the things people mean in uttering sentences are propositions). Sentences of the first sort express so-called 'minimal' propositions, and sentences of the second sort are said to be semantically incomplete.[5] When a speaker utters a sentence with minimal propositional content, what he means is an expansion of that. When a speaker utters a semantically incomplete sentence what he means is a completion of its incomplete propositional content.

The first set of examples to follow contains sentences that express minimal propositions.[6] In each case, what the speaker is likely to mean is expressible by an expanded version of the sentence he utters, perhaps one containing the italicized material in brackets.

Implicit quantifier restriction:

Everyone *[in my family]* went to the wedding.
Lola had nothing *[appropriate]* to wear.
The cupboard *[in this house]* is bare.
Only Bill *[among those present]* knows the answer.
I have always *[since adulthood]* liked spinach.

Implicit qualification:

I will be there *[at the agreed time]*.
I haven't had a coffee break *[this morning]*.
Jack and Jill went up the hill *[together]*.
Jack and Jill are married *[to each other]*.
Jack walked to the edge of the cliff and *[then]* jumped *[off the cliff]*.
Ronnie insulted his boss and got fired *[for insulting him]*.
Ronnie got fired and insulted his boss *[because he got fired]*.

Scalar 'implicature' denial:

It doesn't *[merely]* look expensive – it is.
He didn't *[just]* try to lift the desk – he did it.
Sam doesn't have *[only]* three kids – he has four.

'Metalinguistic' negation:

I didn't trap two *[what are called]* mongeese – I trapped two mongooses.
He's not *[what I'd call]* a shrink – he's a psychiatrist.

In these cases what the speaker means is, in my terminology, an 'impliciture', so-called because it is neither fully explicit nor merely implicated. Here I am avoiding the unfortunate but common tendency to describe the whole thing, even though part of it is implicit, as the 'explicit content' (or 'explicature') of the utterance. Calling it the 'proposition expressed' or 'what is said' by the utterance, as many do, is also inaccurate, since part of it is *not* expressed or said. It has to be inferred as being part of what the speaker meant.

The following are examples of semantically incomplete sentences, sentences that fail to express a proposition, even relative to a context. In each case, what the sentence expresses, as the result of semantically composing the semantic values of its constituents in accordance with its syntactic structure, is an abstract entity that is proposition-like but falls short of being a full proposition because it is missing at least one constituent. In these examples, complete propositions would have been expressed had the speaker included material that answers the question in parentheses.[7] But since the speaker did not do this, what the speaker means is partly implicit, so that the hearer must figure what needs to be added to complete the proposition that is meant but not fully said.

Argumental incompleteness:

Danielle just FINISHED a novel. (doing what: reading, writing, editing, typing, eating?)
Gentlemen PREFER blondes. (to what: brunettes, sheep?)
Brad is TOO old/not young ENOUGH. (for what?)
Psychological facts are not RELEVANT. (to what?)
Spinach TASTES GREAT. (to whom?)
Vladivostok is FAR AWAY (from where?)
John is READY/LATE/EAGER. (to or for what?)

Parametric incompleteness:

That statue is SHORT/CHEAP/OLD. (relative to what?)
That player is GOOD/TALENTED/VALUABLE. (in what respect?)
EVEN cowgirls sing the blues. (in addition to who?)
Gregor was MERELY a bookkeeper. (as opposed to what?)
Arnold MIGHT (for all who knows?) be in Los Angeles.

The examples of semantic incompleteness given so far are cases in which what the sentence expresses requires an additional constituent to comprise a proposition. In other cases the incompleteness is due to a particular term or phrase that does not determinately express one property (or relation), but not because of ambiguity or vagueness.[8] Here are some examples:

Lexical underdetermination (not ambiguity):

GET, PUT, TAKE; AT, BEFORE, IN, ON, TO

Phrasal underdetermination (not syntactic ambiguity):

HAPPY girl/face/days
CONSCIOUS being/state
child/drug ABUSE
FAST car/driver/engine/tyres/fuel/track/race/time
Willie ALMOST robbed a bank (he refrained, failed, robbed something else instead?)

A different kind of underdetermination involves unspecified scope relations. I will not argue for this, but a case could be made that the logical form (as a level of syntax) of each of the following sentences does not specify the relevant scope relations. If so, these sentences are not structurally ambiguous but semantically underdetermined.

Scope underdetermination:

The NUMBER of planets MAY be even.
FIVE boys ate TEN cookies.
I love you TOO. (interpretable in four distinct ways)[9]

3. nine misdirected ideas

I will sketch out a sequence of moves each of which in one way or another commits something like the error made by the ordinary language philosophers more than fifty years ago. Each of these ideas is a way of confronting the fact that a great many of the sentences used in everyday speech, typified by the examples above, either does not express the proposition the speaker is likely to mean or does not express a proposition at all. The error is to suppose that this requires bringing something pragmatic into semantics.

3.1 contextualism

The first idea is that if a sentence expresses a minimal or an incomplete proposition and the speaker means more than that, then context fills the gap – by 'supplying' the sentence with additional or more specific content. So, according to this idea, the context somehow manages to fill out, restrict, or complete the 'proposition expressed' by 'providing' needed constituents or by tightening, loosening, or otherwise modulating concepts expressed by particular constituents of the sentence.

The trouble with this idea is that context is incapable of doing these things. It can play the limited semantic role of fixing the references of whatever pure indexicals occur in the sentence, but otherwise it cannot endow a sentence with additional semantic content, content not derived from the semantic values of its constituents in accordance with its syntactic structure. As mutually salient information, context can play merely the pragmatic, epistemic role of providing information for the *hearer* to use to infer what the speaker means in uttering the sentence.

This first idea conflates the broad, pragmatic role of context with its limited semantic role, by confusing being determined (= ascertained) in context with being determined (= constituted) by context, and thus credits context with something it is incapable of.[10] Context cannot determine, in the sense of constitute, what a speaker means. For example, if Alice says to Trixie, 'Ralph hasn't taken a bath', and means that Ralph hasn't taken a bath today, it is not the context that makes this the case. After all, Alice could have meant something else, however far-fetched, e.g. that Ralph hasn't taken a bath since he found a dead rat in his bathtub. Of course, Alice could not reasonably mean this – she would have no reason to expect her communicative intention to be recognized.

3.2 intentionalism

The next idea is that the gap, construed as a gap in sentence semantics, is filled by the speaker's communicative intention and, further, that since context, if restricted to mutually salient information, can't fill the gap, context must include the speaker's intention. Since context so restricted is not fit to do that, it must be that the speaker's intention is, and so the intention is part of context, now more broadly conceived.

The trouble with this idea is, first, that the speaker's communicative intention can't endow sentences or particular expressions with semantic contents.[11] Nor is the intention part of the context. After all, this intention is what the hearer has to figure out, partly on the basis of the semantic content of that very sentence (along with mutually salient contextual information, given the presumption that the speaker uttered the sentence with an intention the hearer is to recognize). The speaker's communicative intention can't add to the information the hearer needs to identify that very intention. Its identity is the conclusion, not a premise, of the hearer's inference. Moreover, the sentence doesn't acquire additional semantic properties just by being uttered. Rather, it is by uttering the sentence with the semantic properties it already has that the speaker provides the hearer with the linguistic semantic part of his basis for figuring out the speaker's communicative intention.[12]

3.3 propositionalism

There is one idea that seems to underlie those considered so far, that a declarative sentence has to express a proposition (at least relative to a context). This idea apes the deep-seated grammar school lesson that a complete sentence expresses a complete thought. According to this idea, if a sentence doesn't express a proposition independently of context, then context or the speaker's intention (or something) simply must enable it to do so.

The trouble with this idea is that it overlooks the possibility that some sentences are semantically incomplete or underdetermined and fall short of expressing a proposition at all, even relative to a context. Presumably complete thoughts are fully propositional, but that doesn't mean that any sentence a speaker uses to convey a complete thought must itself have a complete propositional content (even relative to a context). As illustrated in section 2, some well-formed sentences do not. And it is a mistake to suppose that being semantically incomplete is to be context-sensitive.[13]

3.4 utterance semantics

Many radical contextualists claim that most (if not all) declarative sentences do not express propositions, even relative to contexts. Some even regard as misguided the very idea of truth-conditional semantics for sentences. They are moved by the observation that for every true utterance of a given sentence, the speaker could have used the same sentence in the same circumstances to make a false utterance. So, they conclude, it must be the utterance, not the uttered sentence, that expresses a proposition. The idea, then, is that utterances, not sentences, are the primary linguistic items with propositional or truth-conditional contents, in which case utterances are the only available subject matter for truth-conditional semantics, or what Recanati (2004) prefers to call 'truth-conditional pragmatics'. A further rationale is that the semantic contents even of sentences that do seem to express propositions are too skimpy to comprise the stable and robust contents that our so-called semantic intuitions are responsive to.

One trouble with this idea, and with the observation it is based on, is that it implies that thoughts are ineffable. For if they're not, a speaker can always use a more elaborate sentence to make fully explicit the thought he wishes to express. And those more elaborate sentences would have complete propositional, truth-conditional contents, assuming thoughts themselves do.

But there is a simpler trouble with this idea: utterances do not express anything – speakers do.[14] If by *utterance* we mean an act of uttering a sentence rather than the uttered sentence (contextualists suppose sentences generally fall short of expressing propositions anyway), there is nothing for the content of an utterance to consist in other than what the speaker means. It is an illusion to suppose that utterances are linguistic entities over and above sentences.[15] They are speech acts. And their contents are what speakers mean in performing them. So there is nothing in between sentences and intentions (in uttering sentences) also capable of having contents. Accordingly, commonly used phrases like 'the proposition expressed by an utterance' and the 'truth-conditional content of an utterance' are highly misleading. Even more misleading, but just as commonly used, are the bare phrases 'proposition expressed' and 'truth-conditional content'. In any case, there is nothing for the truth-conditional 'semantics' of utterances to be about, and calling it 'truth-conditional pragmatics' doesn't help – it's really about what speakers mean.

The fact that many declarative sentences are semantically incomplete and do not have truth-conditional semantic contents does not begin to suggest that linguistic entities of some other sort do have such contents. But coherent sentence semantics is still possible: the semantic content of a sentence is still a projection of its syntactic structure. Its content can be built up from the semantic contents of its constituents in accordance with its syntactic structure, whether the result is a complete structured proposition or a structure that falls short of being fully propositional. The job for pragmatics is not to provide a surrogate for semantics but to explain how semantically incomplete sentences can be used to convey complete propositions.

3.5 indexicalism

Rather than indulge in the fanciful enterprise of utterance semantics, some philosophers adopt a different strategy for saving Propositionalism. They stick with sentence semantics but suppose that sentences that seem not to express propositions actually do (relative to contexts, of course). Their idea is that such sentences contain either hidden indexicals (variables) in their syntax or overt expressions that, contrary to appearances, actually are indexical. So, for example, in the sentence 'Tom is tall' the claim would be either that there is a hidden indexical whose semantic value is the relevant reference class (or standard) or that *tall* is itself an indexical, whose semantic value depends on the relevant reference class (or standard).

The trouble with this idea is that it collapses semantic incompleteness into context-sensitivity. Otherwise, why fish for inaudible or unobvious context-sensitive sentence constituents whose semantic values complete the propositions expressed by sentences in which they occur? Except for when there is special syntactic or lexical justification, going on this expedition is like fishing in the Dead Sea.[16] It is only by overlooking or dismissing the category of semantic incompleteness that one could suppose that any sentence that appears not to express a proposition actually does express one – by virtue of containing some context-sensitive element, whether hidden or disguised. Moreover, positing hidden or disguised indexicals does not simplify the explanation of how communication is possible when an apparently semantically incomplete sentence is used. After all, what the speaker means still has to be figured out by the hearer, by relying on mutually salient information that he can reasonably take the speaker to have intended him to take into account, and this is an entirely pragmatic matter. The hidden/disguised indexical approach needlessly assumes that whatever more the speaker means in order to convey a proposition corresponds to something in the sentence's syntax and that this is somehow 'supplied' or 'provided' by the context. Proponents of this approach not only fail to explain how context manages to work this trick but also fail to realize that the only plausible account of it would inevitably appeal to the same intentional/inferential processes that the pragmatic approach requires. Adding indexical bells and whistles to sentences does not contribute to the explanation but misdirects it instead.[17]

3.6 positing unarticulated constituents

This idea gives up on the supposition that the semantic value of something in the syntax of a seemingly semantically incomplete sentence completes the proposition the sentence expresses. Rather, this semantic value is 'unarticulated': it is a constituent of the proposition expressed by the sentence even though this constituent does not correspond to anything in the sentence (whether phonologically articulated or merely present in the syntax). In other words, if a sentence seems not to express a proposition but the speaker is using all of its constituents literally and is conveying a proposition, then this sentence, as used in the context, semantically expresses that proposition – despite the fact that this proposition has at least one constituent that is not the semantic value of any constituent of the sentence.[18]

The trouble with this idea is that there is no clear sense to the notion that the proposition with its unarticulated constituent is the semantic value of the uttered sentence. Rather, it is the semantic value of a different sentence, a more elaborate one that the speaker could have uttered, which does contain a constituent whose semantic value is the unarticulated constituent of the proposition in question. But this constituent is not the semantic value of a constituent of the sentence actually uttered. Once again, the mistake is to assume that since a sentence seems not to express a proposition but the speaker is using all of its constituents literally and is conveying a proposition, this sentence, as used in the context, semantically expresses that proposition. It overlooks the fact that there is often a mismatch between what it takes for a declarative sentence to be well formed and what it takes for the sentence to express a proposition. Because the latter is partly a metaphysical matter (of, for example, whether or not what the predicate *is ready* expresses is a property), from a semantic point of view we can only let the propositional chips fall where they may.

3.7 dichotomizing (what is said/implicated)

Another idea appeals to the dichotomy between what is said and what is implicated. It supposes that if the speaker means something he is not implicating, he must actually be saying it.[19] Suppose the semantic content of the sentence a speaker utters is at most a minimal proposition but the speaker is using all of the sentence's constituents literally, so that what he means is an enrichment of its semantic content. Then, it is claimed, what he says is not fully determined by the semantic content of the sentence. What is said in this liberal sense is often described as the 'proposition expressed' by the utterance, or as its 'explicit content'.

The trouble with this idea is that it is based on a false dichotomy. It conflates being implicated with being partly implicit. Of course a speaker can mean something that goes beyond the semantic content of the sentence he utters even if he is using all of its constituents literally. Even if he is not implicating anything, what he means can be an enriched version of the sentence's semantic content, especially if what the sentence expresses is merely a minimal proposition or even no proposition at all. In the first case what he means is an expansion of what he says, in the second case a completion of it. In either case, part of what he means does not correspond to anything in the sentence. So it is not said but merely implicit in the saying of what is said.[20] To regard what the speaker means as the 'proposition expressed', that is, as the (fully) explicit content of the utterance, is to treat something that's pragmatic as if it were semantic.

The confusion here stems partly from neglecting Austin's distinction between locutionary and illocutionary acts, between saying something and doing something in saying it. This distinction is commonly neglected these days, perhaps because it is so easy to use *say* interchangeably with *state* or *assert*. But stating or asserting is to perform an illocutionary act, of trying to communicate something, and that goes beyond mere saying in the locutionary sense. As I have pointed out previously (Bach 2001, 17–18; Bach 2005, 25), the locutionary notion of saying is needed, along with the correlative, strictly semantic notion of what is said, to allow for cases in which the speaker does not say what he intends to say, as in the misuse of a word or a slip of the tongue, (intentionally) says one thing but is not speaking literally and means something else instead, means what he says but means something else as well (cases of implicature and of indirect speech acts in general), or says something but doesn't mean (intend to communicate) anything at all. These are all cases in which the speaker says something that he does not mean.

3.8 intuitionism

The next idea takes a different route towards an expansive conception of what is said. It supposes that the business of semantics is to explain intuitions about what is said. This allows enrichments of strictly semantic contents to count as what is said. So if such intuitions are responsive to pragmatic contributions to the contents of utterances, then so much the worse for a purely semantic conception of what is said, and what we need is a 'pragmatics of what is said' (as in the title of Recanati 1989).

The trouble with this idea, insofar it is accurate about what the relevant intuitions are,[21] is that it puts too much credence in them. Of course, semantics must reckon with supposedly semantic intuitions, but it doesn't have to take them at face value, much less have to explain them. It can explain some of them away, to the extent that they are found to be responsive not just to semantic contents but also to pragmatic regularities. Pragmatic regularities include default assumptions about the speaker's likely intent, standardized implicitures involving particular forms of words, and general facts about efficient communication. They all involve streamlining stratagems on the part of speakers and inferential heuristics on the part of listeners. These regularities count as pragmatic because it is the speaker's act of uttering the sentence, not the sentence itself, that carries the additional element of information. Intuitions are tainted also by the fact that when we consider a sentence in isolation, we make stereotypical assumptions about the circumstances of utterance. So we tend not to discriminate between the semantic content of a sentence and the likely import of uttering a sentence with that content. This is just what you'd expect if speakers typically don't make fully explicit what they mean and exploit the fact that it's obvious what they've left out. Accordingly, we should not equate the semantic content of a (declarative) sentence with what it is normally used to assert (see Bach 2005 and Soames forthcoming).

3.9 meaning as use again: pragmatic intrusionism

The final idea is that pragmatics intrudes into semantics, not because intuition says so but for cognitive psychological reasons. Pragmatics contributes to what is said, so the argument goes, because what many sentences express in the would-be strict semantic sense – a miminal proposition or an incomplete proposition – plays no psychological role in understanding, and moreover, because implicatures are often calculated before the strict semantic content is calculated, if indeed the latter is calculated at all.

The trouble with this idea is that it effectively conflates competence with performance, calculability with actually being calculated, and interpretation in the abstract semantic sense with interpretation in the pragmatic, epistemic sense. Claims about the semantics of a sentence and the information it encodes do not have specific implications for how that information is utilized. The argument fails to appreciate that what is said can play a psychological role even if it is not calculated, and that the relevant 'implicatures' are really implicitures, which can be calculated during the course of sentence processing (see the experimental work of Storto and Tanenhaus (forthcoming) on the case of (so-called) scalar implicatures). So, for example, if the speaker says, 'John has three wives and seven children', and means that John has exactly three wives and exactly seven children, this can be understood without first representing the proposition that John has three wives and seven children, a proposition that is compatible with his having more than three wives and more than seven children. Moreover, the speaker does not mean two things, explicitly asserting this last proposition while implicating the distinct proposition that John has exactly three wives and exactly seven children. He means only one thing, the latter, and this is an impliciture, an expansion of what he says.

4. bottom line

Many sentences are semantically incomplete, and many others express propositions that speakers are not likely to mean. There is no need either to bemoan this fact or to make something of it, at least from the standpoint of sentence semantics. The only consequence this fact has for semantics is that the semantic contents of many sentences are not propositions (even relative to contexts) or are not the propositions people may intuitively suppose. Sentence semantics does not need bolstering from context or from speaker intentions, which are instead relevant to the pragmatics of communication. There is no need to divert the attention of semanticists from sentences to utterances, for that would give them nothing to do. Nor is there any need to give them more to do, by finding, wherever semantic incompleteness lurks, hidden variables behind every syntactic bush or unarticulated constituents under every semantic stone.

The implications for pragmatics are straightforward. Allowances can be made for the fact that even if a speaker is using all of a sentence's constituents literally, he can mean, without merely implicating, something beyond what sentence semantics predicts. The additional element(s) are implicit in his saying what he says, and what he means is an enriched version of what he says. If the sentence is semantically incomplete, what he means includes a completion of what he says; if it expresses a minimal proposition, it includes an expansion of what he says. The fact that some linguists and some philosophers have intuitions that lead them to treat completions and expansions as explicit, as part of what is said, attests only to the fluency of their inferential abilities as speaker-hearers. And the fact that inferences about what speakers mean often do not include explicit representations of the semantic content of the uttered sentence, because they can operate locally on particular sentence constituents, does not suggest any sort of intrusion of pragmatics upon semantics. Rather, it suggests the need for enforcing the distinction between competence and performance, insofar as cognitive processes can be sensitive to available information without having to represent all of it explicitly.

There are many specific linguistic and psychological issues here that I have not taken up. For example, in many cases it is debatable whether a given lexical item is semantically underdetermined or ambiguous and, similarly, whether a given phrase or sentence is structurally underdetermined or ambiguous. In some instances, such as relational words like *local* and *enemy*, there may be a good case for positing hidden variables in syntactic structure. It may turn out that in some cases sentences that seem to be semantically incomplete are actually indexical. As for psychology, there are legitimate questions concerning how speakers manage to come up with sentences that make their communicative intentions evident and, when what speakers mean are enriched versions of what they say, how hearers manage to identify speakers' communicative intentions, given that the speaker said what he said in the context in which he said it. And there is the question of delineating the constraints on what a speaker can plausibly be supposed to mean in uttering a given sentence. These and related issues can be addressed without committing new versions of the speech act or assertion fallacies.

notes

1. This leaves open the possibility that there is something fundamentally problematic about their contents. Perhaps such statements are factually defective and, despite syntactic appearances, are neither true nor false. But this is a metaphysical, not semantic, issue about the status of the properties ethical predicates purport to express.

2. Of course, in denying that meaning is use, I am not denying the platitude that linguistic meaning is ultimately grounded in use. I do deny that individual uses (other than effective stipulative definitions) endow expressions with new meanings.

3. Grice anticipates that this may seem 'to involve a reflexive paradox', but insists that 'it does not really do so' (1957/1989, 219). The audience does not have to already know what the speaker's intention is in order to figure what it is, but merely that he is intended to figure this out.

4. So it is not a 'standard Gricean assumption ... that any material derived via conversational principles constitutes an implicature' (Carston 2002, 100). For one thing, the maxims come into play in resolving ambiguities and determining references. Indeed, they can even bear on figuring out what the speaker uttered, as when one doesn't hear the utterance clearly.

5. The term 'minimal proposition' was introduced by François Recanati (1989, 304), but the term has been used recently by Cappelen and Lepore (2005) slightly differently, for what they take to be the propositions expressed by sentences that almost everyone else takes to be semantically incomplete.

6. To keep matters relatively simple, I will limit the discussion to declarative sentences, the ones that are generally assumed to express propositions.

7. I am assuming that the highlighted term in the sentence (*finished, prefer*, etc.) does not have associated with it a hidden variable, whose value is the constituent in question, and that the term itself is not a disguised indexical. For present purposes it does not matter if this assumption is wrong about particular terms, so long as there are plenty of other good examples (contrary to the idea discussed in section 3.5 below).

8. It is important to understand that semantic underdetermination in particular and semantic incompleteness in general is a case of not fully expressing a proposition. It is not a case, as is sometimes supposed, of the sentence underdetermining the proposition explicitly expressed by the sentence, since the sentence doesn't express a proposition. Nor is it a kind of indexicality, in which the linguistic meaning provides for variable semantic content.

9. Well worth noting are examples like *The cat is on the mat*, *John cut the grass*, *The kettle is black*, and *The ball is round*, which Searle (1978) and Travis (e.g. 1997) think are semantically underdetermined – and to be typical of most sentences. Their reason is that whether we'd count the sentence as true or false depends partly on the context. However, perhaps what we're really evaluating is what the speaker would mean in uttering the sentence. Maybe the sentence is not really semantically underdetermined, but in uttering it a speaker is likely to intend something more specific than its semantics predicts, something that includes a perhaps elaborate but implicit qualification on what he says. But if Searle and Travis were right, including more words would rarely suffice to make one's thought fully explicit – and most thoughts would be inexpressible.

10. The narrow, semantic role of context is to provide values for the parameters set by the 'character' of an indexical (Kaplan 1989).

11. I'm not talking about the speaker's linguistic intention to use an ambiguous expression in one of its senses rather than another. But even that intention does not endow the expression with a meaning – it just makes operative a particular meaning the expression already has.

12. A special case of Intentionalism concerns reference by demonstrative pronouns and phrases. The idea is that since the reference of a demonstrative is not determined by the context of utterance, it can only be determined by the speaker's referential intention in using it. And, since demonstrative reference is a matter of sentence semantics, the speaker's intention must be semantically relevant after all. The trouble with this idea is that it conflates what the demonstrative itself does with what the speaker does in using it. Yes, the speaker's referential intention, as part of his communicative intention, determines what he is using the demonstrative to refer to, but this intention does not thereby endow it with referential properties itself. Demonstratives suffer from a character deficiency – they do not refer, even as a function of context. Their meanings can only impose constraints on speakers' referential uses of them. See Bach 1987/1994, 186–92; Bach 2005, 39–41; and Soames (forthcoming).

13. Interestingly, even critics of semantic contextualism, notably Cappelen and Lepore (2005), buy into this idea. They agree with contextualists that if a given sentence did not express a proposition it would be context-sensitive, even if it contains no obvious indexicals, but they deny that there are any such sentences and suppose instead that sentences that seem to everyone else to be semantically incomplete actually express a complete but very weak proposition. Clearly they assume that being semantically incomplete entails being context-sensitive.

14. This is also the trouble with Levinson's (2000) contention that generalized conversational implicature establishes the need for a level of utterance-type meaning intermediate between sentence meaning and speaker meaning.

Without actually giving an argument for this contention, Levinson seems to assume that because GCIs are associated with forms of words but are not literal meanings (he calls them 'presumptive meanings' because, like particularized conversational implicatures, they are cancellable), they comprise a distinct level of meaning. However, the only difference between GCIs and PCIs is that GCIs do not require special contextual triggering. This difference bears on the hearer's inference, not on the meaning of anything.

15. It won't help to invoke sentence tokens, as if they have autonomous semantic properties. Token semantics is, well, token semantics (see Bach 1987/1994, 85–8).

16. One proponent of this idea, Jason Stanley (2000), claims that there is syntactic justification for hidden variables. He relies on a 'Binding Argument', due originally to Barbara Partee (1989), for the existence of hidden variables in the syntax. The idea is that in a sentence like 'Every species of mammal has members that are tall', *tall* picks out a different property with respect to each species, hence that either it is bindable or has a bindable variable associated with it. However, Recanati (2004, 110–14) has argued that this argument is fallacious (not that his appeal to unarticulated constituents is any more warranted – see section 3.6 below), and, as Cappelen and Lepore have argued (2005, ch. 6), this argument overgenerates, leading to an absurd proliferation of variables. I would add that the likely use of the above sentence involves an impliciture: Every species of mammal has members that are tall for that species.

17. I am not denying that there can be lexical grounds for attributing implicit arguments to particular expressions, such as *local*, *foreign*, and *enemy* (see Bach 2001, 38). But one must be judicious in using such arguments.

18. It should be noted that John Perry (1986), when introducing the notion of unarticulated constituents, claimed that certain utterances, not sentences, express propositions with unarticulated constituents. However, as argued above (section 3.5), there is no job for utterance semantics to do.

19. Worth noting here is the common misconception that what is implicated is inferred from what is said. What is inferred is what it is that is implicated, and what this is inferred from is the fact that the speaker said what he said. See Bach (2006) for a discussion of other misconceptions about implicature.

20. Here I am assuming what I have called the Syntactic Correlation Constraint and what Carston calls the Isomorphism Principle (Carston 2002, 22).

21. Psychological research suggests otherwise. Experimental work by Gibbs (2002) indicates that many subjects count the contents of metaphorical utterances as what is said.

references

Bach, Kent (1987/1994). *Thought and Reference*, paperback edition. Oxford: Oxford University Press.

— (1994). 'Conversational impliciture'. *Mind and Language* 9: 124–62.

— (1999). 'The semantics-pragmatics distinction: What it is and why it matters'. In Ken Turner (ed.). *The Semantics-Pragmatics Interface from Different Points of View*. Oxford: Elsevier. 65–84.

— (2001). 'You don't say?' *Synthese* 128: 15–44.

— (2005). 'Context *ex machina*'. In Z.G. Szabó (ed.). *Semantics versus Pragmatics*. Oxford: Oxford University Press. 15–44.

— (2006). 'The Top 10 Misconceptions about Implicature'. In B. Birner and G. Ward (eds). *Drawing the Boundaries of Meaning: Neo-Gricean Studies in Pragmatics and Semantics in Honor of Laurence R. Horn*. Amsterdam/Philadelphia: John Benjamins.

Bach, Kent and Robert M. Harnish (1979). *Linguistic Communication and Speech Acts*. Cambridge, Mass: MIT Press.

Cappelen, Herman and Ernie Lepore (2005). *Insensitive Semantics*. Oxford: Blackwell.

Carston, Robyn (2002). *Thoughts and Utterances*. Oxford: Blackwell.

Gibbs, Raymond W., Jr. (2002). 'A new look at literal meaning in understanding what is said and implicated'. *Journal of Pragmatics* 34: 457–86.

Grice, Paul (1957/1989). 'Meaning'. In *Studies in the Way of Words*. Cambridge, Mass: Harvard University Press. 213–23.

— (1961). 'The causal theory of perception'. *Proceedings of the Aristotelian Society* 35 (suppl.): 121–52.

— (1975/1989). 'Logic and conversation'. In *Studies in the Way of Words*. Cambridge, Mass: Harvard University Press. 22–40.

Kaplan, David (1989). 'Demonstratives'. In J. Almog, J. Perry, and H. Wettstein (eds). *Themes from Kaplan*. Oxford: Oxford University Press. 481–563.

King, Jeffrey and Jason Stanley (2005). In Z. Szabó (ed.). *Semantics versus Pragmatics*. Oxford: Oxford University Press. 111–64.

Levinson, Stephen C. (2000). *Presumptive Meanings: The Theory of Generalized Conversational Implicature*. Cambridge, Mass: MIT Press.

Moore, G.E. (1942). 'A reply to my critics'. In P.A. Schilpp (ed.). *The Philosophy of G.E. Moore*. Evanston, IL: Northwestern University Press. 535–677.

Partee, Barbara (1989). 'Binding implicit variables in quantified contexts'. In C. Wilshire, B. Music, and R. Graczyk (eds). *Papers from CLS 25*, Chicago, IL: Chicago Linguistics Society. 342–65.

Perry, John (1986). 'Thoughts without representation'. *Proceedings of the Aristotelian Society* 60 (suppl.): 263–83.

Recanati, François (1989). 'The pragmatics of what is said'. *Mind and Language* 4: 295–329.

— (2004). *Literal Meaning*. Cambridge: Cambridge University Press.

Searle, John R. (1969). *Speech Acts*. Cambridge: Cambridge University Press.

— (1978). 'Literal meaning'. *Erkenntnis* 13: 207–24.

Soames, Scott (forthcoming). 'The gap between meaning and assertion: Why what we literally say often differs from what our words literally mean'. In M. Hackl and R. Thornton (eds). *Asserting, Meaning, and Implying*.

Stalnaker, Robert (1999). *Context and Content*. Oxford: Oxford University Press.

Stanley, Jason (2000). 'Context and logical form'. *Linguistics and Philosophy* 23: 391–424.

Storto, Gianluca and Michael Tanenhaus (forthcoming). 'Are scalar implicatures computed online?'. *Proceedings of WECOL 2004*.

Travis, Charles (1997). 'Pragmatics'. In B. Hale and C. Wright (eds). *A Companion to the Philosophy of Language*. Oxford: Blackwell. 87–107.

4

constraints, concepts and procedural encoding

diane Blakemore

1. introduction

As it was first understood, the relevance-theoretic notion of procedural meaning was limited to expressions which were shown to contribute to interpretation by constraining the way in which utterances containing them were interpreted as relevant (cf. Blakemore 1987). In fact, the term 'procedural' did not feature in this early research: the meanings these expressions encoded were simply described as 'constraints' on relevance. The emergence of the term 'procedural' is linked to the recognition that the phenomenon was not exhausted by expressions which constrained implicit content. However, the term 'constraint' continues to feature in discussions of procedural meaning. Thus while expressions such as *so* are said to constrain implicit content, pronouns are said to constrain explicit content. Or, to take an example which is more central to this chapter, the Sissala 'hearsay' particle *ré* is described as encoding a constraint on a 'higher-level' explicature in which the proposition expressed is embedded under a higher-level description (cf. Blass 1990).

The problem is that the idea that an expression may *constrain* the interpretation of the utterance in which it appears has also featured in analyses of expressions and constructions which relevance theorists would analyze in conceptual terms.[1] For example, speech act theoretic analyses of sentence adverbials and parenthetical verbs, even if they don't actually use the word *constraint*, are couched in closely related terms: their function, according to these analyses, is to show how the utterance is to be taken or understood. In fact, it seems that relevance-theoretic analyses of similar phenomena may be construed in similar terms. For example, Ifantidou (2001), who argues that an illocutionary adverbial such as *frankly* in (1) encodes conceptual information, also claims that its function is to 'indicate the manner in which some speech act is being performed' (Ifantidou 2001, 201). Similarly, she describes the function of the conceptual adverbial *allegedly* in the utterance in (2) as 'marking' the proposition expressed as being interpretively used:

(1) Frankly, I am not impressed.
(2) Allegedly, she has resigned.

More generally, she argues that parenthetical comments have 'a "fine-tuning" function, narrowing down the interpretation of the speech act to which [they are] appended' (200).

It seems that this idea of a fine-tuning function might be extended to certain parentheticals which do not explicitly communicate information about how the host utterance should be interpreted. For example, the parenthetical clauses in (3) and (4) can be interpreted as constraining the interpretation of their hosts by implicitly communicating information about the degree of commitment that the hearer is expected to have towards the host proposition:

(3) What is obvious – and we have the reports – is that they were killed
     (from a discussion of the causes of the destruction of the population
     of Easter Island, BBC Radio 4, 26 August 2005)
(4) As our eye-witness accounts show, they were killed.

Indeed, as I shall show, there seems to be a variety of ways in which parenthetical constructions can achieve relevance by constraining or fine-tuning the interpretation of their hosts.

It might seem that, if there is a problem here at all, it is simply ter-minological – one we could solve by using different terms for different phenomena, or by ensuring that we distinguish between 'conceptual constraints' (that is, constraints which are communicated by an expression which encodes a constituent of a conceptual representation) and 'procedural constraints' (that is, constraints which are imposed by an expression which encodes a procedure). However, it is not clear that terminology alone will help us understand the different ways in which a parenthetical expression or construction may contribute to the interpreta-tion of their hosts or the difference between the sort of information which is encoded by expressions such as the sentence adverbials in (1)–(2), on the one hand, and that which is encoded by expressions such as the

Sissala *ré*, on the other. In fact, I hope to demonstrate that it is misleading to describe expressions such as *frankly* or *apparently* as 'constraining' the interpretation of their hosts or as 'indicating' or 'marking' how the host proposition should be interpreted. Strictly speaking, if we wish to admit the existence of constraints on interpretation which are communicated by expressions which encode conceptual content, then we must recognize that what they communicate is communicated at the level of conceptual (propositional) representation rather than at the level of linguistically encoded meaning.

2. concepts and comments

2.1 comments and 'asides'

According to relevance theory, the explicatures of an utterance are derived by means of the same relevance-theoretic comprehension strategy that is involved in the derivation of implicit content:

(5) *Relevance-theoretic comprehension strategy*
    a. Follow a path of least effort in computing cognitive effects.
    b. Stop when the expected level of relevance is reached.

The difference between the inferences involved in the derivation of explicatures, on the one hand, and those involved in the derivation of implicatures, on the other, is that the former take a decoded semantic representation as input, whereas the latter take (pragmatically derived) explicit content as input. This should not be taken to mean that the inferences involved in the derivation of explicatures must take place before the inferences involved in the derivation of implicatures. As Carston (2002) has emphasized, hypotheses about both types of communicated assumption are 'made in parallel and adjusted to achieve a final state of sound inference' (Carston 2002, 146). Thus a hypothesis about an implicature (an implicated premise or implicated conclusion) may be made before a logical form is inferentially enriched for the derivation of a hypothesis about the communicated explicit content. The point is that this mutual parallel adjustment of explicit content and implicit import is constrained by the assumption that a satisfactory level of relevance can be achieved.

However, if the expectation of relevance is seen as an expectation about the positive cognitive effects that may be gained for the amount of processing effort invested, then it might seem that the concepts encoded by parenthetical sentential adverbials are not constituents of propositional representations which feature in this mutual adjustment process. For it is not clear that these propositions yield cognitive effects in the same way as the explicatures communicated by the host utterance do. For example, according to Ifantidou's (1993, 2001) analysis, the illocutionary adverbial *frankly* in (1) encodes a concept which is a constituent of a *higher-order explicature* such as the one in (6):

(1)   Frankly, I am not impressed.
(6)   The speaker is saying frankly that the speaker is not impressed.

Intuitively, it seems that the relevance of (1) lies in the cognitive effects that are derived from the lower-order explicature in (7), and that the assumption in (6) plays no role in the derivation of either this explicature or the cognitive effects that are derived from it.

(7)   The speaker is not impressed.

The idea that parenthetical constructions do not contribute to the process of establishing relevance is inherent in Potts' (2005) analysis of parentheticals as conventional implicatures, which he analyzes as 'non-at-issue entailments', that is, as secondary entailments which contrast with the 'regular assertive content' or 'at issue entailments' in that they are 'rarely used to express controversial propositions or main themes of a discourse' (Potts 2003). Thus according to Potts, the parenthetical in (8) would contribute a 'non-at-issue' entailment and is not part of the assertive content:[2]

(8)   It is, as you know, a very long book.

However, it seems that there is a sense in which we can judge one utterance of a parenthetical to be more relevant than another, or in other words, that the relevance of a parenthetical varies from context to context. Compare (9) and (10):

(9)   Receptionist at medical centre: And what was your date of birth?
       Speaker: As my brother should know, it's 26 October 1955.
(10) Biographer: I asked your brother what your date of birth was, but
       he couldn't remember.
       Speaker: As my brother should know, it's 26 October 1955.

The contrast between the responses in these examples would seem to suggest that even if there is a sense in which a parenthetical clause is an 'aside', there is also a sense in which an appropriate parenthetical aside such as (10) must have some relevance. It is this property, I believe, which distinguishes genuine parentheticals from interruptions such as the one in (11):

(11) My date of birth? It was – whoops I nearly dropped the phone – 26 October 1955.

This raises the question of how a parenthetical achieves relevance if it does not contribute to what Potts describes as the 'at-issue' content. As we shall see, even if we consider just a small number of parentheticals, it becomes clear that there is more than one answer to this question. Not only is there a variety of ways in which a parenthetical clause may contribute to relevance by affecting the interpretation of the host, but also there are parentheticals which, although connected to their hosts in some way, do not affect their interpretation. However, before we turn to the different ways in which parentheticals achieve relevance, let us return to Ifantidou's (2001) analysis of sentential adverbials, which provides a framework for describing their function.

2.2 multiple speech acts and the interpretation of evidential adverbials

Ifantidou's (1993, 2001) analysis of parenthetical sentential adverbials suggests a picture in which an utterance is a collection of sub-utterances or speech acts each of which may communicate a variety of explicatures.[3] For example, the utterance in (12) can be regarded as two sub-utterances – the host or basic utterance which communicates the explicatures in (13a) and the parenthetical utterance which communicates the explicature in (13b):

(12) Unfortunately, Jo has no intention of leaving.
(13)   a. The speaker believes that Jo has no intention of leaving.
           The speaker is saying that Jo has no intention of leaving.
           Jo has no intention of leaving.
       b. The speaker believes that it is unfortunate that Jo has no intention of leaving.

This conceptual analysis of parenthetical expressions and structures entails that they are constituents of propositional representations which enter into the inferential computations involved in satisfying the hearer's expectation of relevance. In this section I shall show, first, parenthetical sub-utterances can make a contribution to relevance even if they do not themselves yield positive cognitive effects, and second, there are cases in which one might say that a parenthetical sub-utterance yields cognitive effects of its own which are independent of those yielded by the host.

In fact, there are many utterances in discourse whose contribution to relevance does not lie in the cognitive effects they yield themselves. Consider, for example, the first segment of the sequence in (14):

(14) a. Remember saying that you thought Tom and Mary's marriage wouldn't last? b. Well, Jo saw him with a woman last night and it wasn't Mary.

It is not difficult to imagine these utterances being produced in a context which includes the assumption that the hearer does remember saying that Tom and Mary's marriage wouldn't last. But then, it seems, the speaker would not be understood to be communicating that she would find the proposition interpreted by the question relevant. Instead, it seems that the point of (14a) is to ensure that the intended interpretation is recovered from (14b) by ensuring that it is highly accessible for its interpretation. In other words, it seems that the point of the utterance is to ensure that the hearer is able to derive the intended cognitive effect from (14b) for a minimum cost in processing.

However, this sort of phenomenon contrasts with the evidential adverbials analyzed by Ifantidou and the parentheticals in (3)–(4) which communicate information about the way in which the explicit content of their hosts should be interpreted. (14a) contributes to the interpretation of (14b) only in the sense that it communicates an assumption which the speaker intends the hearer to use as a contextual premise which he combines with the host proposition for the derivation of a cognitive effect (in this case, strengthening). In other words, it functions in the same way as any utterance in discourse whose interpretation yields assumptions which are used as contextual premises in the interpretation of subsequent utterances (for further discussion, see Blass 1990; Blakemore 2001, 2002). The only difference is that it has no relevance beyond this.

Let us return, then, to the hearsay and evidential adverbials analyzed by Ifantidou (2001). According to her analysis, the so-called 'hearsay' adverbial in (15) should be analyzed as encoding a constituent of the higher-level explicature in (16b) which 'marks' the 'ground-floor' proposition in (16a) as being interpretively rather than descriptively used (Ifantidou 2001, 148):

(15)   Allegedly, John is a spy.
(16)   a. John is a spy.
        b. Someone alleges that John is a spy.

In other words, the relevance of the higher-level explicature in (16b) lies in the fact that it ensures that the hearer recognizes that the proposition in (16a) is a representation not of the speaker's thoughts, but of some other (unspecified) person, and therefore comes with a guarantee of faithfulness rather than truthfulness (cf. Sperber and Wilson 1995, 224–43; Wilson 2000).

The evidential adverbial *seemingly* in (17) encodes a constituent of the higher-level explicature in (18b) which makes it clear what the degree of the speaker's commitment to the 'ground-floor' proposition in (18a) is (Ifantidou 2001, 148, 152):

(17)   John is, seemingly, a spy.
(18)   a. John is a spy.
        b. It seems that John is a spy.

The point of communicating the explicature in (18b) is to ensure that any inference which the speaker makes from (18a) will yield a conclusion which inherits a reduced degree of strength.[4]

It might seem that sentence adverbials such as *apparently* or *evidently* are ambivalent between an evidential interpretation and a hearsay interpretation. Compare, for example, the utterances in (19) and (20):

(19)   [A has just attempted to fix an electrical appliance with disastrous results]
        A: I'm really sorry. I thought I knew how to fix it.
        B: Well, evidently, you didn't.
(20)   [Speaker has just finished a telephone call]
        Evidently, Sam is in love again.

However, as Ifantidou (2001) points out, the different interpretations of these utterances do not result from the ambiguity of the adverbial but result from the way in which the linguistically encoded logical form it contributes to is pragmatically enriched. For example, given the context described in (19), the hearer will derive (something like) the higher-level explicature in (21a), while the context in (20) will lead the hearer to derive (something like) the higher-level explicature in (21b):

(21) a. It is evident from the loud bang that the hearer did not know
          how to fix the appliance.
      b. It is evident from what Sam said to the speaker that he is in
          love again.

I return to this point in the final section.

As Ifantidou (2001) points out, so-called 'illocutionary' sentence
adverbials seem to play a different sort of role. Thus while the sentence
adverbials in (15) and (17) contribute explicatures which affect the interpretation of the proposition expressed by the host utterance, an adverbial
such as *unfortunately* 'simply expresses the speaker's attitude to the fact
that [the host proposition] is true' (Ifantidou 2001, 147). Ifantidou's
point is that it is not surprising that, in contrast with evidential and
hearsay adverbials, illocutionary adverbials are not perceived as making
an essential contribution to truth conditions. Thus while the illocutionary
adverbial does not fall under the scope of *although* in (22), the hearsay and
evidential adverbials are perceived as falling within its scope in (24) and
(26). The speaker of (22) is committed to the truth of the propositions
in (23), whereas the speaker of (24) is committed to the propositions in
(25), and the speaker of (26) to the propositions in (27) (examples are
from Ifantidou 2001):

(22) Although John is, unfortunately, a spy, he is very charming.
(23) John is a spy.
      It is unfortunate that John is a spy.
      Although John is a spy, he is very charming.

(24) Although John is, allegedly, a spy, he is very charming.
(25) It is alleged that John is a spy.
      Although it is alleged that John is a spy, he is very charming.

(26) Although John is, seemingly, a spy, he is very charming.
(27) It seems that John is a spy.
      Although it seems that John is a spy, he is very charming.

This is not to say that the higher-level explicatures understood to be
communicated by the use of illocutionary sentence adverbials yield no
cognitive effects at all. For example, the higher-level explicatures in (28)
communicated by *unfortunately* in (12) (repeated below) will achieve
relevance in a context which includes the assumption in (29):

(12) Unfortunately, Jo has no intention of leaving.
(28) The speaker believes that it is unfortunate that Jo has no intention of leaving.
(29) If the speaker believes that it is unfortunate that Jo has no intention of leaving, then she must not approve of the company's policy of sacking employees who do not leave voluntarily.

Ifantidou's argument is that any cognitive effects derived in this context derive from an explicature which simply expresses the speaker's attitude to the fact that the host proposition is true, whereas the explicatures communicated by the use of the hearsay and evidential adverbials in examples such as (22) and (24) affect the truth conditional status of their hosts.

2.3 the implicit communication of evidential information

In some cases, a parenthetical clause may combine with a sentential adverbial in order to support the point being made by the higher-level explicature that is communicated. Thus in (30) the *and*-parenthetical combines with the hearsay adverbial not only to emphasize the information it communicates about the interpretation of the host proposition – namely, that it is not a representation of the speaker's own thoughts – but also to provide more information about the source of the information represented by the host. Similarly, in (31) the *and*-parenthetical interacts with an evidential adverbial in order to emphasize the fact that the speaker should not be understood to be strongly committed to the truth of the host-proposition.

(30) Apparently, and this is only what I've read, their marriage is over.
(31) Perhaps, and this is only an idea, words don't actually encode concepts.

However, it seems that, since these parenthetical clauses are not themselves responsible for altering the truth conditional status of their hosts (by marking it as a case of interpretive use or by affecting the strength of the recommended degree of commitment) but only elaborate on the information already given, they will not be perceived as contributing to the truth conditions of the utterance in the same way as the sentence adverbials. In the case of (30) the hearer will have already hypothesized that the host proposition, once recovered, will be relevant as an interpretive representation before she interprets the parenthetical. Similarly, in (31), she will have already constructed the hypothesis that the proposition which is being explicated by the host is being put forward with a reduced degree of strength by the time she interprets the *and*-parenthetical.

In other cases, however, it seems that an *and*-parenthetical or an *as*-parenthetical may be used to implicitly communicate hearsay or evidential information about the host proposition without the help of a sentence adverbial. Recall (3):

(3)   What is obvious – and we have the reports – is that they were killed
      (from a discussion of the causes of the destruction of the population
      of Easter Island, BBC Radio 4, 26 August 2005).

The utterance in (3) was produced in the context of a discussion which would have led the hearer to understand that the reports referred to in the parenthetical clause were eyewitness reports. In this context, the speaker will be understood to be communicating the explicatures in (32):

(32) It is obvious that the population of Easter Island were killed.
      The speaker and his colleagues have eyewitness reports of what
      happened to the population of Easter Island.

Clearly, the proposition that the speaker and his colleagues have eyewitness reports of what happened to the Easter Island population does not entail anything about the strength of commitment that the hearer is expected to have towards the host proposition. The hearer is expected to derive an assumption about the strength of commitment that is being communicated on the basis of particular contextual assumptions about the eyewitness reports (e.g. that they constitute the best evidence that a historian might provide). In other words, this parenthetical does not *explicitly* communicate an assumption which provides information about the strength of the speaker's commitment to the host proposition, but communicates this information *implicitly*. Similar remarks can be made about the *as*-parenthetical in (4) which explicitly communicates the proposition that the host proposition resembles an assumption communicated by the eyewitness reports.

As Carston (2002, 128) observes in her discussion of similar examples, parenthetical clauses which implicitly communicate assumptions about the evidential status of the host proposition may achieve relevance in their own right. Consider the example in (33), which is a variation on Carston's example:

(33) As Chomsky says, the human language capacity cannot be explained
      by natural selection.

In explicitly communicating that the host proposition resembles one
which has been endorsed by Chomsky, the speaker might simply be
taken to be implicating that the host utterance does not represent a
thought for which she can claim responsibility. Alternatively, depending
on the reader's assumptions about the validity of Chomsky's views, it
might be interpreted as implicating that the host proposition is being
communicated with a high degree of strength. However, it is also possible
that it will interact with other assumptions for the derivation cognitive
effects which have nothing to do with the interpretation of the host
proposition at all – for example, that Chomsky will be committed to
certain other assumptions.

2.4 other interpretations of *as*- and *and*-parentheticals

My discussion of the implicit communication of evidential information
has focused on *as*- and *and*-parentheticals. In this section, I would like
to show, first, that *as*-parentheticals may be used to communicate other
sorts of information about the interpretation of their hosts, and second,
that there are *and*-parentheticals which play a different kind of role in
the interpretation of their hosts.

First, let us consider (34), an utterance which will actually occur later
in this section:

(34) As we have seen in example (14) (repeated below), an utterance may
      achieve relevance in virtue of contributing a contextual assumption
      which the hearer is expected to use in the derivation of the implicit
      content of the following utterance:

By explicitly communicating that the host proposition is a representation of a proposition which has already been established (by the example
cited), I can be understood to be implicating that the host proposition is
relevant only in virtue of resembling an assumption which the reader/
hearer is expected to have in memory. In other words, I will be understood
to be communicating that the host proposition is relevant in virtue of the
role that it is expected to play as a contextual assumption for the interpretation of subsequent utterances. This means that the parenthetical
achieves relevance by virtue of communicating information about how
the host achieves cognitive effects. The role of the parenthetical in (35)
might be understood in similar terms; however, in this case the point of

the parenthetical utterance seems to be to communicate that the host is relevant by strengthening an assumption already held by the speaker:

(35) (Just) as I predicted/thought, she's given me another pair of socks.

Although the *as-* and *and-*parentheticals discussed so far play a role in the process of interpreting the proposition expressed by their host utterances (whether by communicating information about what kind of commitment the speaker has towards it or by communicating information about how it achieves relevance), none of them actually contribute to the content of the host-proposition itself. However, it seems that in certain cases an *and-*parenthetical may achieve relevance by contributing to the proposition that is understood to be expressed by the host. Consider (36) (from Blakemore 2005):

(36) You wouldn't believe what happened when Kevin and I were at the Kro Bar tonight. We were out in the garden and a big rat – and I mean BIG rat – ran out from under our table.

It seems that the point of the parenthetical here is to ensure that the interpretation of the host clause recovered by the hearer is a faithful representation of the speaker's thoughts. Thus the speaker may have begun her utterance assuming that the hearer will understand the complex concept encoded by *big rat* to be such that it will yield the sort of effects that are intended – e.g. disgust, horror. However, in disrupting the utterance in this way, the speaker is indicating that whatever concept the hearer has recovered from the utterance of *big rat*, it is not the one which the speaker intended to communicate.

The way in which the parenthetical achieves this effect can be explained in terms of Carston's (2002) account of the pragmatics of on-line concept construction. The hearer will have been expected to have used her contextual assumptions about rats to derive an ad hoc concept BIG FOR A RAT* from the conceptual template encoded by *big*, but on processing the parenthetical will search her contextual assumptions further in order to derive an enriched concept (BIG FOR A RAT**) which is a more faithful representation of the sort of rat that the speaker was recalling (i.e. something bigger than any rat she has seen).[5]

As we have seen in example (14) (repeated below), an utterance may achieve relevance in virtue of contributing a contextual assumption which the hearer is expected to use in the derivation of the implicit content of the following utterance:

(14) a. Remember saying that you thought Tom and Mary's marriage wouldn't last? b. Well, Jo saw him with a woman last night and it wasn't Mary.

The same sort of role may be played by an *and*-parenthetical. The host proposition in (37) is a representation of an utterance in a letter that the author had received:[6]

(37) A helicopter, a HELICOPTER – and here was me who'd never even flown in an ordinary plane – would come and pick me up ... (from *Stargazing: memoirs of a young lighthouse keeper*, read on BBC Radio 4, originally cited in Blakemore 2005).

The author's aim in this passage is not simply to communicate the contents of the letter he is talking about, but also to enable the hearer to share his reaction to the letter as he read it. Thus the repetition of *helicopter* (which in this reading was produced with emphatic stress) is intended to encourage the hearer to explore his/her own contextual assumptions further in order to derive (weak) implicatures which capture the excitement of the prospect of a helicopter ride.[7] However, the parenthetical refines this search in the sense that it provides a contextual premise which ensures that these implicatures will include assumptions about the excitement of flying in a helicopter for someone who has never flown in any kind of plane at all.

In contrast with the *as*-parenthetical in (35), the parenthetical in (37) does not communicate information about the sort of cognitive effects the hearer is expected to derive, but simply contributes to the cognitive effects derived from the host by providing a contextual assumption which a hearer who is assuming optimal relevance will use in interpretation. It is not clear whether one would classify a parenthetical which plays this sort of role as a constraint or comment. However, what we call such a parenthetical is not the issue. The point of this (limited) survey of the functions of parenthetical clauses was to show that they may achieve relevance by affecting both the explicit content and the implicit content of the host.[8] The important questions are: first, which aspect of interpretation is the parenthetical contributing to, and, second, how does it make this contribution.

3. constraints and procedures

I began this chapter with the observation that the term 'constraint' has been used by theorists from a variety of theoretical frameworks to describe phenomena which do not necessarily fall into a single category. In particular, the term 'constraint' (along with related descriptions of expressions as 'guiding the hearer towards an interpretation', 'indicating how an utterance is to be interpreted') has been used in the analysis of expressions which would be analyzed within relevance theory as falling on both sides of the divide between conceptual and procedural meaning. It might seem that, from the point of view of those approaches which classify linguistically encoded meaning according to whether it does or does not contribute to truth conditions, there is no issue here: the description of these expressions and constructions as constraints on interpretation simply reflects the fact that they are non truth conditional. However, as Ifantidou (2001) has shown, some expressions which have been treated as constraints on interpretation do in fact affect the truth conditions of the utterances that fall within their scope.

The speech act theoretic distinction between truth conditional and non truth conditional meaning is sometimes represented as a distinction between linguistic meaning which contributes to propositional content and linguistic meaning which contributes to pragmatic interpretation.[9] However, according to relevance theory *all* linguistic meaning provides an input to pragmatic interpretation, including that which contributes to what is traditionally recognized as the propositional content of utterances. The fact that linguistic encoding provides an input to pragmatic inference means that either expressions encode information about the conceptual representations which take part in inferential computations (conceptual meaning) or they encode information about the inferential procedures which yield conceptual representations (procedural meaning). As Sperber and Wilson (1995) and Carston (2002) have shown, pragmatic inference is involved in both the derivation of explicit content (explicatures) and the derivation of implicit content (implicatures). This means that expressions which encode information about pragmatic inference are not restricted to expressions which encode procedures for the derivation of implicit content, as is suggested in my early work on procedural meaning (Blakemore 1987), but also may include expressions which encode procedures for the derivation of explicit content. In particular, it has been argued that expressions which have been analyzed as encoding procedures for the derivation of explicit content include expressions which encode procedures for the recovery of higher-level explicatures which provide illocutionary or evidential information about lower-level or 'ground-floor' explicatures communicated by the utterances that contain them. This would seem to suggest that we need to be able to provide criteria for distinguishing them from the sort of expressions discussed in section 2.2.[10]

Wilson and Sperber (1993) have identified a number of properties of conceptual sentence adverbials which are not shared by expressions which encode procedures. As Iten (2005) has pointed out, these provide a negative characterization of procedural encoding so that we end up knowing more about what procedural encoding is not than what it is. Nevertheless, they have provided a means of distinguishing cases of procedural encoding from cases of conceptual encoding. For example, Ifantidou (2001) has used them as a diagnostic for identifying the Modern Greek particle *taha* as a case of procedural rather than conceptual encoding. Thus she argues that, although *taha* can be translated by the English conceptual adverbials *apparently* or *supposedly*, the Greek particle must be analyzed as encoding a procedure for the recovery of a higher-level explicature. As we will see, this explicature may either communicate the information that the ground-floor proposition is hearsay or it may communicate information about the strength of the evidence that the speaker has for its truth. However, it seems that Ifantidou undermines her case for a procedural analysis of *taha* by arguing that its apparent ambiguity between a hearsay and an evidential interpretation can be explained in exactly the same way as the apparent ambiguity of the English conceptual adverbials *apparently* and *evidently* (see above). My point here will not be that Ifantidou is wrong to argue that *taha* is procedural, but rather that, if it does encode a procedure rather than a concept, then it cannot be treated in terms which assume that it is a constituent of a representation which undergoes inferential computations. Its apparent ambiguity must have another sort of explanation. Moreover, I hope to show that this explanation leads us to a property which is not a property of those expressions which encode concepts, but *is* a property of those expressions which encode procedures.

First, then, let us see how Ifantidou applies Wilson and Sperber's diagnostics for procedural encoding to utterances containing *taha*. As Wilson and Sperber (1993) argue, a speaker's use of a conceptual sentence adverbial may lay herself open to charges of untruthfulness. Consider the following:

(38) A: Unfortunately, Jo is leaving us today.
      B: Come on, tell us the truth. You don't think it's unfortunate at all. You can't wait to get rid of her.

According to Ifantidou, the fact that Mary's objection to John's utterance in (39) is inappropriate suggests that *taha* cannot be analyzed as encoding a concept:

(39) John: Taha itan arosti
               was-3D ill
       'Apparently/She says that she was ill'
       Mary: * Then les   alithia
               do not tell-2SG truth
               Tin ida   dimera k' edihne   mia hara
               her saw-1-SG today and seemed-3SG fine (Ifantidou 2001, 190)

She supports this argument by appealing to another property which Wilson and Sperber (1993) argue distinguishes conceptual encoding from procedural encoding, namely, that whereas conceptual adverbials can be constituents of a semantically complex phrase, procedural expressions cannot combine with other expressions in this way. Thus although *taha* and adverbial *ipothetika* can both be translated as *supposedly*, only *ipothetika* can undergo regular compositional rules:

(40) Ine ohi mono ipothetika plousios, alla pragmatika
       is not   only supposedly rich   but truly so
(41) *Ine ohi mono taha plousios, alla pragmatika
       is not   only taha rich   but truly so (Ifantidou 2001, 191)

   Finally, let us turn to the property of procedural encoding which seems to raise a problem for Ifantidou's analysis of *taha*. As I have already noted, while some uses of *taha* seem to lead a hearer to a hearsay interpretation, others seem to result in an evidential interpretation. Thus Ifantidou claims that the utterance in (42) can be interpreted either as (43a) (the hearsay interpretation) or as (43b) (the evidential interpretation):

(42) O Yiannis itan taha arostos
       the John   was   ill
(43) a It is said that John is ill.
       b. It seems to the speaker that John is ill.

The question is how this apparent ambiguity should be explained.
   As Wilson and Sperber (1993) have pointed out, expressions which have been analyzed as encoding procedural meaning are characteristically very difficult to translate or to paraphrase. Thus, whereas it is

relatively straightforward to establish whether two expressions which encode concepts are synonymous, it is considerably more difficult (if not impossible) to establish whether two apparently related procedural discourse connectives (e.g. *but* and *however* or Japanese *dakara* and *sorede*) are synonymous without checking their intersubstitutability in all contexts of use. Similarly, it is considerably more difficult to say whether a procedural discourse connective from one language (e.g. Japanese *dakara*) is appropriately translated by one from another language (e.g. English *so*) without testing their intersubstitutability in all contexts. The explanation for this difference, argue Wilson and Sperber, lies in the distinction between procedures and concepts: 'conceptual representations can be brought to consciousness: procedures cannot' (Wilson and Sperber 1993, 16).

Blass' (1990) analysis of the Sissala hearsay particle *ré* shows that this point would also seem to apply to expressions which encode procedures for constructing higher-level explicatures. Thus, depending on its context of use, *ré* can be used as a complementiser to mark direct or indirect speech, in constructions containing verbs of propositional attitude, in questions and their answers, in utterances which express an attitude (e.g. of dissociation) towards what is said, to echo thoughts and beliefs of people in general, and to mark irony. It would be difficult to capture all of these uses in analysis which treated *ré* as encoding a particular concept. On the other hand, if *ré* is analyzed as encoding a *constraint* on the higher-level explicature which a hearer is expected to construct on a particular occasion, say, that it must communicate the information that the 'ground-floor' proposition is relevant as an interpretation of a thought, then we can account for the wide range of contexts in which it can be used.

For instance, in a particular context the effect of imposing the constraint encoded by *ré* may be a higher-level explicature which endorses a proposition which is attributed to people in general. However, in another context, it may be an explicature in which the proposition expressed is attributed to a particular person, or an explicature which communicates an attitude of dissociation towards the thought which is being interpreted. Blass' point is that there is no constituent of any of these explicatures which is encoded by *ré*, but that all of them are consistent with the constraint it encodes. In other words, while the constraint encoded by *ré* is present at the level of linguistically encoded semantic representation, it simply drops out of the picture once it has served its purpose and the hearer has recovered what she takes to be the higher-level explicature intended by the speaker in that context.

Now let us return to Ifantidou's (2001) example in (42) and its two interpretations in (43). If, as Ifantidou argues, *taha* does encode a procedure rather than a concept, then one might expect that its apparent ambiguity could be explained in the same way as Blass (1990) has explained the apparent ambiguity of *ré*. That is, in some contexts the effect of imposing the constraint will result in an explicature of the form in (44a), while in others it results in an explicature of the form in (44b):

(44) a. It is evident from what the speaker has seen that *P*.
     b. It is evident from what X has said that *P*.

However, instead, Ifantidou compares this phenomenon to the sort of ambivalence in interpretation one finds in utterances containing the *conceptual* sentence adverbials *apparently* and *evidently*. She explained this ambivalence in terms of the way in which the conceptual constituents encoded by these expressions are *enriched*. Thus she argues that '*taha* may undergo enrichment to mean either "X says that ...." or "it seems to the speaker that ...."' (Infantidou 2001, 192).

If *taha* does indeed encode a procedure for the construction of a conceptual representation, then there cannot be a basis for this analogy between *taha* and conceptual adverbials such as *evidently* and *apparently*. For, by definition, an expression which encodes a procedure does not encode a constituent of a representation which undergoes inferential enrichment. If *taha* encodes procedure, then it would interact with the context by encoding a constraint on the inferential procedures involved in the derivation of higher-level explicatures and the hearer would be expected to derive an explicature which is consistent with this constraint. As we have seen in the examples containing *ré*, this constraint can be satisfied in different ways in different contexts.

In contrast, an expression which encodes conceptual information interacts with the context only in the sense that it contributes to a semantic representation which is enriched through pragmatically constrained inference for the recovery of a conceptual representation. It does not itself encode any information about the direction these enrichment processes must take: the conceptual representation recovered will depend on the context and the principle of relevance. This point can also be illustrated by comparing a parenthetical which communicates an assumption whose relevance lies in the role it plays in the derivation of the implicatures from the host with an expression which encodes a procedure for the derivation of implicatures. As we have seen, the point of the *as*-parenthetical in (35) could be understood to lie in the implicitly communicated assumption that the host achieves relevance by strengthening an assumption already held by the speaker:

(35) (Just) as I predicted/thought, she's given me another pair of socks.

As (e.g.) Blass (1990) has shown, there are discourse markers which indicate that the utterance that contains them achieves relevance by strengthening an existing assumption, for example, *indeed* in (45):

(45) A: It's a lovely day. B: It is, indeed.

However, whereas the interpretation of the proposition which is understood to be communicated by the parenthetical in (35) depends on the context and the principle of relevance, the hearer of (45B) takes an inferential route which results in a strengthened assumption because of information which is encoded by *indeed*.

In conclusion, in contrast with the expressions that have been analyzed in procedural terms, the conceptual parenthetical expressions and constructions considered in this chapter do not themselves *encode* constraints on interpretation. What they encode is simply a constituent of the conceptual representation which achieves relevance in virtue of the information it provides about the interpretation of their hosts. If one wants to use the word 'constraint' to describe the phenomena in section 2 of this chapter, then one must recognize that in contrast with the constraints encoded by expressions and structures which have been analyzed in procedural terms, these are constraints which are imposed at the level of conceptual representation.

notes

1. Bach (1999) dismisses the conceptual-procedural distinction on the grounds that anything a speaker says constrains the inferential phase of the comprehension process. However, as we shall see, this misses the point that conceptual encoding only constrains interpretation in the sense that the encoded concepts must appear in the explicature(s) recovered: in contrast with the expressions which encode procedures, expressions which encode concepts do not provide any information about the inferential processes which must take place for the hearer to recover an explicature from the (often) very skeletal clue provided by the encoded logical form. This point will be developed in section 3. See Blakemore (2002, 78–9) and Hall (2007) for further discussion.

2. Potts (2005) sees the 'on the side' nature of (e.g.) *as*-parentheticals as a consequence of the one-way dependency which, he claims, generally holds between the parenthetical and the host: the logical form must be saturated by

something from the 'at-issue' host proposition. He does not want to make this a definitional property, however, because there are expressions which contribute conventional implicatures but which arrive fully saturated. However, as I have shown (Blakemore 2006), there are examples of parenthetical utterances whose logical forms have unsaturated gaps but which do not receive their interpretation from the host proposition.

3. This multiple utterance approach is derived from speech act theoretic approaches to non-truth conditional parenthetical phenomena. See Grice's (1989) analysis of expressions such as *on the other hand*, Hand (1993), Urmson (1960). See Blakemore (1990/1991) for a multiple utterance analysis of performatives within a relevance-theoretic framework.

4. It seems that Potts (2005, 92) is making a similar point when he distinguishes those constructions described as supplements which give rise to conventional implicatures from those which, although they meet the intuitive syntactic and intonational conditions for supplement-hood, cannot be classified as conventional implicature contributors because they impact on the 'at issue' content. Potts cites (i) and (ii) as examples of the latter type of construction:

(i)   Max, it seems, is a Martian.
(ii)   Max is a Martian, isn't he?

Ifantidou (2001) would argue that the fact that *it seems* in (i) affects the 'at issue' content of its host follows from its evidential function. Like *seemingly* in (17), it encodes a constituent of a higher-level explicature which communicates the degree of the speaker's commitment to the 'ground-floor' proposition. The communication of this explicature ensures that any inference the speaker makes from the 'ground-floor' proposition will yield a conclusion which inherits a reduced degree of strength.

It is possible that the fact that the tag in (ii) affects the 'at issue' content of the host follows from the role which it plays in communicating that this content is being questioned. Within relevance theory, interrogatives are analyzed in terms of interpretative use: they are relevant as interpretations of answers which the speaker believes to be relevant (see Sperber and Wilson 1995, 253–4). This means that the tag marks the 'ground-floor' proposition in (ii) as being interpretively (rather than descriptively) used.

5. (a) This analysis departs from the one given in Blakemore (2005). For further discussion of the pragmatics of on-line concept construction, see Carston (2002, 320–75).

   (b) Kavalova (2005) classifies this type of example as a 'sentence-oriented' parenthetical which has a 'non-propositional emphatic effect'. However, it seems that this suggests that the analysis I have given in terms of on-line concept construction not only explains how this effect is achieved, but also explains the location of the parenthetical in the host structure.

6. The following analysis is based on the one given in Blakemore (2005). Kavalova (2005) also draws attention to *and*-parentheticals which provide backgrounded information.

7. For further discussion of the emphatic effects of repetition, see Sperber and Wilson (1995, 219–22).

8. (a) The analyses sketched here have yet to be applied to other types of parenthetical structures (e.g. appositive NPs and appositive relative clauses).

    (b) This is not to say that the relevance of all parenthetical clauses lies in the way they affect the interpretation of their hosts. As I have argued (Blakemore 2006) so-called 'discourse' parentheticals such as the one in (i) cannot be said to comment on the interpretation of their hosts, but are related to their hosts in the same way as the (a) segment is related to the (b) segment in (ii):

        (i) The driver of Al-Kindi's only remaining ambulance – the other three had been stolen or looted – had disappeared. So the dangerously ill Mr Khassem was bundled into a clapped out rust bitten Moskavivh 408. (The *Independent* 16 May. First cited in Blakemore 2005).

        (ii) (a) There was only one ambulance remaining in the city. (b) The others had been stolen or looted.

    The parenthetical is relevant as an answer to a question which the speaker assumes is raised by the subject NP of the host. In contrast with the parenthetical clauses that are the focus of this chapter, it does not contribute to the interpretation that the speaker expects the hearer to derive from the host.

9. See, for example, Fraser (1996).

10. See for example, Derbyshire (1979), Blass (1990), Itani (1998) and Ifantidou (2001) for discussion of hearsay particles, and Wilson and Sperber (1988, 1993) and Clark (1991) for a discussion of illocutionary force markers.

references

Bach, K. (1999). 'The myth of conventional implicature'. *Linguistics and Philosophy* 22: 367–421.

Blakemore, D. (1987). *Semantic Constraints on Relevance*. Oxford: Blackwell.

— (1990/1991). 'Performatives and parentheticals'. *Proceedings of the Aristotelian Society* XCI 3. 197–213.

— (2001). 'Discourse and relevance theory'. In D. Schiffrin et al (eds). *Handbook of Discourse Analysis*. Oxford: Blackwell. 100–18.

— (2002). *Relevance and Linguistic Meaning: the semantics and pragmatics of discourse markers*. Cambridge: Cambridge University Press.

— (2005). '*and*-parentheticals'. *Journal of Pragmatics* 37: 1165–81.

— (2006). 'Divisions of labour: the analysis of parentheticals'. *Lingua* 116: 1670–87.

Blass, R. (1990). *Relevance Relations in Discourse*. Cambridge: Cambridge University Press.

Carston, R. (2002). *Thoughts and Utterances: the pragmatics of explicit communication*. Oxford: Blackwell.

Clark, B. (1991). 'Relevance Theory and the Semantics of non-declaratives'. University of London PhD dissertation.

Derbyshire, D. (1979). *Hixkaryana*. Lingua Descriptive Series 1. Amsterdam: Elsevier.

Fraser, B. (1996). 'Pragmatic markers'. *Pragmatics* 6.2.

Grice, H.P. (1989). *Studies in the Way of Words*. Cambridge, Mass: Harvard University Press.

Hall, A. (2007). 'Do discourse connectives encode concepts or procedures?' *Lingua* 117.1: 149–74.

Hand, M. (1993). 'Parataxis and parentheticals'. *Linguistics and Philosophy* 16: 495–507.

Ifantidou, E. (1993). 'Sentential adverbs and relevance'. *Lingua* 90: 69–90.

— (2001). *Evidentials and Relevance*. Amsterdam: John Benjamins.

Itani, R. (1998). 'A relevance-based analysis of hearsay particles: with special reference to the Japanese sentence-final particle "tte"'. In R. Carston and S. Uchida (eds). *Relevance Theory: applications and implications*. Amsterdam: John Benjamins. 47–68.

Iten, C. (2005). *Linguistic Meaning, Truth Conditions and Relevance*. Basingstoke: Palgrave Macmillan.

Kavalova, Y. (2005). 'Parenthetical and-clauses'. Paper delivered at PG Conference in Linguistics, University of Oxford.

Potts, C. (2003). 'Conventional implicatures, a distinguished class of meanings'. In G. Ramchand and C. Reiss (eds). *The Oxford Handbook of Linguistic Interfaces*. Oxford: Oxford University Press.

— (2005). *The Logic of Conventional Implicatures*. Oxford: Oxford University Press.

Sperber, D. and D. Wilson (1995). *Relevance: communication and cognition*. 2 edn. Oxford: Blackwell.

Urmson, J.O. (1960). 'Parenthetical verbs'. In A. Flew (ed.). *Essays in Conceptual Analysis*. London: Macmillan. 192–212.

Wilson, D. (2000). 'Metarepresentation in linguistic communication'. In D. Sperber (ed.). *Metarepresentation*. Oxford: Oxford University Press. 411–48.

Wilson, D. and D. Sperber (1988). 'Mood and the analysis of non-declarative sentences'. In J. Dancy, J. Moravcsik, and C. Taylor (eds). *Human Agency: language, duty and valence*. Stanford, CA: Stanford University Press. 71–101.

— (1993). 'Linguistic form and relevance'. *Lingua* 90: 1–25.

5
optimality theoretic pragmatics and the explicature/implicature distinction

reinhard blutner

1. introduction

Communication is not a simple matter of *coding* and *decoding* as certain Cartesian theories of language have claimed. Relevance theory (RT) carefully argues that inference is the basis of all communication, and of all aspects of linguistic communication (Sperber and Wilson 1986). Such inferences conform to certain expectations that are created by communication. The representatives of RT are followers of Grice to the extent that they stress that these expectations play a key role in utterance interpretation and are therefore constitutive of the whole interpretation process. Unlike Grice, however, they don't postulate conversational 'maxims' for providing the standards of rational discourse. Instead, they claim that interpretation is primarily a cognitive phenomenon which depends on how humans process information. The contract-like dimension of human communication is thus external to the interpretation mechanism and is not seen as a consequence of the nature of human cognition.

The identification of explicatures and implicatures as two aspects of the pragmatic dimension of natural language comprehension is an important insight of RT (Sperber and Wilson 1986; Carston 2002, 2004). The former are developments of the logical forms that are encoded by the sentence uttered and determine the propositional content of the utterance (truth-conditional pragmatics); the latter conform to expectations that exploit our encyclopaedic knowledge in order to derive more global, non truth-functional aspects of interpretation. The idea that the encoded semantic system of language is not fully propositional, that is, it is not sufficient for determining propositional content (literal interpretation) crucially deviates from the view of Grice, who identifies the truth-conditional content of an utterance ('what is said') with its encoded sentence meaning. I will take this view of RT as basically correct.

In this chapter I will take the RT stance of seeing NL interpretation as a cognitive phenomenon and thus considering the basic principles of communication as a consequence of the nature of human cognition. However, I will argue that this view does not necessarily conflict with the idea that pragmatic inferences[1] are the product of rational behaviour between cooperative interlocutors. Going back to Zipf (1949), I will show that global, rationalist principles of communication conform to a *diachronic* view of language – describing the forces that direct language change. On the other hand, it is obvious that a cognitive theory has to account for the incremental, automatic mechanism of utterance interpretation, and thus requires the analysis of the actual realization of explicatures/implicatures. There is a connection between the diachronic and the synchronic view, between the global forces that generally direct communication and the actual, automatized inferences that evolve from these forces. In the following I will use the term *fossilization* in order to refer to this relationship. A theory of fossilization describes how pragmatic inferences become automatized and form part of an efficient cognitive system that makes fast on-line interpretation of utterances possible.

Accepting the dualism between a diachronic view and a synchronic view invites us to see the synchronic account as informed by the diachronic account. We should try to explain particular synchronic patterns of behaviour by the pragmatic forces that drive language change. If the distinction between implicatures and explicatures is a crucial distinction in actual language interpretation, then it is important to ask if this distinction can be grounded in these fundamental diachronic forces. I think there is a positive answer to this question: the global, rational view behind these diachronic forces can explain which pragmatic inferences behave like explicatures or implicatures, respectively.

This view contrasts with the view of RT, which rests on the stipulation of two distinct cognitive strategies/styles: one for the calculation of explicatures and the other for the calculation of implicatures. Unfortunately, the stipulation does not *explain* the fundamental distinction, and RT does not give any hints how to overcome this explanatory problem. Since explicatures are derived by pragmatic inference as much as implicatures, the discrimination cannot be derived from the nature of the inferential mechanism.

In this chapter I will propose a rational foundation of the distinction based on basic principles of cultural evolution (a Zipfean/neo-Gricean theory of balancing pragmatic forces). However, this is not enough from the perspective of Cognitive Science. It further needs a theory that explains the actual interpretation process – an on-line account of processing explicatures and implicatures. The theory of fossilization is proposed for filling in this gap.

The theoretical framework I adopt is optimality theoretic pragmatics (Blutner 2000; Hendriks and de Hoop 2001; Blutner and Zeevat 2004; Blutner, de Hoop, and Hendriks 2005). I will show that this framework can be used both for giving an appropriate reconstruction of the implicature/explicature distinction and also for developing the idea of fossilization. Unfortunately, the important phenomenological distinction between explicature and implicature was completely ignored in the early papers on OT pragmatics and also later the importance of the distinction was marginalized (but see the discussion in Blutner et al 2005). The main reason for this weakness was that the proponents of OT pragmatics seldom considered *complex* sentences in calculating invited inferences but were mainly concerned with relatively simple sentences. As a matter of fact, the different behaviour of implicatures and explicatures can best be studied in the context of complex sentences. Hence, an examination of pragmatic inferences in complex sentences is essential. Gazdar (1979) pioneered this, and recently, Chierchia (2004) published a paper that has revitalized the investigation of invited inferences in complex sentences.

In the next section, I will examine the RT distinction between implicatures and explicatures, and I will redefine the distinction in order to find a more adequate basis for theoretical analysis. Needless to say, I don't intend to violate the *spirit* of RT with this clarification. I think my implementation of the distinction fits better with the examples provided by the proponents of RT themselves for illustrating the distinction. Section 3 gives a concise introduction into OT pragmatics. Using ideas of Mattausch (2004) and others, I will further show what a model of fossilization might look like. In section 4 I investigate some examples that provide the empirical basis for my proposed distinction between implicatures and explicatures, and I will sketch how my neo-Gricean view can account for the explicature/implicature distinction. In section 5, finally, I will discuss the consequences of the proposed theory for experimental pragmatics and I will draw some general conclusions.

2. the distinction between explicatures and implicatures

It is not a simple task to give a definition of the explicature/implicature distinction. The school of 'radical pragmatics' (cf. Cole 1981) does not make the distinction, and from the perspective of a basically Gricean mechanism of pragmatic strengthening, the distinction appears not to be significant. As mentioned already, for RT the distinction is essential because RT crucially departs from Grice in that it sees linguistically encoded semantic information as not sufficient for determining the propositional content of an utterance. This relates to RT's underdeterminacy thesis, which gives the pragmatic component a much greater role in deriving communicated assumptions. Hence, it is not surprising that RT comes up with a new classification of pragmatically communicated assumptions. In the words of Carston (2003):

> There are two types of communicated assumptions on the relevance-theoretic account: explicatures and implicatures. An 'explicature' is a propositional form communicated by an utterance which is pragmatically constructed on the basis of the propositional schema or template (logical form) that the utterance encodes; its content is an amalgam of linguistically decoded material and pragmatically inferred material. An 'implicature' is any other propositional form communicated by an utterance; its content consists of wholly pragmatically inferred matter (see Sperber and Wilson 1986, 182). So the explicature/implicature distinction is a derivational distinction and, by definition, it arises only for verbal (or, more generally, code-based) ostensive communication. (9)

As Burton-Roberts (2005) points out, in RT, an implicature is defined negatively – as a communicated assumption that is not an explicature. This contrasts with the original definition of Sperber and Wilson (1986) who have a similar description for explicatures like Carston (2003) but see implicatures as assumptions constructed by 'developing assumption schemas retrieved from encyclopaedic memory' (Sperber and Wilson 1986, 181). Whereas the early Sperber/Wilson definition contrasts the development of (underspecified) *logical forms* with the development of *encyclopaedic assumptions*, the position of Carston (2003) is to contrast the *development* of a linguistically encoded logical form with other ways of deriving communicated assumptions. The definition of Sperber and Wilson (1986) is clearer than the definition of Carston (2003) because it contrasts theoretical concepts that are simpler to understand than the contrasts in Carston's definition. This has to do with the availability of cognitive-linguistic theories which explain the distinction between logical forms and encyclopaedic assumptions. However, there is – so far as I can see – no theory that explains the distinction between communicated assumptions derived by development and communicated assumptions derived by other means. Unfortunately, the problem with the definition of Sperber and Wilson (1986) is that it conflicts with the intuitive classification of several *clear cases*.

(1) John had a drink ⇝ John had an alcoholic drink.
(2) Some students wrote an essay ⇝ not all students wrote an essay.

(1) is considered a clear instance of an explicature (free enrichment) though it includes reference to the encyclopaedia. Conversely, (2) is a clear instance of an implicature (scalar implicature) though it does not include reference to the encyclopaedia (instead it has a metalinguistic character – it requires reference to the lexicon for accessing quantifier alternatives in the language under discussion). Hence, we are in trouble with the earlier definition and are left with the second one. But the problem is that neither Carston nor anybody else offers a definition of 'development'. In the words of Burton-Roberts (2005): '"Development" is a black hole at the centre of the theory' (397).

In cases like this, where there is no proper definition, it is a good strategy to look for some empirical tests that help to clarify the situation and which might be used to operationalize the distinction. Fortunately, there are such tests, and among the candidates that have been proposed are (i) the independency principle (Recanati 1989), (ii) the scope embedding test (Recanati 1989; Carston 2002), and (iii) a test based on cancellability (e.g. Burton-Roberts 2005). I will not go into an explanation of the independency principle since it has been rejected as a useful test by most authors (cf. Carston 2002). The scope embedding test, however, has been considered useful by many authors. Here is a concise presentation of this criterion called scope principle by Recanati (1989):

> Scope principle: A pragmatically determined aspect of meaning is part of what is said (and therefore, not a conversational implicature), if – and perhaps only if – it falls within the scope of logical operators such as negation and conditionals. (Carston 2002, 191)

Obviously, this principle is related to Green's 'Embedded Implicature Hypothesis' (EIH):

EIH: If assertion of a sentence S conveys the implicatum that p with nearly universal regularity, then when S is embedded the content that is usually understood to be embedded for semantic purposes is the proposition S&p. (Green 1998, 77)

We can see an 'implicatum' that regularly satisfies EIH as an explicature and an 'implicatum' that has systematic violations of EIH as an implicature. Carston considers the scope principle and EIH as a helpful tool 'though it should probably not be given the status of a principle' (Carston 2002, 195).[2]

One property that is crucially discussed in connection with the implicature/explicature distinction is cancellability. Carston argues that cancellability cannot be a criterion that distinguishes explicature from implicatures: 'it is pragmatic inference quite generally that is cancellable/defeasible' (Carston 2002, 138). Hence, both explicatures and implicatures are cancellable and this property cannot distinguish them. Burton-Roberts rejects the idea of explicatures that are cancellable because, in RT, explicatures are constitutive of the truth-conditional content of an utterance (satisfying EIH): 'Cancellable explicature, then is a logical impossibility in Carston's own terms' (Burton-Roberts 2005, 401). I think the argument is convincing, and this might suggest that we can take cancellability as the criterion we are looking for. Unfortunately, cancellation is not only difficult to distinguish from *clarification* (as discussed by Burton-Roberts) but also from *contextual change*. With regard to the latter point, van Kuppevelt (1996) has carefully argued that scalar implicatures are topic-dependent, that is, they are dependent on the question being asked in a particular conversational setting.[3] Consider the following example as discussed by van Rooy (2006):

(3)   a. Question: Who has 2 children?
      b. Answer: John has 2 children.
      c. John doesn't have more than 2 children.

In this case, the implicature (3c) does not even arise. This is different from the following situation where the question is focusing on the number of children:

(4)   a. Question: How many children has John?
      b. Answer: John has 2 children.
      c. John doesn't have more than 2 children.

In this case the implicature (4c) arises; however, it cannot be cancelled. Van Kuppevelt (1996) argues that the 'phenomenon of cancellation' that is normally discussed in connection with scalar implicatures has nothing to do with genuine cancellation; instead it has to do with contextual change. In this sense scalar implicatures are *particularized* conversational implicatures. Obviously, the topic-dependency of scalar implicatures is not restricted to numerals but also holds in connection with the Q-implicature triggered by 'or' (cf. van Rooy 2006). The consequence of this finding is that cancellability is ruled out as a criterion that distinguishes explicatures from implicatures. Hence we are left with EIH as the crucial test. This suggests we should take the different projection properties of explicatures and implicatures as defining the distinction.

Since explicatures are derived by pragmatic inference as much as implicatures, RT has to stipulate two distinct cognitive strategies/styles in order to explain the difference between explicatures and implicatures. One strategy/style explains the cognitive mechanism of *developing* a logical form, the other deals with other forms of deriving pragmatic assumptions. In contrast, the present view is neo-Gricean in nature and tries to explain pragmatic inferences as the product of rational behaviour between cooperative interlocutors. I claim that this global account makes it possible to derive the different projection behaviour of explicatures and implicatures and gives, moreover, a detailed description of the embedding contexts where even implicatures project with nearly universal regularity. However, as already mentioned there is a problem with such a global account because it does not apply to the actual, on-line interpretation process. Therefore, we propose to add a theory of fossilization for filling in this gap. We will argue in the following section that this approach relates to a general theory of cultural learning.

3. pragmatics in optimality theory

In this section I will give a concise, but informal introduction into optimality theoretic pragmatics. For a detailed discussion the reader is referred to original literature (e.g. Blutner and Zeevat 2004; Blutner et al 2005). Not surprisingly, the idea of optimization was present in the pragmatic enterprise from the very beginning. Much more than in other linguistic fields, optimality scenarios are present in most lines of thinking: Zipf's (1949) balancing between effect and effort, the Gricean conversational maxims (Grice 1975), Ducrot's argumentative view of language use (Ducrot 1980), the principle of optimal relevance in relevance theory (Sperber and Wilson 1986). Interestingly, more than one optimization procedure is involved in some of these accounts. For instance, the neo-

Gricean framework assumes two countervailing optimization principles called Q and I Principle (Atlas and Levinson 1981; Horn 1984, who writes R instead of I).

Optimality Theory (OT) can be seen as a general framework that systematizes the use of optimization methods in linguistics. One component of OT is a list of tendencies that hold for observable properties of a language. These tendencies take the form of violable constraints. Because the constraints usually express very general statements, they can be in conflict. Conflicts among constraints are resolved because the constraints differ in strength. Minimal violations of the constraints (taking their strength into account) define optimal conflict resolutions. OT specifies the relation between an input and an output. This relation is mediated by two formal mechanisms, GEN and EVAL. GEN (for Generator) creates possible output candidates on the basis of a given input. EVAL (for Evaluator) uses the particular constraint ranking of the universal set of constraints (CON) to select the best candidate for a given input from among the candidate set produced by GEN. In phonology, the input to this process of optimization is an underlying linguistic representation. The output is the form as it is expressed. In syntax, the input is an underlying logical form, and the output is the surface form as it is expressed. Hence, what is normally used in phonology and syntax is unidirectional optimization. Obviously, the point of view of the speaker is taken. This contrasts with OT semantics where the view of the hearer is taken (Hendriks and de Hoop 2001; de Hoop and de Swart 2000).

Bidirectional optimization integrates the speaker's and the hearer's perspective into a simultaneous optimization procedure. In pragmatics, this bidirectional view is motivated by a reduction of Grice's maxims of conversation to two principles: the I/R Principle, which can be seen as the force of unification minimizing the Speaker's effort, and the Q Principle, which can be seen as the force of diversification minimizing the Auditor's effort. The Q Principle corresponds to the first part of Grice's quantity maxim (*make your contribution as informative as required*), while it can be argued that the countervailing I/R Principle collects the second part of the quantity maxim (*do not make your contribution more informative than is required*), the maxim of relation and possibly all the manner maxims. In a slightly different formulation, the I/R Principle seeks to select the most coherent interpretation and the Q Principle acts as a blocking mechanism which blocks all the outputs which can be grasped more economically by an alternative linguistic input (Blutner 1998). This formulation makes it quite clear that the Gricean framework can be conceived of as a bidirectional optimality framework which integrates the speaker and the hearer perspective. Whereas the I/R Principle compares different possible interpretations for the same syntactic expression, the Q Principle compares different possible syntactic expressions that the speaker could have used to communicate the same meaning.

In the so-called strong version of bidirectional OT, a form-interpretation pair $<f, m>$ is called (strongly) optimal iff (I/R) no other pair $<f, m'>$ is generated that satisfies the constraints better than $<f, m>$ and (Q) no other pair $<f', m>$ is generated that satisfies the constraints better than $<f, m>$. I will give a very schematic example in order to illustrate some characteristics of the bidirectional OT. Assume that we have two forms f_1 and f_2 which are semantically equivalent. This means that GEN associates the same set of interpretations with them, say $\{m_1, m_2\}$. We stipulate that the form f_1 is less complex (marked) than the form f_2 and that the interpretation m_1 is less complex (marked) than the interpretation m_2. This is expressed by two markedness constraints F and M for forms and interpretations, respectively – F prefers f_1 over f_2 and M prefers m_1 over m_2. This is indicated in example (5).

(5)

	F	M
$< f_1, m_1 >$		
$< f_2, m_1 >$	*	
$< f_1, m_2 >$		*
$< f_2, m_2 >$	*	*

From these differences of markedness the following ordering relation between form-meaning pairs can be derived as shown in (6). I'm using a graphical notation to indicate the preferences by arrows in a two-dimensional diagram. Such diagrams give an intuitive visualization for the optimal pairs of (strong) bidirectional OT: they are simply the meeting points of horizontal and vertical arrows. The optimal pairs are marked with the symbol ☝ in the diagram.

(6)

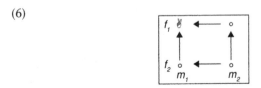

The scenario just mentioned describes the case of *total blocking* where some forms (e.g. *furiosity, *fallacity) do not exist because others do (*fury, fallacy*). However, blocking is not always total but may be partial. This means that not all the interpretations of a form must be blocked if another form exists. McCawley (1978) collects a number of further examples demonstrating the phenomenon of partial blocking. For example, he observes that the distribution of productive causatives (in English, Japanese, German, and other languages) is restricted by the existence of a corresponding lexical causative. Whereas lexical causatives (e.g. (7a)) tend to be restricted in their distribution to the stereotypical causative situation (direct, unmediated causation through physical action), productive (periphrastic) causatives tend to pick up more marked situations of mediated, indirect causation. For example, (7b) could have been used appropriately when Black Bart caused the sheriff's gun to backfire by stuffing it with cotton.

(7) a. Black Bart killed the sheriff.
     b. Black Bart caused the sheriff to die.

To make things concrete we can take f_1 to be the lexical causative form (7a), f_2 the periphrastic form (7b), m_1 direct (stereotypical) causation and m_2 indirect causation.

   Typical cases of total and partial blocking are found in morphology, syntax and semantics. The general tendency of partial blocking seems to be that 'unmarked forms tend to be used for unmarked situations and marked forms for marked situations' (Horn 1984, 26) – a tendency that Horn (22) terms '*the division of pragmatic labour*'.

   There are two principal possibilities to avoid total blocking within the bidirectional OT framework. The first possibility is to formulate so-called bias constraints (Mattausch 2004) and to find the appropriate ranking of the constraints such that partial blocking comes out. The table in (8) formulates four bias constraints besides the two markedness constraints F and M: the bias constraint F→M says that simple (unmarked) forms express simple interpretations (Levinson's I-constraint), the constraint *F→*M says that complex forms express complex interpretations (Levinson's (2000) M-constraint), and the two remaining bias constraints express the opposite restrictions.

(8)

	F	M	F→M	*F→*M	F→*M	F*→M
$<f_1, m_1>$					*	
$<f_1, m_2>$		*	*			
$<f_2, m_1>$	*			*		
$<f_2, m_2>$	*	*				*

Let's assume that the two bias-constraints F→M and *F→*M are higher ranked than the rest of the constraints. This can be depicted as in (9a). Hence, strong bidirection can be taken as describing Horn's division of pragmatic labour when the appropriate bias constraints are dominating.

(9)

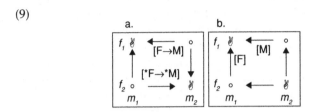

The second possibility is to weaken the notion of (strong) optimality in a way that allows us to derive Horn's division of pragmatic labour by means of the *evaluation procedure* and without stipulating particular bias constraints. Blutner (2000) develops a *weak* version of two-dimensional OT, according to which the two dimensions of optimization are mutually related: a form-interpretation pair $<f, m>$ is called super-optimal iff (I/R) no other *super-optimal* pair $<f, m'>$ is generated that satisfies the constraints better than $<f, m>$ and (Q) no other *super-optimal* pair $<f', m>$ is generated that satisfies the constraints better than $<f, m>$. This formulation looks like a circular definition, but Jäger (2002) has shown that this is a sound *recursive* definition under very general conditions (well-foundedness of the ordering relation). The important difference between the weak and strong notions of optimality is that the weak one accepts super-optimal form-meaning pairs that would not be optimal according to the strong version. It typically allows marked expressions to have an optimal interpretation, although both the expression and the situations they describe have a more efficient counterpart. Consider again the situation illustrated in (7), in the light of this weak version of bidirectional optimization.

It is not difficult to see that the *weak* version of bidirection can explain the effects of partial blocking without the stipulation of extra bias constraints; in particular, it can explain why the marked form f_2 gets the marked interpretation m_2. This is a consequence of the *recursion* implemented in weak bidirection: the pairs $<f_1, m_2>$ and $<f_2, m_1>$ are *not* super-optimal. Hence, they cannot block the pair $<f_2, m_2>$ and it comes out as a new super-optimal pair. In this way, the weak version accounts for Horn's *division of pragmatic labour*. This is demonstrated in (9b). To stress this point again: to get this solution we only have to assume the markedness constraints F and M (alternately, we can assume that all the markedness constraints are higher ranked than the bias constraints). The diagrams (9a) and (9b) describe the same set of solution pairs but the calculation of the solutions is completely different in the two cases. In the case of (9a) unidirectional optimization (either hearer or speaker perspective) is sufficient to calculate the solution pairs. I think this kind of OT system can be used to construct cognitively realistic models of on-line, incremental interpretation (Fanselow et al 1999). But what about the status of weak bidirection (super-optimality) which is illustrated in (9b)? There are implementations of a recursive algorithm to calculate the super-optimal solutions (see various contributions in Blutner and Zeevat 2004). Unfortunately, such a procedure doesn't even fit the simplest requirements of a psychologically realistic model of on-line, incremental interpretation because of its strictly non-local nature (Beaver and Lee 2004; Zeevat 2000).

Another problem is conceptual in nature and is raised by the existence of two notions of bidirectionality. What is the proper notion of optimization in natural language processing? The puzzle can be solved by relating weak bidirection to an off-line mechanism that is based on bidirectional learning. Benz (2003) worked out the formal details of such a theory. His theory is based on the idea that the speaker and hearer coordinate on form-meaning pairs which are most preferred from both perspectives. This theory predicts partial blocking as the result of an associative learning process where speaker and hearer preferences are coordinated. Other approaches ground weak bidirection likewise in repeated processes of bidirectional learning (cf. van Rooy 2004; Jäger 2004). It is remarkable that in this research the solution concept of weak bidirection is considered as a principle describing the direction of language change: super-optimal pairs are tentatively realized in language change. This relates to the view of Horn (1984) who considers the Q Principle and the I/R Principle as diametrically opposed forces in inference strategies of language change. The basic idea goes back to Zipf (1949), and was reconsidered in van Rooy (2004) and Blutner et al (2002). It conforms to the idea that synchronic structure is significantly informed by diachronic forces. Further, it respects Zeevat's (2000) acute criticism against super-optimality as describing an on-line mechanism.

For the sake of illustration, let's go back to example (9). Let's assume a population of agents who realize speaker and hearer strategies based exclusively on the markedness constraints F and M. That is, in this population each content is expressed in the simplest way (f_1) and each expression is understood in the simplest way (m_1). Let's assume further that these agents communicate with each other. When agent x is in the speaker role and intends to express m_1, then expressive optimization yields f_1. Agent y is a hearer who receives f_1 and, according to interpretive optimization, he gets the interpretation m_1 – hence the hearer understands what the speaker intends: successful communication. Now assume the speaker wants to express m_2. With the same logic of optimization he will produce f_1 and the agent y interprets it as m_1. In this case, obviously, the communication is not successful. Now assume some kind of *adaptation* either by iterated learning or by some mutations of the ranked constraint system (including the bias constraints). According to this adaptation mechanism the expected 'utility' (how well they understand each other in the statistical mean) is improving in time. In that way a system that is evolving in time can be described including its special attractor dynamics. In each case there is a stabilizing final state that corresponds to the system (9a) where the two Levinsonian constraints I and M outrank the rest of the constraints. It is precisely this system that reflects Horn's division of pragmatic labour. The only condition we have to assume is that the marked contents are less frequently expressed in the population than the unmarked contents.[4]

Hence, the important insight is that a system that is exclusively based on markedness constraints such as (9b) is evolutionarily related to a system based on highly ranked bias constraints such as (9a). We will use the term *fossilization* for describing the relevant transfer. The mentioned approaches of grounding weak bidirection in repeated processes of bidirectional learning can be seen as concrete realizations of fossilization. Recently, Mattausch (2004) has implemented the idea of fossilization using stochastic OT. In that way he was able to explain the evolution of reflexive marking strategies in English and he was able to show how an optional and infrequent marking strategy like that of Old English could evolve into a pattern of obligatory structural marking like that attested in modern English.

4. embedded implicatures

There are two views of analyzing embedding implicatures. Following Chierchia (2004) I will call them the *global* and the *local view*, respectively. According to the global view one first computes the (plain) meaning of a complete sentence; then, taking into account the relevant alternatives, one strengthens that meaning by adding in all the implicatures. This contrasts with the local view which first introduces pragmatic assumptions locally and then projects them upwards in a strictly compositional way where certain filter conditions apply. Representatives of the global view are Gazdar (1979), Soames (1982), Blutner (1998), Sauerland (2004), and Russell (2006); the local view is taken by Chierchia (2004), van Rooy (2006), Levinson (2000), and RT. Whereas many globalists argue against the local view and many localists against the global view, I think that proper variants of both views are justified if a different status is assigned to the two views: global theories provide the standards of rational discourse and correspond to a diachronic, evolutionary setting; local theories account for the shape of actual, on-line (synchronic) processing including the features of incremental interpretation. My suggestion is to take the proposal of fossilization as a mediator between the two views. However, at the moment this is not much more than an idea since concrete implementations of fossilization have applied for very simple examples only, predominantly in the domain of lexical pragmatics.

In the last section I introduced an OT implementation of the neo-Gricean view. I will illustrate now how this global theory can account for the basic distinction between explicatures and implicatures. I will explain this by considering the projection behaviour of pragmatic inferences in complex sentences. What I will demonstrate is that explicatures regularly satisfy EIH whereas implicatures systematically violate EIH (predominantly in downward entailing contexts). Interestingly, the global theory does more than merely predict the basic distinction. Especially for scalar implicatures, it precisely predicts the projection behaviour's dependence on the surrounding context.

In Blutner (1998) I have proposed an approach to 'scalar implicatures' that has some advantages over the traditional approach based on Horn-scales (cf. Gazdar 1979). For example, it solves a famous puzzle given by John McCawley. In the exercise part of his logic book, McCawley (1993, 324) points out that the derivation of the exclusive interpretation by means of Horn-scales breaks down as soon as we consider disjunctions having more than two arguments. For example, from a disjunctive sentence of the form *John or Paul or Ede is sick* we can conclude that only one of the three is sick. However, the traditional approach predicts that not all the disjuncts can be true, which is too weak. The solution was to admit a whole lattice of alternative expressions constructed by the AND operator in order to block all interpretations with more then one individual sick.

The global solution also works in cases like (10a) where the implicatures are (10b) and (10c):

(10) a. Someone is sick.
    b. The speaker does not know who is sick.
    c. The speaker knows (exactly) one individual is sick (given a set of individuals).

Blocking sentences are of the form *i is sick* in this case, where *i* is the name of an individual. As van Rooy points out a Gazdarian analysis of scalar implicatures predicts that *i is not sick*, for any individual *i*. And this results in an *inconsistency* because we can draw that conclusion for each individual *i* and thus conclude that no one is sick. To resolve this problem Soames (1982) has proposed an alternative account based on a careful consideration of the quality maxim. He concludes that we should weaken the force with which the implicatures are generated. Instead of claiming that the speaker knows that the stronger proposition *i is sick* is not the case we should conclude only that the speaker does not know whether *i is sick* is the case. In that way we get the inference (10b). In order to get the implicature (10c) we can assume a neg-raising account of propositional attitudes (e.g. Horn 1989). In the present context this conforms to an I-inference of the following kind:

(11) $\neg K\varphi \rightarrow K\neg\varphi$, for any proposition φ [K is a belief operator]

Assuming this inference conforms to a default that is realized as long as no conflicts arise, we can derive the expected conclusion (10c). For a related proposal, see Sauerland (2004) and Russell (2006).

Now we are ready to analyze the projection behaviour of scalar implicatures in complex sentences. Compare the simple sentence (12a) and the complex sentence (12b):

(12) a. Mary lives somewhere in the south of France.
    b. If Mary lives somewhere in the south of France, then I do not know where.
    c. Speaker does not know where in the south of France Mary resides.

Obviously, uttering (12a) implicates the proposition (12c). The derivation of this implicature is analogous to the derivation of (10b). However, the implicature does not locally arise in the antecedent of a conditional such as in (12b). Were it to arise, then the whole sentence (12b) would be a tautology, but it is not. Carston (2002, 194) uses this example to show that implicatures can violate EIH. The explanation in our neo-Gricean

framework is straightforward: the expression alternates to (12b) have to
be logically stronger than (12b) itself. Because in (12b) the weak quantifier
somewhere in the south of France occurs in the antecedent of a conditional
(i.e. in a downward entailing context), replacing it by concrete locations
results in a *weaker* expression. Since a weaker expression is not allowed as
an expression alternative the implicature does not arise. We can conclude
that scalar implicatures are indeed implicatures in the sense of RT rather
than explicatures.

Another example confirms this conclusion:

(13) a. I believe that some students are waiting for me ⇝ I believe that
          some but not all students are waiting for me.
      b. I doubt that some students are waiting for me ⇝ I doubt that
          some but not all students are waiting for me.
      c. ?Possibly all students are waiting for me. Hence, I doubt that
          some students are waiting for me.
      d. I doubt that some students are waiting for me ⇝ I believe that
          no students are waiting for me.

In the upward entailing context (13a) the scalar implicature is realized as
expected by the global account. In the downward entailing context (13b),
however, the implicature does not project locally. Otherwise a discourse
such as (13c) should be fine, but it is not. Rather, the implicature is as
indicated in (13d), which relates to the logical negation of the quantifier.
For a formal derivation the reader is referred to Russell (2006). It is essential
that no extra stipulation is required besides those mentioned.

Chierchia discussed many other examples with scalar implicatures
and concluded that only a local view can account for the observed
phenomena. However, as Sauerland (2004) and Russell (2006) have
shown, a Gricean theory can also account for each of the implicatures
Chierchia identified. Hence, I conclude that a global account is possible
for the treatment of scalar implicatures. The important question that
arises now is whether a global account can also explain all the other
pragmatic inferences that are discussed in the literature. In the rest of
this chapter I will show how this account can explain examples typically
treated as *explicatures* in the RT literature.

(14) a. John had a drink ⇝ John had an alcoholic drink.
      b. I believe that John had a drink ⇝ I believe that John had an
          alcoholic drink.

    c. I doubt that John had a drink ⇸ I doubt that John had an alcoholic drink.

This example shows that the inference of free enrichment in (14a) satisfies EIH both in upward entailing contexts (14b) and in downward entailing contexts (14c). Hence, it is an explicature in the sense of RT. The same projection behaviour is visible in the following examples when checking the pragmatic inferences given in parentheses:

Domain restrictions

(15) a. Everyone left early (⇸ everyone at the party left early).
    b. Either everyone left early or the ones who stayed on are in the garden.

Meronomic restrictions

(16) a. This apple is red (⇸ the outside of the apple is red).
    b. I doubt that the apple is red.

Reciprocals and plural predication

(17) a. The girls saw each other (⇸ every girl saw every other girl).
    b. I doubt that the girls saw each other. No girl sees girl No. 5.

(18) a. The cats see the dogs (⇸ every cat sees every dog).
    b. I doubt that the cats see the dogs. No cat sees dog No. 3.

(19) a. The cats are sitting in the baskets (⇸ every cat is sitting in one of the baskets).
    b. I doubt that the cats are sitting in the baskets. Cat No. 1 is not sitting in any basket.

A first observation is that all these examples are based on *I/R-implicatures* according to the neo-Gricean classification. Hence, in order to give an explanation of the projection properties it is essential to have a proper measure of relevance. Van Rooy (2006) lists some candidate definitions found in the linguistic, philosophical and statistical literature. For goal-oriented theories of relevance, but also for the entropy-based version, it is essential that the value of relevance can be positive and negative. The maxim of optimal relevance then means maximizing the absolute amount of relevance.

Building on Merin (1997), van Rooy (2006) identifies two crucial conditions for a local theory of relevance, i.e. a theory of relevance that conforms to a compositional, linear mode of calculating the value of relevance for complex sentences:

(20) a. Rel(A&B) = Rel(A) + Rel(B) if propositions A and B are independent
      b. Rel(A) = $-$Rel($\neg$A)

Using such a local theory of relevance (which hopefully can be extended to other complex forms than those constructed by negation and conjunction), the neo-Gricean approach can explain that the given examples exhibit *explicatures*, that is, they satisfy EIH.

The explanation runs as follows. First, notice that unidirectional optimization (hearer perspective) is sufficient in the present case because blocking does not take place in the examples under discussion. Further, let's assume that GEN generates all possible enrichments of the logical form of the (complex) sentence; my favourite realization for such a mechanism of 'developing logical forms' is abduction (cf. Blutner 1998). Finally, we assume that the evaluation component maximizes the amount of relevance (in absolute terms).

Assume an enrichment m of *LF*. By using a local enrichment mechanism it results that $\neg m$ is an enrichment of $\neg LF$. Assuming the condition (20b), Rel(m) = $-$Rel($\neg m$), yields the following conclusion: if m is an *optimal* enrichment of *LF* then $\neg m$ is an optimal enrichment of $\neg LF$. Hence, it can be concluded that EIH is inherited by negation, i.e. if a structure S satisfies EIH, then also $\neg S$ satisfies it. Since *believe* and *doubt* are related by negation, it is obvious that in these contexts the I/R inferences qualify as explicatures. Assuming that Merin's linear pragmatics can be extended to other complex sentences, then it generally holds that all pragmatic inferences that count as I/R implicatures (neo-Gricean terminology) are explicatures in the terminology of RT. I suggest this claim is empirically supported.

5. consequences and conclusions

This chapter contains some speculation about the possibility of deriving the explicature/implicature distinction within a neo-Gricean framework of optimality theoretic pragmatics. The speculations rest on several assumptions that I will list here once more:

(a) The nature of the distinction has to do with the embedded implicature hypothesis EIH: explicatures regularly satisfy EIH, implicatures regularly violate EIH in a definite class of contexts.

(b) A neo-Gricean theory of scalar implicatures based on a global blocking mechanism.

(c) Soames' reconsideration of the epistemic status of scalar implicatures paired with a default mechanism of neg-raising.

(d) A local theory of relevance.

None of these assumptions has a stipulative character. With the exception of the first assumption they are all motivated by independent evidence that has nothing to do with the explicature/implicature distinction.

However, while claiming that a global theory can explain the distinction, it is essential to state that a global theory cannot count as an on-line mechanism, since it doesn't conform to the principles of incremental interpretation. Rather, a global account describes the general forces that direct communication. It has a diachronic dimension. In order to get a synchronic system which describes the actual pragmatic inferences, the idea of *fossilization* has been proposed (see section 3). A theory of fossilization can be seen as describing how pragmatic inferences become automatized and form part of an efficient cognitive system that makes fast on-line processing possible. In this way, the theory conforms to a memory/instance theory of automatization (cf. Logan 1988).

From the perspective of cultural evolution the presumption of fossilization relates to a theory that realizes Dawkins' (1983) idea of *memic selection*. This idea conforms to the 'universal Darwinist' claim that the methodology of evolutionary theory is applicable whenever any dynamical system exhibits (random) variation, selection among variants, and thus differential inheritance. Related proposals are Steels' recruitment theory of cultural evolution (e.g. Steels 1998) and Kirby's paradigm of iterated learning (e.g. Kirby 2000).

OT is a system of knowledge representation that invites the development of the evolutionary perspective because the manipulation of the different rankings of a given system of constraints is a powerful but computationally simple task. It has been applied in the area of lexical pragmatics, especially in order to explain the phenomenon of broadening and strengthening in connection with the prepositions *om* and *rond* in Dutch (Zwarts 2006).

In this chapter I have proposed applying the theory to phenomena outside the realm of lexical pragmatics. Though real simulation results are missing at the moment, there are some psychological implications of the new perspective of fossilization. Recent data presented by Noveck's experimental pragmatics group (cf. Noveck 2005) suggests that children are sometimes more logical than adults. In one of their experiments they presented children and adults with sentences such as (21) where a relatively weak term is used in scenarios where a stronger term is justified.

(21) Some elephants have trunks.

Surprisingly, younger children are typically more likely than adults to find the utterance acceptable. One way of interpreting this data is to assume that children are pragmatically delayed at young ages. From the fossilization perspective, it can be claimed that scalar inferences become automatic with age and that the experimental results are simply revealing how such inference-making matures. This contrasts with the suggestion made in RT 'that children and adults use the same comprehension mechanisms but that greater cognitive resources are available for adults, which in turn encourages them to draw out more pragmatic inferences' (Noveck 2005).[5]

With regard to binding phenomena many researchers found a delayed principle B effect in comprehension but not in production. Children correctly interpret reflexives like adults from the age of 3;0 but they continue to perform poorly on the interpretation of pronouns even up to the age of 6;6. This contrasts with production data where even the youngest children use the pronoun to express a disjoint meaning while they use the reflexive to express a coreferential interpretation. This is puzzling because, usually, comprehension of a given form precedes production of this form.[6] In unpublished work it has been shown that fossilization theory can explain these data without further stipulation. The pragmatic inferences in this case are explicatures in the sense of RT, and it would be interesting to see how RT can account for these effects.

The present examination sees global and local accounts of analyzing embedding implicatures as complementary. (And the same holds for global and local accounts of lexical pragmatics.) Hence, peaceful coexistence and even collaboration between globalists and localists is possible and desirable.

acknowledgements

I am grateful to Jason Mattausch, Robert van Rooy, Torgrim Solstad and Henk Zeevat for valuable suggestions and comments on earlier versions of this chapter. Special thanks to Noel Burton-Roberts for valuable comments, advice and painstaking editorial help.

notes

1. I use this term collectively for implicatures and explicatures.
2. Recanati (1993) rejects the test because of metalinguistic negation. Indeed, examples like 'I am not his daughter; he is my father' suggest that sometime some property other than propositional content is falling within the scope of negation or other logical operators. However, this does not really undermine the usefulness of the test because of intonational and other cues that indicate the metalinguistic use.
3. Another example is due to a classic paper by Sadock (1978) and discussed in Blutner (1998): 'Grice states explicitly that generalized conversational implicatures, those that have little to do with context, are cancellable. But is it not possible that some conversational implicatures are so little dependent on context that cancellation of them will result in something approaching invariable infelicity? In a paper in preparation, I argue that sentences of the form *almost P* only conversationally entail *not P*, contrary to the claim made by Karttunen and Peters (1979). The implicature is straightforwardly calculable and highly nondetachable but, unfortunately for my thesis, just about uncancellable. The sentence *Gertrude not only almost swam the English Channel, in fact she swam it* is, I admit, pretty strange' (Sadock 1978, 293).
4. There are examples where this condition is violated. For example, Zwarts (2006) considered the case of *om* and *rond* in Dutch where the unmarked term om refers to some strengthening of the frequent de tour interpretation, and the term rond refers to some weakening of the less frequent circle interpretation. The principle of strongest interpretation – taken as a markedness principle – however predicts the opposite pattern.
5. Noveck's data seem to confirm RT, especially the data that show a link between scalar-inference production and task complexity. However, the present fossilization view does not necessarily conflict with these findings since memory-based automatization does not mean that the task complexity cannot have any influence (cf. Blutner and Sommer 1988). Also the idea that context determines in many cases which pragmatic enrichment to make does not necessarily conflict with the fossilization view. This view assumes that fossilized pragmatic implicatures can be context-dependent but they are not cancellable. This contrasts with Levinson's (2000) view, which clearly is refuted by these data.
6. For a summary of the data and an interesting theoretical proposal cf. Hendriks and Spenader (2004).

references

Atlas, J.D. and S.C. Levinson (1981). 'It-clefts, informativeness and logical form'. In P. Cole (ed.). *Radical Pragmatics*. New York: Academic Press. 1–61.

Beaver, D. and H. Lee (2004). 'Input-output mismatches in OT'. In R. Blutner and H. Zeevat (eds). *Optimality Theory and Pragmatics*. Basingstoke: Palgrave Macmillan.

Benz, A. (2003). 'Partial Blocking, associative learning, and the principle of weak optimality'. In J. Spenader, A. Eriksson and Ö. Dahl (eds). *Proceedings of the Stockholm Workshop on Variation within Optimality Theory*. Stockholm: University of Stockholm. 150–9.

Blutner, R. (1998). 'Lexical pragmatics'. *Journal of Semantics* 15: 115–62.

— (2000). 'Some aspects of optimality in natural language interpretation'. *Journal of Semantics* 17: 189–216.

Blutner, R., E. Borra, T. Lentz, A. Uijlings and R. Zevenhuijzen (2002). 'Signalling games: Hoe evolutie optimale strategieen selecteert'. *Handelingen van de 24ste Nederlands-Vlaamse Filosofiedag*. Amsterdam: Universiteit van Amsterdam.

Blutner, R., H. de Hoop and P. Hendriks (2005). *Optimal Communication*. Amsterdam: CSLI.

Blutner, R. and R. Sommer (1988). 'Sentence processing and lexical access: The influence of the focus-identifying task'. *Journal of Memory and Language* 27: 359–67.

Blutner, R. and H. Zeevat (eds) (2004). *Optimality Theory and Pragmatics*. Basingstoke: Palgrave Macmillan.

Burton-Roberts, N. (2005). 'Robyn Carston on semantics, pragmatics and "encoding"'. *Journal of Linguistics* 41: 389–407.

Carston, R. (2002). *Thoughts and Utterances: The Pragmatics of Explicit Communication*. Oxford: Blackwell.

— (2003). 'Explicature and semantics'. In S. David and B. Gillon (eds). *Semantics: A Reader*. Oxford: Oxford University Press. 817–45.

— (2004). 'Relevance theory and the saying/implicating distinction'. In L. Horn and G. Ward (eds). *Handbook of Pragmatics*. Oxford: Blackwell. 633–56.

Chierchia, G. (2004). 'Scalar implicatures, polarity phenomena, and the syntax/pragmatics interface'. In A. Belletti (ed.). *Structures and Beyond*. Oxford: Oxford University Press. 39–103.

Cole, P. (ed.). (1981). *Radical Pragmatics*. New York: Academic Press.

Dawkins, R. (1983). *The Extended Phenotype*. Oxford: Oxford University Press.

Ducrot, O. (1980). *Les Echelles argumentatives*. Paris: Minuit.

Fanselow, G., M. Schlesewsky, D. Cavar and R. Kliegl (1999). 'Optimal parsing, syntactic parsing preferences, and Optimality Theory'. Unpublished ms, University of Potsdam.

Gazdar, G. (1979). *Pragmatics*. New York: Academic Press.

Green, M. (1998). 'Direct reference and implicature'. *Philosophical Studies* 91: 61–90.

Grice, P. (1975). 'Logic and conversation'. In P. Cole and J.L. Morgan (eds). *Syntax and Semantics 3: Speech Acts*. New York: Academic Press. 41–58.

Hendriks, P. and H. de Hoop (2001). 'Optimality theoretic semantics'. *Linguistics and Philosophy* 24: 1–32.

Hendriks, P. and J. Spenader (2004). 'When production precedes comprehension: An optimization approach to the acquisition of pronouns'. Unpublished manuscript, Groningen.

Hoop, H. de and H. de Swart (2000). 'Temporal adjunct clauses in optimality theory'. *Rivista di Linguistica* 12.1: 107–27.

Horn, L. (1984). 'Towards a new taxonomy of pragmatic inference: Q-based and R-based implicature'. In D. Schiffrin (ed.). *Meaning, Form, and Use in Context: Linguistic Applications*. Washington, DC: Georgetown University Press. 11–42.

— (1989). *A Natural History of Negation*. Chicago, IL: University of Chicago Press.

Jäger, G. (2002). 'Some notes on the formal properties of bidirectional optimality theory'. *Journal of Logic, Language and Information* 11: 427–51.

— (2004). 'Learning constraint sub-hierarchies. The bidirectional gradual learning algorithm'. In R. Blutner and H. Zeevat (eds). *Pragmatics and Optimality Theory*. Basingstoke: Palgrave Macmillan.

Kirby, S. (2000). 'Syntax without natural selection: how compositionality emerges from vocabulary in a population of learners'. In C. Knight, M. Studdert-Kennedy and J.R. Hurford (eds). *The Evolutionary Emergence of Language: Social Function and the Origins of Linguistic Form*. Cambridge: Cambridge University Press. 303–23.

Levinson, S. (2000). *Presumptive Meaning: The Theory of Generalized Conversational Implicature*. Cambridge, Mass.: MIT Press.

Logan, G.D. (1988). 'Toward an instance theory of automatization'. *Psychological Review* 95: 492–527.

Mattausch, J. (2004). 'On the Optimization & Grammaticalization of Anaphora'. Unpublished PhD thesis. Humboldt University, Berlin.

McCawley, J.D. (1978). 'Conversational implicature and the lexicon'. In P. Cole (ed.). *Syntax and Semantics 9: Pragmatics*. New York: Academic Press. 245–59.

— (1993). *Everything that Linguists have Always Wanted to Know about Logic*. 2nd edition. Chicago, IL: University of Chicago Press.

Merin, A. (1997). 'If all our arguments had to be conclusive, there would be few of them'. *Arbeitspapiere SFB 340*. Stuttgart: University of Stuttgart. 101.

Noveck, I.A. (2005). 'Pragmatic inferences related to logical terms'. In I.A. Noveck and D. Sperber (eds). *Experimental Pragmatics*. Basingstoke: Palgrave Macmillan.

Recanati, F. (1989). 'The pragmatics of what is said'. *Mind and Language* 4: 294–328.

— (1993). *Direct Reference: From Language to Thought*. Oxford: Blackwell.

Russell, B. (2006). 'Against Grammatical Computation of Scalar Implicatures'. *Journal of Semantics* 23: 361–82.

Sadock, J.M. (1978). 'On testing for conversational implicature'. In P. Cole (ed.). *Syntax and Semantics 9: Pragmatics*. New York: Academic Press. 281–97.

Sauerland, U. (2004). 'Scalar implicatures in complex sentences'. *Linguistics and Philosophy* 27: 367–91.

Soames, S. (1982). 'How presuppositions are inherited: A solution to the projection problem'. *Linguistic Inquiry* 13: 483–545.

Sperber, D. and D. Wilson (1986). *Relevance*. Oxford: Blackwell.

Steels, L. (1998). 'The origins of syntax in visually grounded robotic agents'. *Artificial Intelligence* 103: 133–56.

van Kuppevelt, J. (1996). 'Inferring from Topics: Scalar Implicature as Topic-Dependent Inferences'. *Linguistics and Philosophy* 19: 555–98.

van Rooy, R. (2004). 'Signalling games select Horn strategies'. *Linguistics and Philosophy* 27: 493–527.

— (2006). 'Relevance of complex sentence'. *Mind and Matter* 4: 195–278.

6
varieties of semantics and encoding: negation, narrowing/loosening and numericals[1]

noel burton-roberts

1. varieties of semantics?

Semantics is 'conceptual-intentional'. It articulates the connection between a language and the world. As such, it is truth-theoretic, dealing with the truth-conditions of truth-evaluable entities. Thoughts are semantic in this sense. The language in which thoughts are couched is the 'Language of Thought' (LoT).

This much, I believe, is generally agreed upon, if only because it skates over much we don't understand. It is certainly part of the picture assumed in relevance theory (RT). But RT makes two claims that, taken together, are difficult to fathom.

Claim 1 is that LoT is not just a locus, but the (only) locus, of semantic properties. Taken seriously, this implies that the particular languages we speak don't have semantics. However, RT's second claim at least obscures Claim 1. Claim 2 is that particular languages do in fact have semantics. RT seeks to reconcile these claims by distinguishing two varieties of semantics, 'real' and 'linguistic'. Particular languages, for RT, have only 'linguistic', not 'real', semantics.

While 'real semantics' is clear enough – it's semantics as outlined above – it is less clear what 'linguistic semantics' is. The force of RT's 'linguistic'-'real' semantics distinction is essentially negative: to withhold 'real' (truth-theoretic) semantic properties from the expressions of particular languages. The oft-repeated claim of RT is that the sentences of particular languages like English are not truth-evaluable, don't 'encode'/express any

90

proposition. This is consistent with Claim 1, but it only tells us what 'linguistic semantics' isn't.

On the other hand, when RT offers more positive hints regarding 'linguistic semantics', these seem to undermine the distinction, and thus Claim 1, by attributing to expressions of particular languages properties that seem 'really' semantic. Robyn Carston offers a representative RT view:

A: The decoding process is performed by an autonomous linguistic system.... Having identified a particular acoustic (or visual) stimulus as linguistic, this system executes a series of deterministic grammatical computations ... resulting in an output representation which is the semantic representation, or logical form, of the sentence or phrase employed in the utterance. It is a structured string of concepts, with certain logical and causal properties. (Carston 2002, 57)

This attributes conceptual and logical – i.e. real semantic – properties to expressions of particular languages. Equally, Sperber and Wilson (1986, 72–3) allow that the semantic representation of the English sentence (a) *She carried it* enters into logical relations. For example, it contradicts (b) 'No one ever carried anything'. But this cannot be unless at least part of what is encoded in (a) is a truth-evaluable proposition ('Someone carried something at some point in the past'), false when (b) is true. See Burton-Roberts (2005) for further discussion.

RT's 'linguistic semantics', in short, is 'unstable' in the sense of Cappelen and Lepore (2005). By 'linguistic semantics', I suggest, RT attributes either too little or too much in the way of semantics to particular languages. It is too little to be consistent with the traditional assumption that particular languages have semantics as ordinarily understood, and too much to be consistent with LoT being the sole locus of real semantic properties.

This instability is reflected in the following passage from Fodor (1998, 9), which Robyn Carston (personal communication) quotes as representing the RT position:

English inherits its semantics from the contents of beliefs, desires, intentions, and so forth that it's used to express.... Or, if you prefer (as I think, on balance, I do), English *has no semantics*. Learning English isn't learning a theory about what its sentences mean, it's learning how to associate its sentences with the corresponding thoughts. (Fodor's italics)

It seems to me that this hardly clarifies relevance theory's distinction between 'linguistic' and 'real' semantics. Either English 'inherits' semantics as per Fodor's first disjunct – in which case what it inherits (and therefore has) is the real semantics of LoT – or, as per the second disjunct, it does not. Furthermore, it is not clear to me that RT's position amounts to either of Fodor's disjuncts.

Given this instability, I propose we admit of just the one – real – variety of semantics. Assuming LoT has semantics so understood, this gives us two options:

Option A: Attribute genuine semantic properties to the expressions of particular languages (e.g. English) as well as to LoT (Fodor's first disjunct).

Option B: Maintain LoT as THE locus of semantics and deny that expressions of particular languages have semantics – of any variety (Fodor's second disjunct).

Option A is the traditional one of course. But we should at least entertain Option B, notwithstanding its prima facie improbability. This is what I propose to do. In aid of this, I will appeal to a conceptual project that I and colleagues have been developing: the representational hypothesis (RH). The RH offers a perspective from which it can be seen to be not only unnecessary but incorrect to suppose that expressions of particular languages have semantics. Here I can only sketch the idea briefly.[2] Presented so baldly, it will seem rather startling. From an unlikely angle, it points in the direction of the strongest of Recanati's (2004, ch. 9) forms of Contextualism: 'Meaning Eliminativism'. It follows from the RH that English (for example) indeed has no semantics. So it can't inherit semantics from LoT. Nevertheless, it follows naturally from the RH that English will – though only to speakers of English – *seem* to inherit semantics from LoT. Seeming-to-inherit and actually inheriting are different and call for different theoretical models.

Having presented the RH, I will explore the semantic instability in RT by pointing up a crucially related instability in its notion of 'encoding'.

2. the representational hypothesis

A supposed truism of linguistic theory – Saussurian and Chomskian at least – is that it is necessary to posit entities having properties relating to both sound and 'meaning'. In Minimalism for example it is assumed that, when a lexical item is selected by the syntactic computation, what's selected is a (Saussurian) object constituted both by syntactico-semantic and phonological/phonetic properties. At a point in the computation (called 'Spell-Out'), the phonological properties of expressions are stripped out and fed to the phonology. This takes them to PF (Phonetic Form), the interface with articulatory-perceptual systems. What's left in the computation continues on to LF (Logical Form), the interface with the conceptual-intentional system (LoT).

This – and the general idea of 'sound with a meaning' – is Chomsky's 'DOUBLE INTERFACE' view of expressions and the computation (Chomsky 1995, 2). The computation compositionally projects sound-meaning correspondences encoded in lexical items onto an array of more complex expressions. This double-interface view is thought to be necessary if linguistic communication is to be possible (Chomsky 1995, 221). What has syntactico-semantic properties, it is assumed, must also have phonological properties if it is to be utterable – 'tokened' or 'realized' – in the acoustic medium of speech.

I'll mention here just two reasons for questioning this picture of things. The first is this. If the computation compositionally projects lexical sound-meaning correspondences (Saussurian signs), we should expect it to preserve those correspondences and thus expect isomorphism of phonology and syntactico-semantics in the complex expressions it generates. But, as is well known, this expectation is comprehensively defeated – by 'the fact that objects appear in the sensory output in positions "displaced" from those in which they are interpreted' (Chomsky 1995, 221–2). The very oddity of this way of expressing the matter reflects the problem posed by the double-interface assumption. How can one and the same single object be heard in one position and yet be interpreted as in another position? If, as Cormack and Smith (1997, 224) put it, 'a lexical item does not necessarily appear at Spell Out as a Saussurian sign', we need to question the existence of lexical items as double-interface objects (Saussurian signs). See Burton-Roberts and Poole (2006b) for detailed discussion.

A related reason for questioning the Saussurian (double-interface) sign is even more fundamental. It concerns arbitrariness. The arbitrariness of the Saussurian sign is universally acknowledged. What is not addressed is WHY it should be arbitrary. It is arbitrary because it is a relation between things that, ultimately, are SORTALLY incommensurable (Thomason 1972): acoustic phenomena and conceptual structures. This sortal incommensurability is acknowledged in Minimalism, by its assumption that what is PF-interpretable is not LF-interpretable and conversely. Given this sortal rationale of the arbitrariness, surely, no single entity could possibly be constituted by both sets of properties. But Saussurian signs – lexical items – consist precisely in the conjunction, within a single object, of both sorts of property. For this reason too we should question the very possibility of the Saussurian sign, the double-interface notion of linguistic expression.[3] Can we really think of expressions figuring in or generated by the cognitive syntactico-semantic system as utterable, as tokened in acoustic phenomena? Acoustic phenomena, I have suggested (Burton-Roberts 2000, 44–6), are tokens of acoustic types, not of syntactico-semantic types. Syntactico-semantic types, surely, are tokened in and only in syntactico-semantic structures. On these terms, syntactico-semantic expressions cannot be regarded as 'realized' or tokened in speech. We need some other way of conceiving 'sound-meaning' relations.

The central idea of the RH is very simple: speakers produce phonetic phenomena in aid of REPRESENTING expressions manipulated/generated by the syntactico-semantic computation. Ultimately, this boils down to the intuitive and unoriginal idea that speakers utter sounds as a way of perceptually representing – and thus communicating – their thoughts. But, from the RH's reconstruction of this idea, a picture emerges that contrasts sharply with standard generative assumptions. In explanation, I need to discuss what I mean by 'represent(ation)'.

'Representation' is not intended here in the sense usual in linguistics, where '"representation" is not to be understood relationally, as "representation OF"' (Chomsky 2000, 159–60). In Chomsky's sense, what-is-represented is not distinct from the representation itself. A 'syntactic representation', for example, is not a representation OF anything; it simply IS the syntax.

In the RH, by contrast, 'representation' IS intended 'relationally': a representation emphatically is a representation-OF something – something ELSE. To emphasize this, I use the term 'M-representation'. 'M' stands for Magritte, a reminder of his painting *La Trahison des Images*, in which the image of a smoker's pipe is accompanied by the warning 'Ceci n'est pas une pipe'. This points up the *distinction* between a representation (Peircian sign) and what it is a representation (or sign) OF. Simply, a representation-of-a-pipe is NOT (and does not include) a pipe. The RH takes seriously C.S. Peirce's counter-Saussurian stricture that 'a sign must be OTHER than its object'. (By contrast, the Saussurian sign – as [*signifiant+signifié*] – is partly CONSTITUTED by what it is a sign of, namely *signifié*.) On both sortal and semiotic grounds, the RH distinguishes fundamentally between a phonetically constituted M-representation R on the one hand, and, on the other, the structured conceptual (syntactico-semantic) object that R is an M-representation *of*.

Viewed from this perspective, the traditional double-interface view conflates *representans* and *representatum*: by including phonology – along with structured semantics – within the generative system, it conflates facts concerning WHAT-is-represented with independent facts concerning HOW-it-is-represented in the acoustic medium. Notice, too, that the double-interface Saussurian sign treats as a (further) ENTITY what is in reality just a (semiotic) RELATION between entities.

I can now explain my earlier scare quotes round 'sound-meaning relation'. In that phrase, the relational term 'meaning' suggests that whatever-it-is-that-sounds-relate-to should be thought of as a property-of the sound (cf. Chomsky's 'sound with a meaning'). The RH, by contrast, seeks to emphasize that what the sounds relate to is an independent object, with an independent rationale. It is a conceptual-intentional (C-I) structure, an object not defined by (and innocent of) the fact that sounds relate to it – and not a property of sound. It is the C-I structure that HAS semantics; it is not the case that the C-I structure IS the semantics-OF anything (let alone sounds).

Let me emphasize here that I don't deny that relevant sounds 'have meaning' (for someone). I am denying that they HAVE SEMANTICS – a different matter.[4] The notoriously vague term 'meaning' covers both 'significance' and 'semantics'. All sorts of things have significance (for someone) – and thus have meaning – without having semantics: black clouds, red litmus paper, green lights, ringing bells, raised eyebrows....

In the light of this, consider again the quote from Fodor. The significance – 'meaning' – of utterances in English consists in the fact that (for English speakers) they function as M-representations of the kinds of contents that Fodor refers to (thought contents). Given that, speaker-hearers of English will inevitably 'read into' a given phonetic M-representation what they assume it is an M-representation *of*. That's only natural. But it does not follow that English actually inherits the semantics of LoT. The closest we can come to saying this is to say that English will *seem* to inherit the semantics of LoT. But why drag in 'semantics' here? It is enough to say that, for speakers (of English), the 'meaning' (significance) of utterances in English derives from the thoughts they are used to express. It is the thoughts that have semantics.[5] Speakers get to express/communicate thoughts by producing phonetic (merely phonetic) M-representations of thoughts (though the M-representations themselves radically under-determine the thoughts).

The RH, then, identifies the generative computation as dealing in purely syntactico-semantic properties. Conversely, it identifies utterance phenomena as purely phonetic. The claim is that we don't utter/hear expressions generated by the computation (they are not such as to be utterable/hearable). What we utter/hear are merely PHONETIC M-REPRE- SENTATIONS OF those expressions. Rather than (realizationally) EMANATING FROM the computation, as in traditional generative thought, PFs are (M- representationally) TARGETED AT that computation. Since the respective properties of *representans* and *representatum* are sortally distinct, the relation is, of necessity, wholly conventional ('symbolic' for Peirce, 'arbitrary' for Saussure).

As a simple illustration, consider NEGATION. Tradition has it that the English word *not* is a Saussurian double-interface object, constituted by both phonological/phonetic and syntactico-semantic properties. Its semantic properties are supposed to be those of the logical operator. The RH, by contrast, distinguishes sharply between the logical operator and the English word *not*. The operator (a) is logically-but-not-phonetically constituted, the word (b) is phonetically-but-not-logically constituted. The two are DISTINGUISHED not only sortally but also in how they are RELATED: conventional M-representation, in English, OF (a) BY (b). There is just one such operator but (inevitably, given conventionality) many different phonetic M-representations of it in the speakable languages of the world.

That, distilled, is the representational idea. And here, also distilled, are a couple of its more radical implications, as they appear to me. The first concerns the relation between Chomsky's Human Faculty of Language (HFL) and LoT. For Chomsky, HFL is recursive, interpretable in conceptual-intentional terms, invariant across the species, innate, and wholly mind-internal. These are generally agreed to be the properties of LoT itself. However, as conceived of by Chomsky, HFL must be distinct from LoT because HFL includes phonology (it being a double-interface system). Here's the implication then. Having excluded phonology FROM HFL – on grounds of its M-representational relation TO HFL – the RH asks why HFL (thought of as a 'real object of the natural world' – Chomsky 1995, 11) and LoT should not be identified. That they are one and the same is the most parsimonious assumption. And Chomsky's claims about HFL seem most clearly sustainable if HFL and LoT are indeed the same. I'll assume without further ado that they should be identified, sometimes calling the result 'L'.[6]

The second implication is really a cluster of implications – for 'phonology' and 'particular languages'. It is, or should be, uncontrover- sial that a phonological system is a system that determines what counts as a well-formed phonetic string. Now, for the RH, relevant phonetic strings are M-representational. For the RH, then, a phonological system is a system that determines what counts as a well-formed phonetic M-representation. Of course, what counts as a well-formed M-representational phonetic string differs from language to language. It depends on the particular language – i.e. on its particular representational conventions. Now, arguably, a particular language just IS the set of its particular conventions. Accordingly, the RH identifies particular languages AS phonological systems. More specifically, each particular (spoken) language is a distinct, phonologically constituted, Convention System for the Phonetic (M-)Representation of the same single system, L – a $CSPR_{(L)}$. See Burton-Roberts and Poole (2006b) for further discussion of implications of this idea for 'phonology', cross-linguistic variation and what generally passes for language-particular 'syntax'.

In the light of this, the RH insists that a particular language's M-representations have only phonetic properties. The (sortally incorrect) assumption that they also have syntactico-semantic properties arises from theorists agreeing with naïve speakers in projecting onto the M-representations what pertains only to what-they-are-M-representations OF (namely, properties of L). Consider 'parsing' in this connection. Phonetic M-representations of L require parsing – and parsing is fallible (not 'deterministic' as Carston suggests in Quote A above) – precisely because they DON'T possess syntactico-semantics. Parsing is a matter of putting (a) what LACKS syntactico-semantic structure into correspondence with (b) what HAS such structure – on the assumption that (a) was produced with the intention of M-representing (b).[7]

The RH offers a fleshing out of Fodor's contention that 'learning English isn't learning a theory about what its sentences mean [i.e. their putative semantics – NBR], it's learning how to associate its sentences with the corresponding thoughts' (quoted above). What's learnt is a system of (phonologically constituted) conventions for the phonetic M-representation of the syntactico-semantic properties of LoT.

3. varieties of 'encoding' in relevance theory

I want here to explore relevance theory's notion of 'encoding' in the light of the above and thereby show that the RH is considerably more consistent with the quote from Fodor than RT itself is.

The RH was developed in response to problems at the syntax-phonology interface in Minimalism. But it is consistent with – indeed implies – RT's claim that the Language of Thought ('L') is the sole locus of semantic properties. I think the RH clarifies that claim and obviates the 'real' vs 'linguistic' 'semantics' qualification. It acknowledges the intuition that the phonetically constituted expressions of particular languages have – in some loose sense – 'meaning' on occasions of use, but without attributing to them objective semantic (conceptuo-logical) properties. Construed as M-representational of what does have such properties, they are indeed SIGNIFICANT (for the construer, at least).

The tension surrounding 'linguistic semantics' arises, I believe, from RT's reluctance to abandon the Saussurian/Chomskian 'double interface' tradition despite RT's view of LoT as the sole locus of semantics. This tension is reflected in RT's 'encoding'.

Carston (2002, 57–8) refers to David Lewis' (1970/1983) distinction between the 'genuinely semantic' (conceptual-intentional) relation between some symbolic system and the world of NON-symbols on the one hand and, on the other, the relation of 'encoding'. Encoding deals merely with (non-conceptual-intentional) relations between one symbolic system and another. RT's 'linguistic semantics' refers to a system of utterable symbols and its encoding relation to L. As with Morse code, all that is needed or appropriate here is not a SEMANTICS for the encoding system but a set of CODING CONVENTIONS. On these terms, particular languages, as mere codes, don't have semantics.

The force of Lewis' (important) distinction rests crucially upon a further distinction, however: that between the ENCODING with WHAT IS ENCODED. To maintain Lewis' encoding/semantics distinction, we must be careful not to conflate the encoding and what is encoded. That would risk attributing the genuine ('real') semantic properties of L (LoT) to mere encodings of them in the (utterable) symbols of particular languages. If we maintain these distinctions, then no remotely semantic properties can be attributed to the utterable encodings of a particular language.

All this suggests something similar, even identical, to the representational hypothesis. 'Encoding' on these terms amounts to the RH's 'M-representation'. On that assumption, call it 'M-ENCODING'.

All this notwithstanding, RT generally operates with a quite different notion of 'encoding', one inherited from the double-interface tradition. That is, when it characterizes an expression E as 'encoding' some conceptual-logical property f, RT attributes f to E, as a property-of E. Let's call this notion of encoding 'C-ENCODING'. 'C-' is for 'Constitutive'. C-encodings are CONSTITUTED by the properties they encode (as well as by phonetic properties – i.e. by how they encode it). This 'C-' notion of encoding, I suggest, completely undoes the appeal to Lewis and undermines Claim 1. It also gives rise to a range of problems which I will illustrate by reference to negation, narrowing, and numerals.

3.1 problems with C-encoded negation

Carston (2002, ch. 4, especially 311) conceives of *not* in C-encoding terms: for her, the word HAS (is constituted by) the logical properties of the operator that it 'encodes'. The first problem here is that, if *not* C-encodes (rather than M-encodes, or M-represents) the logical operator, then we have to accept that the (real) operator itself – a function from true(false) to false(true) – figures in the domain of 'linguistic encoding'. This is surely not consistent with RT's claim that the 'linguistic encoding' is a non-truth-theoretic domain.

Furthermore, if the English word *not* C-encodes – and thus is – a logical operator, there must be scope-of-negation WITHIN THE LINGUISTIC ENCODING. Where real negation is, there also is scope of negation. Against this, it is often unclear from the linguistic encoding what the scope of negation is. This is suspicious: if the linguistic encoding were such as to C-encode and thus include the logical operator, and thus have a genuine logical form, we should expect it to wear scope-of-negation on its sleeve. We can't say the encoding is scopally ambiguous if it C-encodes (and thus has) a logical form. Logical form, by definition, is *not* ambiguous. To admit that the linguistic encoding could be semantically ambiguous would be to concede that the linguistic encoding and logical form are distinct – that the latter isn't a property of the former – in short, that logical form is NOT C-encoded. Ambiguity indeed is a central plank in RT's argument that truth-theoretic properties are not in the linguistic encoding but ELSEWHERE (in the C-I structures of LoT).

But for Carston (2002, ch. 4), negation – and hence scope-of-negation – is C-encoded. And, notwithstanding the unclarity of the encoding, she wants to avoid scopal ambiguity. How to square this circle? She does it by insisting that (C-)encoded negation always has wide scope. When this doesn't square with the thought communicated, narrow scope is derived by pragmatic inference. Well, this does the trick, but it is somewhat stipulative. The point is that cases in which this strategy is available are precisely cases in which there IS nothing in the linguistic encoding that indicates scope.

That scope of negation is ALWAYS pragmatically inferred is Jay Atlas' (1989, 2005) scope neutrality thesis. For Atlas, there IS no scope of negation in the linguistic encoding (the sentence). However, it is difficult to accept this if the word *not* is a linguistic C-encoding of, and thus HAS, logical properties. To repeat, where real negation is, there also is scope-of-negation. Although Atlas (1989) opens with a suggestive discussion of representation (effectively – for him as for me – 'M-representation'), he doesn't invoke it in connection with negation. He too assumes C-encoding rather than M-encoding here. At least, he never suggests that *not* doesn't have logical properties, indeed he refers to it (Atlas 1989, 80) as 'one of our language's most basic logical words'. And, while assuming that semantics IS semantics-of-sentences, he gives no account of what his scope-neutral sentence-semantics actually consists in. See Burton-Roberts (1991, 170–2) and Carston (2002, 287–8) for discussion.

I believe that M-encoding – M-representation – offers a framework within which Atlas' proposal and Carston's (2002, 287) 'basic thesis' can be properly realized. Operating with M-encoding, we can (must) say that the encoding includes nothing with logical properties, but merely phonetic material (*not*) which, by the conventions of English, is used to M-represent (M-encode) something else, namely a logical operator located in and only in LoT. 'Scope neutrality' follows automatically – or something stronger since, if the operator simply isn't there in the (M-) encoding, it's beside the point to say the encoding is 'sense general' or 'neutral' with respect to scope of negation.

On these terms – and as Atlas suggested – pragmatics is required, not on SOME occasions nor in order to narrow C-encoded wide-scope negation, but on ALL occasions, to infer the logical properties of the thought intended to be communicated by some – ontologically purely phonetic, but functionally M-representational – utterance.

It might be thought the RH is committed to the linguistic M-encoding being scope ambiguous. In fact this makes no sense in RH terms, if 'ambiguity' is understood (as it standardly is) as a SEMANTIC property. To repeat, it follows from the RH that linguistic encodings – as M-encodings, or M-representations – DON'T HAVE semantic properties. So they can't be semantically ambiguous. This is not to say they can't be subjectively 'ambiguous'. But that simply means that it – scope of negation in thought, or whatever – can be UNCLEAR to a particular hearer on a particular occasion. Subjective 'disambiguation' is a matter of the hearer escaping this subjective state by ascertaining what the speaker intended. This is not what linguists generally mean by 'semantic ambiguity' – which, as objective, is supposed to remain in the absence of subjective ambiguity.[8] The very possibility of subjective ambiguity arises precisely because linguistic encodings, as purely phonetic, are – as a matter of ontological necessity – M-representationally indeterminate with respect to the thoughts they are intended to evoke.

3.2 lexical loosening and narrowing

I am suggesting that, while RT operates (in the light of Lewis' semantics-encoding distinction) with M-encoding at a general level, when it comes to the analysis of particular phenomena (e.g. negation) it in fact operates with C-encoding. This is particularly apparent in RT's approach to lexical matters.

It is clearly C-encoding that underlies the distinction between pragmatic narrowing (enrichment) and loosening (broadening) – Carston (2002, ch. 5). That is, it is assumed that there are two conceptual domains: (a) C-encoded in words – these are 'lexical concepts' – and (b) in LoT, actually entertained in thought. Loosening and narrowing are involved in getting from conceptual domain (a) to conceptual domain (b). Take loosening first. Examples are *bald* and *raw*. These words are assumed to C-encode the non-gradient, absolute concepts HAIRLESS and UNCOOKED respectively. However, it is not generally (indeed hardly ever) the lexical concept that's actually entertained in thought but one of a range of distinct, looser, gradiently related concepts.

Now it could be argued that it is empirically incorrect (i) to pick the non-gradient concept as the (C-)encoded lexical concept and posit loosening when necessary, rather than (ii) pick a gradient concept and posit narrowing when necessary. My contention, rather, is that choice is arbitrary. As Robyn Carston (personal communication) notes, the availability of *He wasn't strictly speaking bald* suggests (i). Against this, the non-tautological feel of *completely/totally bald* suggests (ii). And what about the acceptability of the phrase *very bald*? Does it indicate that the lexical concept is gradient or that it is non-gradient but can be used loosely? I don't think this is empirically decidable. But, given C-encoding (and thus a domain of 'lexical concepts' distinct from the conceptual domain of LoT), there's no escape: we must decide.

More on loosening below. It is really narrowing that concerns me here. Carston assumes that the English word *tired*, for example, C-encodes a single, extremely general, highly abstract concept. In thought, by contrast, there is a 'virtually indefinite range of finely distinct [highly specific] concepts' – from slight lassitude to total exhaustion, from [ENOUGH TO MAKE WALKING THE DOG MORE ATTRACTIVE THAN JOGGING] to [IMPOSSIBLE TO MAKE IT TO BASE-CAMP THOUGH THAT'S THE ONLY CHANCE OF SURVIVAL]. This disparity – between the single, highly general, lexically C-encoded concept and the multiplicity of highly specific concepts in thought – calls for narrowing.

Carston (2002) vividly delineates a fundamental and very relevant problem in connection with narrowing: in many cases, the lexical semanticist will need to posit 'lexical concepts' that are so extremely general and so abstract that it is difficult to imagine that any actual thought could actually involve them. *Open* is a classic case. As Carston notes, we use this verb to talk of John 'opening' a window, his mouth, a book, a briefcase, the curtains, a package, a wall, a wound. Think also of: his fingers, his dog's mouth, his bowels, a drawer, a bottle, the throttle, a computer file, the bidding, a chess game, a shop (for the first time, or as usual at 9.00 am) or Parliament. As Carston puts it:

> B: [W]hen we try to think about the general concept OPEN and to have a thought in which such a general concept features, as opposed to any of the more specific concepts that we grasp, ... the experience is an odd one, as we seem to have no definite thought at all.... [W]hat is not at all clear is whether we actually have (hence sometimes try to communicate) thoughts in which this very general lexicalised concept features as a constituent....But surely if the word *open* encodes a concept we should be able to have thoughts which include that concept... (Carston 2002, 361–2)

Exactly. When an English speaker says that Max opened a book, it's not part of what she says or means that Max did anything in common with the Queen opening Parliament, Kasparov deploying the Queen's Pawn Gambit, my use of a corkscrew or.... The putative C-encoded lexical concept doesn't just envelop us, as analysts, in a cloud of unknowing – it's hard to accept that it figures even in any ordinary use of the word.

An admittedly strong intuition underlying the search for a unitary semantics for *open* might go like this: 'Surely, since we use the same word for all those activities, they must have SOMETHING in common – and, surely, that 'something' constitutes the semantics of the word.' Strong though this intuition is, we need to resist it. Everything has something in common with everything else but we don't use the same word for everything. More significantly, few if any other languages use one and the same word for exactly the range of activities (i.e. all and only the activities) that in English we use *open* for (Bowerman and Choi 2003; Young 2006). That intuition is in danger of leading to a 'rightly-are-they-called-pigs' school of lexical semantics. Like the Argument from Design, this gets it round the wrong way. What all and only those activities have in common is that – in English – we use the same word for them.[9]

3.3 the problem of N

The problem – the fugitive character of lexical semantics – arises with numerical expressions. In use, *N* can mean any of:

(a) [EXACTLY N]
     i.   Q: How many children do you have? A: *Three*.
     ii. No creature has *five* legs.
     iii. A triangle (but not a quadrilateral) has *three* sides.
(b) [AT LEAST N]
     i.   You must be *eighteen* to vote.
     ii. If you have *four* children, you qualify for benefit.
(c) [AT MOST N]
     i.   I must pare that article down to *sixty* pages.
     ii. We're allowed *thirty* days' holiday a year.

The favoured (neo-Gricean) analysis is that N is lower-bounded semantically – has (b) as its (C-encoded) semantics – and upper-bounded by implicature (Horn 1989, ch. 4). This pragmatically derives (a) from (b). However, as Carston (1988) notes, this doesn't accommodate (c). Conversely, were N semantically upper-bounded, as (c), and lower-bounded pragmatically, yielding (a), this wouldn't accommodate (b). Sadock (1984) favoured (a) as the semantics, suggesting that (b) and (c) arose from loose use of N, by analogy with 'France is hexagonal'. But, as Carston notes, loose use of N is quite different from (b)–(c). The true analogy is between 'France is hexagonal' and examples in which N is used to convey [APPROXIMATELY N], which corresponds to none of (a)–(c).

On the basis of such considerations, Carston (1998) suggests that the semantics of N (what N C-encodes) cannot be any of (a)–(c). For her – and Atlas (1992) – its semantics is more general than any of those. But, as with *open*, the question is: what could that semantics possibly amount to? Logically, the inclusive disjunction [[AT LEAST N] ∪ [AT MOST N]] might do the trick. However, possibly because it comes too close to polysemy, Carston doesn't consider it. And Atlas (1989) explicitly rejects a disjunctive analysis of sense generality.

Instead, Carston's account of the concept C-encoded by *three*, for example, is '[X [THREE]]'. Here the value for 'X' is chosen from {[AT LEAST], [AT MOST], [EXACTLY]} and must be supplied pragmatically (a case of saturation?). Now, arguably, this just transfers variability in the (putative) semantics of *three* onto 'X'. And there is a more serious problem. On C-encoding terms, we're looking for a SEMANTIC DEFINITION of *three* – and, considered as such, '[X [THREE]]' surely won't do. Independently of, or prior to, assigning a value to 'X', we still have '[THREE]'. Notwithstanding the typographical distinction (small caps), '[THREE]' can hardly figure (non-circularly) in a semantic definition of *three*.

The point is that C-encoding commits us to identifying a SINGLE ('lexical') concept consistent with a VARIETY of uses. But, again, even when

– as with *N* – the variety isn't huge, we seem to be facing a concept that's quite inscrutable. This is the general problem posed by the (C-encoding) assumption that a particular language constitutes a conceptual, semantic domain (of 'lexical concepts') distinct from and in addition to the conceptual semantic domain constituted by LoT.

I return to *three* below, where I pursue Jerry Sadock's more recent observation that 'If sometimes the cardinal numbers are upper bounded by implicature and sometimes lower bounded, we are lead to conclude that they have no semantic content at all' (2005).

4. carston's response

In responding to the problem (in connection with *open*), Carston comes tantalizingly close to entertaining a notion of M-encoding, the M-representational relation of the RH.

> C: Could it be that the word ... does not encode a concept, but rather 'points' to a conceptual region ... in memory? (Carston 2002, 360)

As I interpret this, Carston is here (effectively) questioning the notion of C-encoding and entertaining the possibility of M-encoding. Indeed, the pointing idea (borrowed from Sperber and Wilson 1998, 196–7) exactly captures the Magrittian/Peircian representational distinction I'm after. A pointer, [α], is OTHER THAN what-it-points-to, [β]. [α] does not, in virtue of pointing to [β], partake of any of [β]'s properties (conceptual, in our case).

In the event, however, it appears that M-encoding – and thus the denial of any conceptual property (semantics) located in utterable words – is not what Carston has in mind. Instead, she replaces talk of 'encoding a concept' with talk of 'encoding a concept schema or pro-concept' (363) – and continues using 'encoding' in the 'C-' sense. I deal here just with 'concept schema', returning to 'pro-concept' below. Carston writes:

> D: Suppose it is right that there is a sizeable class of words that do not encode particular concepts (senses) but rather concept schemas or pointers, or addresses in memory (which of these is the best metaphor remains unclear)... (Carston 2002, 363)

It seems that, for Carston, 'pointer' is just another metaphor along with 'concept schema'. But these – for me, at least – are utterly different. To repeat, using a phonetic pointer to (phonetically M-encoding/M-representing) a conceptual region in thought doesn't require us to attribute ANY conceptual property to the word (the pointer) itself – quite the reverse. Carston's notion of 'concept schema', by contrast, seems called for precisely by the perceived need to attribute SOME kind of conceptual property to the word – a need that arises only on C-encoding assumptions. Carston herself (363) alludes to the parallelism between 'concept schema' and her 'schema or template for a range of propositions'. But the latter, I've suggested (Burton-Roberts 2005, 396), precisely IS a proposition, albeit a very general one. By the same token, I suggest a 'concept schema' just IS a very general, highly abstract concept.[10] Despite the change in terminology, this brings us right back to the problem we started with (quote B above) – and, furthermore, the task of specifying the concept schema's content, and thus offering a substantive semantics for *open* (i.e. more substantive than just '[OPEN]').

On these C-encoding terms, we are going to have to admit of what Carston (very honestly) describes as 'a whole additional population of mental entities' distinct from the concepts actually entertained or entertainable in thought, which 'don't seem to have any function in mental life except to mediate the word/concept relation' (363). Furthermore, we face

E: [a] challenging question that arises concerning acquisition: if word meanings are these abstract schematic entities that do not feature in our thinking about the world, how do we ever manage to acquire (learn) them? (363)

She writes

F: There must be some process of abstraction ... from the particular concepts associated with the phonological form /open/ to the more general 'meaning', which then functions as a gateway both to the existing concepts of opening and to the materials needed to make new OPEN* concepts which may arise in the understanding of subsequent utterances. (364)

Carston is persuaded (in contrast to Hintzman's (1986) multiple trace memory model) that the multiple traces left by experience of particular uses resolve themselves into a distinct general conceptual representation (rather like those multiple images that, seen from a distance, compose a picture of the Mona Lisa). The difficulty here is not so much how the abstraction arises – assuming that it does – but what cognitive function it serves. Its function couldn't be to enable 'understanding of subsequent utterances', precisely because it arises post hoc. That is, it arises FROM, and presupposes, a prior understanding of relevant utterances (Hintzman 1986, especially 422–3).

5. biting the M-representational bullet

Carston has vividly articulated a genuine problem, implied by the very idea of 'lexical' or 'linguistic semantics' and the C-encoding she assumes. Given these problems, and our overarching endeavour of identifying LoT as the sole locus of conceptuo-logical (semantic) properties, I suggest we unequivocally jettison C-encoding in favour of M-encoding, deny that words have conceptual properties, and thereby deny the existence of 'lexical semantics' – on the grounds of the Magrittian/Peircian DISTINCTION between properties of the phonetic *representans* (the word) and those of the conceptual *representatum*.

What we have in *bald, tired, open, three* is, in each case, a single *representans* and, quite distinctly, a multiplicity of conceptually related *representata* in thought, on occasions of their use. The singularity we have in each of these is not conceptual but phonetic. The multiple traces resolve themselves round a PHONETIC attractor (or 'address'). This disposes of the problem of identifying a single, context-invariant, cognitively suspect ('lexical') concept as the 'semantics of the word'.

A major consequence of this is a Fodorian 'emptying' of the lexicon (Fodor and Lepore 1998) and, I believe, a dismantling of the distinction between logical entries for words and encyclopaedic knowledge/presuppositions (Searle 1980). I believe this resolves a fundamental tension in Carston's work in this connection: while she explicitly endorses (Carston 2002, 141, 321) Fodor's arguments against lexical decomposition (essentially, arguments against the analytic-synthetic distinction), Carston (with Sperber and Wilson 1986, 86) nevertheless posits, in addition to encyclopaedic entries for words, logical entries designed (contra Fodor) to 'capture certain analytic implications of the [lexical] concept'. See Burton-Roberts (2005), Groefsema (this volume), and Vincente (2005) for further discussion.

In fact, the M-representational approach goes further than Fodor. Fodor has it that WORDS have denotations (surely not consistent with the Fodor quote above). I suggest that it is particular USES of words that have denotations (Recanati 1998). And even then, what I really mean here is that it is just the CONCEPTS (in thought – where else?) M-represented by such word-uses that in fact have denotations.

5.1 'three' again

On these terms, rather than look for a semantic definition of the word *three*, we might attempt to say something about the range of concepts that *three* can be used to point to, or M-represent. Here is my attempt.

On some occasions, the concept actually entertained in thought and M-represented by the use of *three* is [THREE OR MORE]. And the concept [THREE] that figures there is [EXACTLY THREE]. This gives [EXACTLY THREE OR MORE THAN EXACTLY THREE]. Those are occasions of use on which *at least three* would be a more precise M-representation. On other occasions – when *at most three* would be more precise – the entertained concept is [EXACTLY THREE OR LESS THAN EXACTLY THREE]. And on others again, it is [EXACTLY THREE].

Given the distinction between the M-representation and the concept it M-represents – so we're not talking of any conceptual property of *three* itself – the circularity of using '[THREE]' to explicate a putative semantics for *three* doesn't arise. It is the concept [(EXACTLY) THREE] that has semantics. What is the semantics of that concept? The semantics of this concept consists in its denoting a NUMBER – for example, the number of dots in a 'therefore' sign (∴).

Notice that this captures the unity of uses of *three* (i.e. what all uses of *three* have in common). For what those different concepts all have in common is the fact that [EXACTLY THREE] figures in their composition. It is [EXACTLY THREE], then, that defines the conceptual range of (and constrains) the use of *three*. So, presumably, the convention governing the use of *three* effectively says: use *three* to M-represent any cardinal concept in thought in which the concept [EXACTLY THREE] figures.[11]

This proposal has an important implication, which I think could only emerge on an M-encoding/representational approach: it allows us to acknowledge that [EXACTLY THREE] defines the conceptual range of uses of the word – and is the concept referred to in the relevant convention – WHILE SIMULTANEOUSLY DENYING THAT [EXACTLY THREE] IS THE SEMANTIC DEFINITION OF THE WORD. This strikes me as a highly satisfactory result because – even if we allow that the word has a semantic definition, which I don't – we already know that [EXACTLY THREE] is not, and cannot be, that definition.

I suspect that Sadock's earlier (1984) proposal – that the word *three* means [EXACTLY THREE] – would be the intuitive/pretheoretical definition-of-choice for most ordinary speakers. If I am right in that, then the M-representational approach has the merit of reconciling that pretheoretical intuition with the (later) conclusion of Sadock (2005) that the word in fact has no definition. Indeed, in identifying [EXACTLY THREE] as the concept involved in all uses of *three*, while (correctly) denying that [EXACTLY THREE] constitutes the definition of *three*, this approach could be seen as actually explaining that intuition.

What all this shows, more generally, is that identifying the conceptual range of uses of a word *W* is NOT THE SAME AS identifying *W*'s putative semantics. It is possible, then, that the more daunting task of identifying the conceptual range of uses of the word *open* (which I won't attempt) wouldn't anyway yield anything that could be regarded as its semantics.

5.2 narrowing-loosening and conceptual-procedural

Carston (2002, ch. 5) seeks to unify loosening and narrowing as a single (symmetric) process of 'concept adjustment' resulting, across the board, in explicature (see also Wilson and Carston, this volume). This, she suggests, departs from the previous RT (asymmetric) view that only narrowings – as enrichments or 'developments' – are explicated, and that loosenings, by contrast, are implicated.

However, if (as Carston assumes) there are two conceptual domains, (a) C-encoded in words and (b) entertained in thought, then – like it or not – some inferences from (a) to (b) will result in 'narrowings' and others in 'loosenings'. With C-encoding (and thus 'concept adjustment'), we are not going to disband the loosening-narrowing distinction. In which case, it is difficult to see how the results of ALL such inferences could be explicated. Of course it depends on the criterion for 'explicature' (as against 'implicature'). This is unclear in RT, since 'explicature' is defined in terms of 'development' (of the logical form of the sentence uttered) but 'development' itself is not defined – see Burton-Roberts (2005). If we go with Carston (1988), we might take a proposition *P* to be a 'development' of the LF – and thus explicated – if *P* unilaterally entails the LF. True, this doesn't cover all cases that RT has claimed to be explicatures (and is not consistent with 'linguistic semantics' being non-truth-theoretic – see Burton-Roberts 2005, 398) but it is at least clear conceptually and seems pretheoretically consistent with explicatures being 'enrichments' of the linguistically encoded LF.

On these terms, explicatures are conceptually/logically MORE SPECIFIC than what is encoded. But then, only narrowings could count as developments, and thus as explicated, not loosenings – just as in the asymmetric account that Carston seeks to reject. What makes 'development' and 'enrichment' pretheoretically appropriate in describing those concept adjustments that result in narrowings – and thus allows us to see narrowings as explicated – is that the narrowed concept INCLUDES AND BUILDS ON the content of the lexical (C-encoded) concept. In 'loosening', by contrast, the lexical concept is not included – it is DROPPED AND REPLACED. But then how could any concept adjustment that resulted in a loosened concept count as an 'enrichment' or 'development' of the lexically encoded concept? As long as we HAVE a distinction between loosening and narrowing, I suggest, we are not going to be able to say that concept adjustment results (across the board) in explicature, as Carston proposes.

But, again, it depends on what 'development' is – and that's the problem. The problem is not resolved – but rather intensified – when Carston suggests:

> G: The characterization of an 'explicature' as a communicated assumption which is a *development* of a logical form of the utterance … can be maintained provided that the notion of a 'development' of a logical form is understood to include pragmatic adjustments to linguistically encoded concepts which may involve dropping logical or definitional elements of the encoded concepts. (Carston 2002, 342, original italics)

I believe the RH can make a positive contribution here. Narrowing and loosening are forms/results of 'concept adjustment'. The clearest way to disband the narrowing-loosening distinction is to deny the existence of 'concept adjustment'. Such a denial follows directly from the M-encoding/M-representation idea. If words aren't conceptual C-encoders in the first place – but merely phonetic M-representational pointers to conceptual regions in thought – then there IS no lexical conceptual domain (a). So there can't be any conceptual disparity between (a) and (b), the conceptual domain constituted by LoT. There are, in short, no 'lexical concepts' to be 'adjusted' – or, therefore, either narrowed or loosened.

Instead, and across the board, we have a single inferential process from a speaker's 'phonetic effort' (Searle 1965) to a thought – assuming those efforts were M-representational. Now a speaker's M-representational 'phonetic effort' is what RT calls an 'ostensive acoustic stimulus'. The inference is from just such a stimulus to a thought – and it makes no sense to say that some but not all of these inferences yield 'enrichments' or 'developments' of what was 'encoded'. In fact, it makes no sense – in M-encoding terms – to say ANY of them do. So, if relevance theory wants to say that the result of the inference is EVER explicated, we have no reason not to say that it ALWAYS is. Whatever you 'meant' – whatever concept you had in mind and were M-representing – in using *tired, bald, three* or *open*, that's what you 'said', 'explicated', 'expressed' and were committed to.

In this connection, we might dismember the notion of 'pro-concept', discarding the '-concept' bit and developing the 'pro-' bit. As is well known, pro-forms (such as *she* and *it* in *She carried it*) are now treated in RT as having 'procedural meaning', not 'conceptual meaning'; they encode procedures that a hearer should engage in to infer explicated conceptual-intentional properties. Recall that it was precisely the attribution of 'conceptual meaning' (as against procedural meaning) to the linguistic encoding that called for the qualification embodied in Claim 2 and led to the undermining of Claim 1.

Speculating: if we want to allow that linguistic encoding ever C-ENCODES anything, we might allow that what it C-encodes is procedural. That is, since the phonetically constituted expressions of particular languages function (for those aware of the M-representational conventions of the given language) as M-representations of the conceptual-intentional structures in terms of which thought is couched, it is not unreasonable to think of those expressions as C-encoding (i.e. constituting) instructions to construct such conceptual-intentional structures. In which case, the representational hypothesis might be expressed in terms of the conceptual-procedural distinction – by saying that the words of particular languages function as CONCEPTUAL M-ENCODERS in virtue of being PROCEDURAL C-ENCODERS. On these terms, all linguistic 'meaning' (encoding) is procedural – M-representationally pointing the hearer towards structures in LoT, the unique locus of conceptual-intentional (i.e. semantic) properties.

6. envoi

Carston's discussion raised the general question of how we get to understand other people's uses of words. For her it is the question of how abstract lexical semantics arises (in a given I-language) and is an 'acquisition' question. The position advanced here is that there are no abstract schematic lexical concepts to 'acquire'. Whatever is going on here, it is not a process of acquisition and it doesn't involve abstraction. It seems, rather, to be a process of LEARNING – learning to USE bits of phonetic material in roughly the same ways as others in the community. This, we have seen, presupposes some understanding of the utterances of the community. The circularity that threatens here can be avoided by positing a lively capacity for pragmatic inference and mind-reading (Carston 2002, 30).

The 'representational conventions' that I've been alluding to may be nothing other than – in one sense of 'conventional' – the conventional (i.e. habitual) use of words in a community. In this sense of 'convention', the conventions DETERMINE use precisely because they are themselves DETERMINED BY use (Pelczar 2000, 503).

When I started teaching pragmatics, I used to contrast Gricean ideas with the Wittgensteinian slogan 'Don't ask for the meaning, ask for the use', suggesting that Wittgenstein operated in a benighted world with no semantics-pragmatics distinction. Well, perhaps Wittgenstein should rather be thought of as the father of radically radical pragmatics. Certainly Hintzman's multiple trace theory – appositely cited by Recanati (1998) – points towards a Wittgensteinian concept of lexical understanding.[12]

notes

1. I am grateful to Jay Atlas, Diane Blakemore, Phil Carr, Robyn Carston, Marjolein Groefsema, Ruth Kempson, Begona Vincente, Deirdre Wilson, and David Young for discussion and/or comments on previous drafts. I gratefully acknowledge an AHRC Research Leave award in support of this work.
2. See Burton-Roberts (2000); Burton-Roberts and Carr (1999); Burton-Roberts and Poole (2006a, 2006b); Chng (1999) for more detail.
3. Jackendoff (1997, esp. 41, 83) is in part motivated by essentially the same thought.
4. Notice that, in the earlier quote, Fodor follows the general practice of effectively equating '(having) semantics' and '(having) meaning'. Notice also that, if we make a distinction between the two, as I maintain we need to, then 'Meaning Eliminativism' (Recanati 2004, ch. 9) is not what I am after. What I am after is 'Semantic Eliminativism', the denial that the utterable expressions of English (for example) have a semantics.
5. Thoughts do not, *in virtue of* having semantic content, have meaning in the sense of having significance (or communicating), though they may have significance (communicate) in giving rise to further thoughts.
6. Bickerton (1996, 73–4, 107–12) too, argues for this. However, it is difficult to sustain if you hold – as Bickerton (with Chomsky) does – that HFL is INSTANTIATED in particular languages: for, if HFL = LoT, then LoT must be thus instantiated. This is surely untenable (Pinker 1992). For the RH, by contrast (see below), the relation of particular languages to HFL/LoT is M-representational. An M-representation-of-X is NOT an instantiation-of-X.
7. Dynamic Syntax (Kempson et al 2001) doesn't appeal to (M-)representation, but its process of building structure on the basis of string information is consistent with the representational idea.
8. If *bank* is ambiguous as a matter of C-encoded (semantic) fact, it should be ambiguous regardless of context. But everyone concedes that 'ambiguity' is generally resolvable in context – in other words, that ambiguity is context-dependent. This suggests that, when semanticists/pragmaticists purport to be addressing an objective, semantic phenomenon, they are in fact addressing a subjective, pragmatic phenomenon. See Burton-Roberts (1994).

9. Consider Denham's 'Lines on the Thames' (quoted by Richards 1936, 121): 'O could I flow like thee, and make thy stream/My great exemplar, as it is my theme!/Though deep, yet clear; though gentle, yet not dull;/Strong without rage; without o'erflowing full.' As Richards notes, Dr Johnson praised this on the grounds that 'the particulars of resemblance are so perspicuously collected' – displaying what for Aristotle was 'an eye for resemblances'. But this assumes the lines are an exercise in natural history, reporting on supposed resemblances (between a river and a mind) out there, rather than a work of literary – that is, linguistic – art. The resemblances hold only 'under a description'.

10. The alternative interpretation – that, in positing 'concept schemas', Carston (2002) is indeed denying that words have conceptual properties – would leave the notion of 'concept schema' quite unclear. And, in fact, responding to Recanati (1998), she makes it clear she is not pursuing 'the radical claim that there is no lexical meaning in the sense of stable encoding' but a 'more conservative one ... on which words do encode something, albeit something very schematic...' (Carston 2002, 375).

11. What about 'approximately three'? [APPROXIMATELY EXACTLY THREE] sounds contradictory, I concede. But [APPROXIMATING TO EXACTLY THREE] is good and indeed accurate.

12. In fact, if Wittgenstein was suggesting that meaning and use are one, asking for the use of expressions amounts to asking for their meaning. Given the distinction between 'meaning' (of expressions in a particular language) and 'semantics' (of thoughts) argued for in this chapter, the slogan should perhaps be 'Don't ask for the semantics of expressions in a language, ask for their use'.

references

Atlas, J. (1989). *Philosophy without ambiguity*. Oxford: Clarendon Press.

— (1992). ms. 'Why three does not mean 3'. Claremont, CA: Pomona College.

— (2005). *Logic, meaning and conversation*. New York: Oxford University Press.

Bickerton, D. (1996). *Language and human behaviour*. London: UCL Press.

Bowerman, M. and S. Choi (2003). 'Space under construction: language specific spatial categorization in first language acquisition'. In D. Gentner and S. Goldin-Meadow (eds) *Language in Mind*. Cambridge, Mass: MIT Press. 387–427.

Burton-Roberts, N. (1991). 'Review of Atlas 1989'. *Mind and Language*. 6: 161–76

— (1994). 'Sentence, utterance and ambiguity: a representational approach'. *Transactions of the Philological Society* 92: 179–212.

— (2000). 'Where and what is phonology? A representational perspective'. In N.Burton-Roberts, P. Carr and G. Docherty (eds). *Phonological knowledge*. Oxford: Oxford University Press. 39–66.

— (2005). 'Robyn Carston on semantics, pragmatics and encoding'. (Review of Carston 2002). *Journal of Linguistics* 42: 389–407.

Burton-Roberts, N. and P. Carr (1999). 'On speech and natural language'. *Language Sciences* 21: 371–406.

Burton-Roberts, N. and G. Poole (2006a). 'Syntax vs phonology: A representational approach to stylistic fronting and verb-second in Icelandic'. *Lingua* 116: 562–600.

— (2006b). '"Virtual conceptual necessity", feature-dissociation and the Saussurian legacy in generative grammar'. *Journal of Linguistics* 42: 575–628.

Cappelen, H. and E. Lepore (2005). 'Radical and moderate pragmatics: does meaning determine truth conditions?' In Z. Szabo (ed.). *Semantics vs. Pragmatics*. Oxford: Oxford University Press. 45–71.

Carston, R. (1988). 'Implicature, explicature and truth-theoretic semantics'. In Kempson, R. (ed.). *Mental Representations*. 155–81. Reprinted in S. Davis (ed.) (1991). *Pragmatics: a reader*. Oxford: Oxford University Press. 33–51.

— (1998). 'Informativeness, relevance and scalar implicature'. In R. Carston and S. Uchida (eds). *Relevance theory: implications and applications*. Amsterdam: John Benjamins. 179–236.

— (2002). *Thoughts and utterances: the pragmatics of explicit communication*. Oxford: Blackwell.

Chng, S. (1999). 'Language, thought and literal meaning'. PhD thesis. University of Newcastle.

Chomsky, N. (1995). *The minimalist program*. Cambridge, Mass.: MIT Press.

— (2000). 'Language from an internalist perspective'. In N. Smith (ed.). *New horizons in the study of language and mind*. Cambridge University Press. 134–63.

Cormack, A. and N. Smith (1997). 'Checking features and split signs'. *Working Papers in Linguistics* 8. University College London. 223–322.

Fodor, J. (1998). *Concepts: where cognitive science went wrong*. New York: Oxford University Press.

Fodor, J. and E. Lepore (1998). 'The emptiness of the lexicon: reflections on James Pustejovsky's *The Generative Lexicon*'. *Linguistic Inquiry* 29: 269–88.

Groefsema, M. (2007). 'Concepts and word meaning in relevance theory'. This volume.

Hintzman, D. (1986). '"Schema abstraction" in a multiple-trace memory model'. *Psychological Review* 93: 411–28.

Horn, L. (1989). *A natural history of negation*. Chicago, IL: University of Chicago Press.

Jackendoff, R. (1997). *The architecture of the language faculty*. Cambridge, Mass.: MIT Press.

Kempson, R., W. Meyer-Viol and D. Gabbay (2001). *Dynamic syntax*. Oxford: Blackwell.

Lewis, D. (1970). 'General semantics'. *Synthese* 22: 18–67. Reprinted in D. Lewis (1983). *Philosophical papers*. Vol. 1. New York: Oxford University Press. 189–229.

Pelczar, M. (2000). 'Wittgensteinian semantics'. *Noûs* 34.4: 483–516.

Pinker, S. (1992). 'Review of Bickerton, D. *Language and species*' (1990 University of Chicago Press). *Language* 68: 375–82.

Recanati, F. (1998). 'Pragmatics'. *Routledge encyclopaedia of philosophy*. Vol. 7. 620–33.

— (2004). *Literal meaning*. Cambridge: Cambridge University Press.

Richards, I.A. (1936). *The philosophy of rhetoric*. New York: Oxford University Press.

Sadock, J. (1984). 'Wither radical pragmatics?' In D. Schriffin (ed.). *Meaning, form and use in context*. Washington, DC: Georgetown University Press.

— (2005). Abstract for 'Math according to GARP.' Available at <http://www.lcs. pomona.edu/JayFest/abstract.htm>.

Searle, J. (1965). 'What is a Speech Act?' In M. Black (ed.). *Philosophy in America*. London: Allen & Unwin.

— (1980). 'The background of meaning'. In J. Searle et al (eds). *Speech act theory and pragmatics*. Dordrecht: Reidel. 221–32.

Sperber, D. and D. Wilson (1986). *Relevance: communication and cognition*. Oxford: Blackwell.

— (1998). 'The mapping between the mental and the public lexicon'. In P. Carruthers and J. Boucher (eds). *Language and thought*. 184–200.

Thomason, R. (1972). 'A semantic theory of sortal incorrectness'. *Journal of Philosophical Logic* 1: 205–98.

Vincente, B. (2005). 'Meaning in relevance theory and the semantics/pragmatics distinction'. In S. Coulson and B. Lewandowska-Tomaszczyk (eds). *The literal and non-literal in language and thought*. Frankfurt am Main: Petr Lang.

Young, D.G. (2006). 'The problem of semantic underdeterminacy: a representational approach'. PhD thesis. University of Newcastle.

7

relevance theory and shared content

herman cappelen and ernie lepore

Speakers share content when they make the same assertion (claim, conjecture, proposal, etc.). They also share content when they propose (entertain, discuss, etc.) the same hypothesis, theory, and thought. And again when they evaluate whether what each says (thinks, claims, suggests, etc.) is true, false, interesting, obscene, original or offensive. Content sharing, so understood, is the very foundation of communication. Relevance theory (RT), however, implies that content sharing is impossible; or at least, we will argue as much in what follows.

This chapter is divided into three sections. In section 1, we amplify on what we mean by 'shared content' and its roles in how we think about language and communication; we discuss various strategies RT might invoke to account for shared content and why all these strategies fail. Section 2 is exegetical; there we show why RT *must* deny the possibility of shared content. The denial is a direct consequence of some of the most central tenets of RT. It is, however, a consequence downplayed by RT proponents. Our goal in section 2 is to show how central the denial of shared content is to RT. In section 3 we outline how we think a pragmatic theory should account for shared content.

question: good enough?

According to RT, interpreters follow 'the least effort strategy' (LES):

> (LES) Check interpretive hypotheses in order of their accessibility, that is, follow a path of least effort, until an interpretation which satisfies the expectation of relevance is found; then stop. (Carston 2004, 822)

In section 2 we elaborate on how exactly to interpret (LES) and its RT defence. For now, we assume (LES) and ask: How does pursuing (LES)

115

help the interpreter work out which proposition a speaker intends to communicate (i.e. which proposition she endorses, believes, etc.)? Here's Carston's reply:

> It [i.e. the procedure described in (LES)] provides a reliable, though by no means foolproof, means of inferring a speaker's meaning. As a patently non-demonstrative inference process, it sometimes fails and doesn't come up with the intended meaning. And when it is successful what is achieved is *seldom* a perfect replication in the hearer's mind of the very assumptions the speaker intended to communicate. An utterance, like any ostensive stimulus, usually licenses not a single interpretation, but any one of a number of interpretations with *very similar* import; provided the addressee recovers one of these, comprehension is successful, that is, *it is good enough.* (Carston 2004, 823; emphasis added)

Carston's view then is this: A speaker utters a sentence S intending to communicate the proposition that q; the interpreter 'typically' ends up with a range of propositions p1...pn, none of which is identical to q. But that's no problem, says Carston, because as long as p1...pn are similar to q, then that *is good enough.* In this respect, Carson agrees with Bezuidenhout:

> Since utterance interpretation is always in the first place colored by one's own cognitive perspective, we think we should reject the idea that there is an intermediate stage in communication which involves the recovery of some content shared by speaker and listener and which is attributed by the listener to the utterance. In communication....[w]e *need recognize only speaker-relative utterance content and listener-relative utterance content and a relation of similarity holding between these two contents...* This does not mean that we have to deny that literal interpretation requires the preservation of something. But this something need simply be a relevant degree of similarity between the thought expressed by the speaker and the thought expressed by the listener. (Bezuidenhout 2002, 212–13; emphasis added)

Sperber and Wilson, in their classic work (1986), do not make this explicit, but they do say:

> ... communication can be successful without resulting in an exact duplication of thoughts in communicator and audience. *We see*

communication as a matter of enlarging mutual cognitive environments, not of duplicating thoughts. (Sperber and Wilson 1986, 192–3; emphasis added)

All these writers are committed to a version of the following non-shared content principle (NSC):

(NSC): When a speaker utters a sentence, S, thereby intending to communicate the proposition that p, the audience will not grasp p. Instead, she will interpret the speaker to have intended to communicate some proposition (or set of propositions) R-related to p.

According to Carston and Bezuidenhout, the R-relation is similarity. In section 2, we argue that this is too optimistic; there's no non-trivial sense of 'similarity' in which the explicatures arrived at by using the Principle of Optimal Relevance will be similar to the proposition that the speaker intended to communicate. They will, if RT is correct, be developments of the same logical form LF, but an LF can be developed into *radically different* propositions, and there is, for example, no guarantee that the different developments will even have the same truth-value, much less the same truth conditions. So, only in a trivial sense are we, according to RT, guaranteed similarity between, on the one hand, the proposition the speaker intends to communicate and, on the other, the interpretation the interpreter will come up with by following the procedures RT claims we as a matter of fact do follow.

We leave the question of how to understand the R-relation for section 2. For now, we assume that R-relation is some kind of similarity relation (though the arguments we use in section 1 have even greater force if the R-relation isn't even similarity, in any interesting sense).

We'll argue that (NSC) is not, in Carston's terminology, *good enough.* We have three main arguments:

a. Theories that incorporate (NSC) fail to account for our reporting practices, i.e. our practice of reporting on what others say (assert, claim, suggest, propose, etc.). We consider two main strategies RT can exploit to explain what we do in such reports, and both, we argue, fail.

b. Theories that incorporate (NSC) fail to explain our practice of assessing what others assert (claim, suggest, propose, conjecture, etc.): if we (typically) don't grasp the proposition that they intended to express (but only one sufficiently similar), we can't evaluate the proposition they intended to express. At best, we will evaluate some proposition similar to the one they are committed to, and not the one they are actually committed to.

c. Theories that incorporate (NSC) create self-referential problems – they are what we will call 'Communicatively Self-Defeating' – a view is communicatively self-defeating if its truth implies that it can't be communicated (and hence, not evaluated).

Before moving to criticism, we make one more introductory remark: RT isn't the only theory that endorses NSC. It is a view in common among all theorists that Cappelen and Lepore (2005) call *Radical Contextualists*. Slightly more precisely, it's a feature of every theory that adheres to some version of (RC1)–(RC3):

(RC1): No English sentence S ever semantically expresses a proposition. Any semantic value assigned to a sentence S can be no more than a propositional fragment (or radical), where the hallmark of a propositional fragment (or radical) is that it does not determine a set of truth conditions, and hence, cannot take a truth-value.

(RC2): Context sensitivity is ubiquitous in this sense: Fixing for linguistic context sensitivity will never, no matter how widespread, issue in more than a propositional fragment.

(RC3): Only an utterance can semantically express a complete proposition, have a truth condition, and so, take a truth-value.

Searle (1978, 1980), Travis (1985, 1989, 1996), Recanati (2001, 2004), and a whole range of neo-Wittgensteinians, are all Radical Contextualists in this sense. Many of the objections raised against RT below apply also to all Radical Contextualists, but our focus here is on the specific version of NSC found in RT.

1. relevance theory vs shared content

(NSC) is treated as an interesting corollary of RT – it's presented more or less as an afterthought, 'Oh, by the way, if you buy into our story, you'll have to give up that old fashioned Fregean idea that in successful communication we share thoughts.' We suspect one reason for this is that (NSC) is seen as a *philosophical thesis* with *no direct empirical import*. But that's a serious error. (NSC) has direct consequence for how we should expect speakers to behave linguistically. In particular, (NSC) requires RT proponents to provide an explanation of what speakers do (how we as theorists should understand what they do) when they report on each other's speech, when they attribute beliefs to each other, and when they evaluate each other's speech and beliefs.

We discuss these in turn.

data 1: speech reports

Imagine someone, Naomi, uttering a sentence, S. To say what she said, we paradigmatically utter sentences like (1):

(1) Naomi said that p.

We end up having the belief expressed by such sentences because we interpret Naomi's utterance as having asserted that p. If (NSC) is correct, the proposition attributed to Naomi will (typically) be similar to, but not identical to, the proposition that Naomi intended to communicate with her utterance. That is, our utterances of sentences like (1) will attribute to Naomi the endorsement of a proposition different from the one she originally intended to communicate. A proponent of (NSC) has to tell us how to understand this kind of metalinguistic activity. She has but two options: (a) she can say that reports like (1) are literally false, or (b) she can say that (1) can be true even though Naomi did not intend to communicate the proposition that p. Both options are problematic for reasons discussed below.

To see the scope of this problem, consider sentences like (2) (with 'that' demonstrating Naomi's utterance of S):

(2) That's what Sally said too.

According to RT, what we've been doing is the following: we've reached an interpretation of Naomi that yields a proposition similar (but not identical) to the one Naomi intended to communicate; we've reached an interpretation of Sally that yields a proposition similar (but not identical) to the one that Sally intended to communicate, and in uttering (2), we're claiming that there's a single proposition such that both Sally and Naomi asserted it. Again, (NSC) proponents must tell us whether (NSC) implies that sentences like (2) (and more generally claims about speakers having made the same assertoric commitments) are false or should be interpreted in such a way that they come out true. Both options are criticized below.

data 2: from assertion to belief attributions

Often we exploit our conclusions about what people say in order to attribute beliefs to them. We're not mind readers, so we go from asserted contents to beliefs. In at least some context, the following is true: if we believe (1) to be true (and we also believe that Naomi was sincere, etc.), then we infer that Naomi believes that p. So in some contexts, the truth of (1) and (2), will enable us to infer that Naomi and Sally both believe that p.

If (NSC) were correct, this procedure would, at a minimum, be questionable. Remember, the proposition that we end up with in interpretation, is typically not the proposition that the speaker intended to communicate. It is a proposition similar to the one that she intended to communicate. We certainly do not believe all of the propositions similar to the ones we believe. (If we did, we would believe everything.) So, if (NSC) were true, then our practice of (sometimes) going from asserted content to belief attributions would be in jeopardy. Again, two strategies present themselves to the (NSC) proponent: (a) Agree that the attributions we end up with using this procedure are false, or (b) claim that belief reports – 'A believes that p' – can be true even though A doesn't endorse p, but only a proposition relevantly similar to p. Both of these options are evaluated below. At this point we don't mean to rule out either of these options. We just want to earmark that endorsing (NSC) has implications and so, its defence requires work.

data 3: assessments of assertions

There's a pretheoretic presumption, we think, in favour of the view that in speech and belief reports we share contents with the reportee. That presumption is even more salient in our evaluations of others' assertoric commitments and beliefs. Consider sentences like (3)–(6) (where the 'that' in (4)–(6) demonstrates Naomi's utterance):

(3)   I agree with Naomi.
(4)   That's true.
(5)   That's questionable/inflammatory/unacceptable/irrational/clever.
(6)   There's no evidence for that.

Again, there's tension between (NSC) and (3)–(6):

- There's tension between (3)–(4) and (NSC) because in uttering either (3) or (4) the speaker doesn't mean to express agreement just with a proposition similar to the one endorsed by Naomi's utterance;

the speaker of (3) or (4) means to express agreement with the very proposition/thought that Naomi expressed.

- There's a tension between (5)–(6) and (NSC) because in uttering (5) or (6) the speaker doesn't mean to evaluate a proposition similar to the one asserted by Naomi's utterance; the speaker of (5) or (6) means to evaluate the very proposition/thought that Naomi expressed.

1.1 revisionism and conservativism

The challenge for (NSC) proponents is to explain what the implications of their theory are for our practices of describing others' speech act contents, of going from such descriptions to belief attributions, and then, for evaluations of the attributed contents. We imagine (NSC) proponents responding to this data in one of two ways. (These strategies mirror the responses philosophers who advocate apparently counter-intuitive positions in other areas of philosophy make use of.)

1. Revisionist Strategy: RT implies that the statements we make (and the thoughts we have) about shared content (described in (1)–(6) above) are false. When we utter sentences like (1)–(6) (or think the thoughts they express), we make false claims (and have false thoughts). The Revisionist Strategy can be compared to an error theory about moral statements: Our moral language presupposes there are moral facts. It turns out that there are none. So, what we say when we make moral claims is false. Similarly: The concepts we use for talking about content presuppose that contents can be shared across contexts, but, according to the Revisionists, contents aren't shared across contexts. So, we end up making false statements and having false thoughts about content. Normal speakers not initiated into RT think that they can duplicate thoughts and that successful communication requires matching of propositions, but they are entirely wrong. RT reveals this pretheoretic prejudice for what it is.

2. Conservative Strategy: The Conservative Strategy says that when correctly interpreted, Data 1–Data 3 are *not* incompatible with (NSC). It's a confusion, the Conservative says, to think our common sense beliefs about shared content are incompatible with (NSC). When these pretheoretic beliefs (and the sentences used to express them, like (1)–(6)) are properly interpreted, they are, on the whole, true. The particular version of this we consider below says that utterances of the form 'A said that p' are true just in case A said something similar to p. That, the Conservative points out, is compatible with (NSC).

The discussion of these strategies has three parts: First, we present some objections to the Revisionist Strategy; then some objections to the Conservative Strategy. These first objections focus on how the two strategies deal with speech and belief reports. Then finally we discuss the ways in which both positions fail to provide an adequate account of our practice of evaluating others' sayings and beliefs.

1.2 objections to the revisionist strategy

Revisionists, as we have described them, imagine their revisionism limited to certain metalinguistic sentences and thoughts, those instantiated by (1)–(6). In their judgement, rejection of our belief in (1)–(6) is not too high a price to pay for a psychologically adequate theory of interpretation. The Revisionist thinks of herself as eliminating a non-theoretical dogma about content – a Fregean myth the denial of which has very little cost.

That impression is, however, quite mistaken. Our practice of content sharing is inextricably intertwined with other practices that figure centrally in our non-linguistic lives. If our beliefs about shared content are false, as the Revisionist claims, then our basic foundational beliefs about, and our understanding of, these non-linguistic practices are also in jeopardy. Here's what we have in mind:

- Coordinated action: Often, people in different contexts are asked to do the same thing, e.g. pay taxes. They receive the same instructions, are bound by the same rules, the same laws and conventions. For such instructions to function, we must assume a wide range of utterances express the same content.
- Collective deliberation: When people over a period of time, across a variety of contexts, try to find out whether something is so, they typically assume content stability across those contexts. Consider a CIA task force concerned with whether Igor knows that Jane is a spy. They are unsure whether or not he does. Investigators, over a period of time, in different contexts study this question. If what they are trying to determine, i.e. whether Igor knows that Jane is a spy, changes across contexts, contingent, for example, on their evidence, what is contextually salient, the conversational context, etc. collective deliberation across contexts would make no sense.
- Intra-personal deliberation: Suppose Igor, on his own, is trying to determine whether p is so. Suppose its being so makes a difference to his life, but he's unsure. Sometimes he thinks the evidence, on balance, supports p, sometimes not. It depends on how he looks at

the evidence, on what he takes to be the relevant considerations. Just as in the inter-personal case, this presupposes a stable content he's deliberating about.

- Justified belief: Much of our knowledge of the world is based on testimony. Hearing a trustworthy person assert that p can provide good reason to believe that p. If we think everything Jason says is true and he says naked mole rats are blind, we have good reason to believe naked mole rats are blind. But this is possible only if we can say what he said, viz. that naked mole rats are blind. We need to understand (and remember) what he said. We have to be in a position to agree with it. This is possible only if content can be shared across contexts.
- Responsibility: We hold people responsible for what they say, ask, request, claim, etc. We can do so only if we, in another context, can *understand* what they said (suggested, ordered, claimed, etc.), *say* what they said, and *investigate* what they said.
- Reasons for actions: A closely connected phenomenon is this: What others say often provides reasons for action. What people said in another context can provide reason for action only if we can understand what they have said, investigate it, trust it, etc.

These interconnections and mutual dependencies between content stability and non-linguistic practices are significant because any theory that implies content is *not* shared across contexts must account for the potentially devastating implications that this view has for these non-linguistic practices. To endorse a view that implies that what we do in all these cases is based on a fundamental confusion we harbour about the nature of our own language is an awfully high price to pay to protect relevance theory.

In sum, to accept (NSC) isn't just to reject some cutesy and fluffy philosophical dogma. It has direct implications for some of the most important aspects of our non-linguistic social practices. It implies that these practices are based on fundamentally mistaken beliefs. We believe we can give the same orders to many people, that what others say can justify our beliefs, that we can hold others responsible for what they have said, etc. But there's no such thing as shared content to underwrite these practices. Of course, we could be fundamentally mistaken about ourselves in just these very ways, but at least this much is clear: If you are inclined to bite this bullet, then you had better provide an alternative account of these non-linguistic practices. Absent some such story, we have, we think, some very good reasons for staying far away from this particular kind of revisionism.

1.3 objections to the conservative strategy

At the heart of the Conservative Strategy is the idea that sentences like 'A said that p', 'A said what B said', 'I agree with what A said', 'I understand exactly what A said', and the other such locutions do *not* require for their truth content *identity* across contexts. All that they require is content *similarity* across contexts. The details can be elucidated in various ways, one version of which is:

- 'A said that p' means the same as 'A said something similar to p'.
- 'A said what B said' means the same as 'A said something similar to what B said'.
- 'A and B agree' means the same as 'A and B endorse similar thoughts'.
- 'A understands what B said' means (something like) 'A grasped a proposition similar to the one expressed by B'.

And so on for other cases. According to this similarity view (SV), we do not make false claims when reporting or repeating others. Our practice has, wisely, factored in that there is no cross-contextual content identity.

We discuss four concerns we have about this strategy:

criticism 1: identity is transitive; similarity is not.

The most obvious and most serious problem for the Conservatives is this: Similarity is not transitive. Transitivity is, however, built into the 'said that' locution. Consider first (T1):

(T1): If A said what B said, and B said what C said, then A said what C said. If, however, A said something similar to what B said, and B said something similar to what C said, it simply doesn't follow that A said something similar to what C said.

(T1), according to the similarity theory, could be false. Since T1 can't be false, the similarity theory fails. 'A said that p' simply does not mean the same as 'A said something similar to p'. The same point is brought out by (T2):

(T2): If A said that p, and B said that p, then A and B said the same (or: A said what B said).

Again, the similarity theory implies that (T2) can come out false: If A said something similar to p, and B said something similar to p it doesn't follow that what A said is *identical* to what B said (or that what B said is similar to what A said).

As far as we can tell, this is about as close to a conclusive objection to the view that 'A said that p' means the same as 'A said something similar to p' that anyone will ever come up with. So, we could just end the critical discussion here. But there are three other philosophically revealing objections worth mentioning.

criticism 2: SV doesn't explain our distinction between saying exactly what someone said and saying something similar but not identical.

If 'A said that p' means 'A expressed a proposition similar to p', then how do we interpret sentences like:

- He almost said that p, but didn't.
- He came very close to saying that p, but didn't.
- What he said was similar to p, but not exactly p.

The easiest way to focus this criticism is to think about (SA):

(SA): A didn't say that p, but she said something similar to p.

In uttering (SA), we don't mean what the similarity theory predicts. According to the similarity theory, 'said that' means 'said something similar to', so (SA) should mean:

(SAS): A didn't say something similar to p, but he said something similar to something similar to p.

That is not what (SA) means. Suppose A asserted q. Suppose q is similar to p. Under those conditions, SAS would be false. SA would clearly be true. So SA can't mean what SAS means.

In sum: If content similarity is employed to explain what's meant by 'saying the same', it becomes impossible to explain what's meant by 'saying something similar, but not identical'.

criticism 3: claims about degrees of similarity and comparative similarity are unintelligible in connection with 'said that' claims.

We can make intelligible and even true similarity judgements of the form:

- A is more similar to B than to C.
- A is a little bit like B.
- A is like B in some respects.

According to SV, 'A said that p' means 'A expressed a proposition that's similar to p' but that predicts we should not only be able to make sense of, but also make, true judgements of the form:

- A said p very much.

The only reading we can get of this is that he said p over and over again. We clearly cannot get the reading predicted by the similarity theory.

criticism 4: similarity without identity.

The following seems plausible: to understand what it is to say a proposition similar to p, we must understand what it is to say that p. Similarity is parasitic on identity, in at least that respect. If the similarity theory were correct, then language would leave us with no linguistic device for talking about sameness of sayings, but only with a device for talking about the derivative phenomenon. But, if, in general, talk about F's being similar to G's requires that we can talk about F's and G's directly, then wouldn't it be exceedingly surprising if our language had *no* device whatsoever, for talking about what people say rather than what's similar to what people say? (Of course, if their view is correct, there should be no way to interpret the previous sentence in the way we are sure you, our reader, as a matter of fact, interpreted it.)

1.4 nsc and evaluations of speech acts

So far we have focused on Conservativism's and Revisionism's failures to account for our reporting practices. We turn now to their implications for our *assessments* of what others say. There's an obvious connection between these two issues: to evaluate what someone has said (asserted, suggested, etc.), we have first to determine what she has said (asserted, suggested, etc.). So RT's failure to account for our practices of reporting what others have said has direct implications for our ability to assess reported contents. The way this plays out depends on whether we are considering a Conservative or Revisionist version of RT. There are three main worries:

1. *Massive verbal disagreement*: The most obvious worry is this: If (NSC) were true, then when we think we're evaluating what Naomi intended to communicate, we're really just evaluating some proposition similar to that proposition. When we think we're evaluating what Naomi said, we're not. When we think we're collecting evidence and arguments against her claim, we're not. Our evaluations are always off their mark. We never really agree or disagree – we always miss our real target. There can be no doubt that our real target is the proposition that the speaker intended to communicate – what she intended to commit herself to.

It should be obvious that neither Conservativism nor Revisionism can alleviate this problem. The Revisionist, it would seem, endorses this view. She says this is one of the things we'll see clearly once we realize RT is true; it's a view we should embrace. Again, we hope it is clear that this is no minor cost of RT. It certainly is not a view that can be endorsed in passing, as an interesting corollary. It needs an account of the point of evaluation, on the assumption that evaluations are always off target. (Indeed, if what we argue in section 2 is correct, they are typically *way off target*.)

The situation is no better for the Conservative. According to her, it is true to say that Naomi said that p, even though the proposition she intended to communicate is q. It follows that an utterance of 'What Naomi said is true' can be true, even though the proposition she intended to communicate, i.e. that q is false (on the assumption that p and q are R-related). This is in itself an extremely counter-intuitive and unattractive implication of (NSC).

2. *Varying truth-values*: Here's another unattractive implication of Conservativism: If the Conservative were correct, it could be true, in a context of interpretation, C1, to utter 'What Naomi said is true' and in another context of interpretation, C2, false to utter the very same sentence (assuming the demonstrative demonstrates the same utterance by Naomi). Imagine a context of utterance, C, in which A utters S intending to communicate q. In C1, p is sufficiently similar to q, and q is true, so in C1, it is true to say, 'What A said is true'. In another context of interpretation, C2, p is sufficiently similar to r, and r is false. So, in C2 it is false to say 'What A said is true'. So, in C1, what A said is true, while in C2, what she said is false. The truth-value of her utterance will vary from one context of utterance to another.

These are two intrinsically problematic implications of (NSC). But they also lead RT into various positions best described as weakly self-defeating.

3. *NSC is communicatively self-defeating*: Hawthorne (2004) describes a position as 'weakly self-defeating' if the truth of the position implies that we should not believe it. (NSC) has a related problem: Let's say a position is 'Communicatively Self-Defeating' if it follows from the truth of the position that it can't be communicated. If a position is communicatively self-defeating, then it implies that no one can understand it or that no one can evaluate whether it is true or false (rational or irrational, well supported or not, etc.).

(NSC) is communicatively self-defeating: it implies, first, that what the proponents of (NSC) think and intend to communicate will not be communicated to their intended audience. Some proposition R-related to what they intend to communicate might be communicated, but this might be very different from what the proponents of (NSC) have in mind. As a consequence, it implies that those who try to evaluate (NSC) (like us) will provide evidence and arguments against a position different from the position (NSC) proponents intended to communicate.

2. relevance theory and nsc

Our attribution of (NSC) to RT proponents has been based primarily on a passage in Carston (2002), where she endorses something much like it. That passage does not, however, reveal the full extent of relevance theorists' commitment to (NSC). It does not make clear just how radical a version of (NSC) follows from taking relevance-theoretic principles. In what follows we will argue:

a. (NSC) is a direct implication of central tenets of RT.
b. RT does not guarantee significant similarity between the proposition the speaker intended to communicate and the explicatures the audience reaches by using the procedure described by RT.

In this respect, we think, RT proponents misrepresent their theory to a significant extent. The discussion of specific examples by RT proponents essentially ignores (NSC). It gives the impression that we can say and grasp what's said by an utterance.

2.1 optimal relevance and contextual effects

According to RT, an interpreter encounters an utterance of a sentence with a certain logical form; she then looks for a development of that logical form that is *optimally relevant*. A development of a logical form is optimally relevant just in case it is 'at least relevant enough to warrant the addressee's attention and, moreover, as relevant as is compatible with the communicator's competence and goals' (Carston 2004, 822). More specifically:

optimization of relevance

> A speaker (or more generally, an ostensive communicator) calls for an expenditure of mental effort from an addressee (an outlay of attentional and inferential resources) and that licenses an expectation of a worthwhile yield of cognitive effects and no gratuitous expenditure of effort. This is captured by the 'Communicative Principle of Relevance': every act of ostension communicates a presumption of its own optimal relevance; that is, a presumption that it will be at least relevant enough to warrant the addressee's attention and, moreover, as relevant as is compatible with the communicator's competence and goals. (Carston 2004, 822)

The presumption of optimal relevance leads us to utilize the least effort strategy (LES) for interpretation (which we repeat here):

> (LES) Check interpretive hypotheses in order of their accessibility, that is, follow a path of least effort, until an interpretation which satisfies the expectation of relevance is found; then stop. (Carston 2004, 822)

Carston spells out the reasoning in the following passage:

> The least effort strategy follows from the presumption of optimal relevance in that the speaker is expected to have found an utterance for the communication of her thoughts which minimizes the hearer's effort (modulo her own goals and abilities); the justification for the addressee stopping processing as soon as an interpretation satisfies his expectation of relevance follows similarly, in that any other interpretation that might also achieve the requisite level of effects will be less accessible and so incur greater processing costs. (Carston 2004, 822)

To understand this, we need to understand the central notion in RT: *Relevance*. The notion of relevance is intertwined with that of a *Contextual Effect*. Sperber and Wilson write:

> The notion of a contextual effect is essential to a characterization of relevance. We want to argue that having contextual effects is a

necessary condition for relevance, and that other things being equal, the greater the contextual effects, the greater the relevance. (Sperber and Wilson 1986, 116)

The connections between relevance and cognitive effects are spelled out in the following two conditions:

> *Extent Condition 1*: An assumption is relevant in a context to the extent that its contextual effects in this context are large.
> *Extent Condition 2*: An assumption is relevant in a context to the extent that the effort required to process it in this context is small. (Sperber and Wilson 1986, 125)

Carston summarizes the notion of a contextual (or cognitive) effect, as follows:

> Cognitive effects (or contextual effects) include the strengthening of existing assumptions of the system, by providing further evidence for them, the elimination of assumptions that appear to be false, in the light of the new evidence, and the derivation of new assumptions through the interaction of the new information with existing assumptions. (Carston 2004, 822)

On this view, a new assumption (or a new piece of information) can have three kinds of contextual effects: (a) it can *combine* with old information to derive new information (that couldn't have been derived before); (b) it can provide new evidence *for* old assumptions; and (c) it can provide new evidence *against* old assumptions. An interpretation is relevant to the extent that it has contextual (or cognitive) effects.

2.2 from optimal relevance to nsc

When an interpreter looks for an interpretation that satisfies the principle of optimal relevance, she checks for cognitive (i.e. contextual) effects. The cognitive effects of an utterance on a person at a time t will depend, essentially, on the beliefs the interpreter has at t. These vary between interpreters. They vary for a single interpreter over time. Here is an example: The sentences of this chapter have certain logical forms. The readers of this chapter will develop these until they satisfy the Principle of Optimal Relevance. Which development satisfies that principle for a particular reader R will depend on the contextual effects these logical forms have on R. We have no way to predict in advance which development of these logical forms various readers will end up with. There are infinitely many such developments and common sense dictates that readers will all end up in different places. There's not even a guarantee that these places will be similar – developments of these logical forms can be radically different and it would be a minor miracle if they were not.

When Carston and Bezuidenhout tell us to relinquish the very idea of shared content, they proffer the prospect of similarity as a substitute, but what does that really amount to and what in RT guarantees it? Any interpretation of an utterance u of a sentence S will be a development of the logical form of S – so in that sense, there's similarity. But what counts as a 'development' is unconstrained in this sense: whatever you end up with as a result of applying (LES), starting from the logical form of the sentence you're interpreting, will be a development of that logical form. What you end up with depends on what cognitive effects the utterance has on you, and that again on what beliefs (etc.) that the interpreter has. Even if we fix a standard of similarity, there's no guarantee that what radically different interpreters would end up with is similar were they to use (LES).

The way we just put this point assumes that there's some fixed standard of similarity that RT can appeal to. That assumption is false. It's a basic fact about similarity that what counts as similar to what depends on contextually determined standards of similarity. So if the relevance theorist tells us that the process she describes ends up guaranteeing similarity between the results reached by different conversational participants, she needs to tell us *by what standard of similarity* this is supposed to be so. There is trivially no guarantee that what we end up with will be similar *by all such standards*. Of course, there will always be *some* standards by which what interpreters and speakers end up with is similar, but that's hardly comforting (since this standard could be absurdly loose – e.g. explicatures will all be similar in that they are developments of logical forms). The relevance theorist could try to suggest that the interpretative results in C will be similar by the similarity standards of C. But again, given the radical variability in standards between contexts, what could possibly guarantee this claim? Certainly nothing in relevance theory itself guarantees it.

In sum, the claim that what conversational participants end up with will be similar, has no basis in relevance theory. For a most radical illustration of this, consider Carston's notion of *ad hoc concept construction;* these are 'cases where any one of a wide range of related concepts might be communicated by a single lexical item' (Carston 2004, 641). She gives the following examples:

> ... think of all the different kinds, degrees and qualities of feeling that can be communicated by each of *tired, anxious, frightened, depressed, well, happy, satisfied, sweet*, etc. In one context, an utterance of *I'm happy* could communicate that the speaker feels herself to be in a steady state of low-key well-being, in another that she is experiencing a moment of intense joy, in yet another that she is satisfied with the outcome of some negotiation, and so on. The general concept HAPPY encoded by the lexical item *happy* gives access to an indefinite number of more specific concepts, recoverable in particular contexts by relevance-driven inference. (Carston 2004, 644)

There is, in Carston's view, an indefinite number of concepts that could be communicated by an utterance of a sentence containing *happy*. She doesn't tell us how many 'an indefinite number' is, but it's probably a lot. Which one an interpreter latches on to, depends on what is relevant to that interpreter and that depends on which cognitive effects the utterance has on her. That, again, depends on what beliefs and other cognitive states she's in at the time of interpreting the utterance. For the reasons given above, it is not only hard to imagine an argument that could establish that a speaker and number of audience members will invariably end up with similar results after going through such a process, it is also hard to understand what 'similar' could mean in such a claim.

In conclusion: Proponents of RT should endorse a particularly extreme version of (NSC), according to which speaker and audiences might faultlessly interpret each other, and nonetheless end up with explicatures that are radically different from each other.

3. pluralistic minimalism

A central challenge in pragmatics is to develop a theory of communication that reconciles two fundamental facts: we can share contents across contexts and communicated content is deeply context sensitive. Both sets of data are robust: what ends up in a speaker's mind when hearing an utterance depends on an extraordinarily wide range of features both of the speaker's context of utterance and the context of the audience. At the same time, the idea that speakers and audiences, variously situated, should be incapable of sharing contents runs counter to equally fundamental features of our linguistic self-understanding (if that sounds too metaphorical, what we mean by it is spelled out in section 1).

Here, in summary form, is our solution to this apparently paradoxical data set (presented in more detail in Cappelen and Lepore 2004): The crucial step is to relinquish what we call Speech Act Monism. This is the view that each utterance of a sentence says (asserts, claims, etc.) just one thing (one proposition, one thought). It is Speech Act Monism that generates even the appearance of tension between content stability and variability: If utterance u_1 of S says just one thing, e.g. p, and utterance u_2 of S says something else, e.g. q, and if $p \neq q$, then how could u_1 and u_2 say the same? Here's the solution: Drop the idea that an utterance expresses one proposition, i.e. endorse a combination of what we call Speech Act Pluralism and Semantic Minimalism. (We call the combination Pluralistic Minimalism.)

According to Speech Act Pluralism, any utterance can be used to express a plurality of propositions. Accordingly, u_1 of S expresses a set of propositions, say, C1, and u_2 of S expresses a set of propositions, say, C2; and it may be that C1 $\neq$ C2, i.e. they don't share the exact same members. This, however, does not prevent an overlap. If C1 and C2 do overlap, then there is an obvious explanation of how u_1 and u_2 can both say different things and yet say the same. When we speak of two utterances of S saying the same, we are focusing on the area of overlap, and when we speak of two utterances saying different things, we are focusing on the area of non-overlap.

Two utterances of S might express different sets of propositions. We claim that if you adjust for obviously context sensitive expressions (i.e. hold the semantic value of these stable), then these sets will have at least one proposition in common. Call this *the semantic content of S*, i.e. one way (not the only) to characterize the semantic content of S is as that content which all utterances of S have in common (once we adjust for obvious context sensitivity). The view that there is such a common content we call *Semantic Minimalism* ('minimalism' because the contextual influence is minimal).

What's our argument for Semantic Minimalism, i.e. that there is such an overlap between different utterances of S? In earlier work, we presented three kinds of arguments (for more details, see Cappelen and Lepore 2004, ch. 10):

1. Semantic Minimalism helps explain how we can share contents across contexts. If we accept that theory, we can explain why contents are not contextually trapped. If our arguments above are right, then this

is our only protection against what can be called contextual content solipsism. Semantic Minimalism guarantees a level of content that enables speakers whose conversational, perceptual and cognitive environments are very different to agree and disagree. It's a kind of inference to the best explanation.

2. There's a related argument (in some sense the flip side of the last one), but it appeals more directly to intuitions: When we encounter a range of utterances of S in diverse contexts (or just one utterance in a context we are ignorant of), we're often inclined to use S to say what was said by these utterances. When we do that, i.e. when we focus on what they all share (or what was said by a single utterance in an unknown context), we have a kind of direct access to the minimal content. It's not something we focus on (or care about) in most contexts, but when we do, it's right there and we have direct cognitive access to it.

3. Finally, we argued that the view that there's no common content is internally inconsistent. We will not present that argument here because it requires saying much more about our opponent's position, but for an extended discussion see Cappelen and Lepore (2005, ch. 9).

Pluralistic Minimalism has two important corollaries:

1. A Pluralistic Minimalist must reject the Speech Act Conception of Semantics. The Speech Act Conception of Semantics can be characterized as follows:
   - According to the Speech Act Conception of Semantics variability in what speakers say by uttering S in different contexts is relevant to semantics of S because the goal of semantics is, roughly speaking, to account for the content of speech acts performed by utterances of sentences. So, if S is a sentence of L and S is used to say that p (to assert that p), then the semantics for L should explain how that could be. On this view, there must be a close explanatory connection (this connection can be spelled out in various ways) between the semantic content of S and the content of speech acts involving S. As a corollary, if what is said by utterances of S varies between contexts of utterance, then the semantic content of S should be context sensitive.

2. Pluralistic Minimalists must also reject the Semantic Conception of Indirect Reports, according to which: If 'A said that p' is a true indirect report of an utterance of S, then the semantic content of p (as it occurs in that report) should be identical to the semantic content of S. In short, they reject that view that indirect reports report on semantic contents.

Both (1) and (2) have important implications for how one thinks about the methodology of semantics (for more details, see Cappelen and Lepore 2004, chs 1–4). Even with these pieces in place, we should emphasize that Pluralistic Minimalism is a research project, not a completed theory. The challenges for this project fall into three main categories:

- Say more about the nature of speech act content.
- Say more about semantic contents.
- Say more about the relationship between speech act content and semantic content.

We have started some of that work in Cappelen and Lepore (2006) and (forthcoming), but we have no doubt that the framework is in need of considerable additional refinement.

references

Bezuidenhout, A. (2002). 'Truth-Conditional Pragmatics'. *Philosophical Perspectives* 16: 105–34.

Cappelen, H. and E. Lepore (2004). 'Context Shifting Arguments'. *Philosophical Perspectives*. 25–50.

— (2005). *Insensitive Semantics*. Oxford: Basil Blackwell.

— (2006). 'Reply to Critics'. *Mind and Language* 21.1: 50–73.

— (forthcoming). 'Reply to Critics'. *Philosophy and Phenomenological Research*.

Carston, R. (2002). *Thoughts and Utterances: The Pragmatics of Explicit Communication*. Oxford: Blackwell.

— (2004). 'Explicature and Semantics'. In S. Davis and B. Gillon (eds). *Semantics: A Reader*. Oxford: Oxford University Press.

Hawthorne, John (2004). *Knowledge and Lotteries*. Oxford: Oxford University Press.

Recanati, F. (2001). 'What is Said'. *Synthese* 128: 75–91.

— (2004). *Literal Meaning*. Cambridge: Cambridge University Press.

Searle, John (1978). 'Literal Meaning'. *Erkenntnis* 13: 207–24.

— (1980). 'The Background of Meaning'. In J. Searle, F. Kiefer and M. Bierwisch (eds). *Speech Act Theory and Pragmatics*. Dordrecht: Reidel. 221–32.

Sperber, D. and D. Wilson (1986). *Relevance*. Oxford: Blackwell.

Travis, Charles (1985). 'On What is Strictly Speaking True'. *Canadian Journal of Philosophy* 15.2: 187–229.

— (1989). *The Uses of Sense*. Oxford: Oxford University Press.

— (1996). 'Meaning's Role in Truth'. *Mind* 100: 451–66.

8
concepts and word meaning in relevance theory[1,2]

marjolein groefsema

1. introduction

In the context of relevance theory, Sperber and Wilson (1986/1995) propose that the meaning of a word is a concept. A concept in their view is a psychological object consisting of a label or address (86), which performs two different and complementary functions:

1. It may appear as a constituent of a logical form.
2. It appears as an address in memory, a heading under which different types of information can be stored and retrieved.

Concepts have different entries for the different types of information:

> The *logical* entry for a concept consists of a set of deductive rules which apply to logical forms of which that concept is a constituent. The *encyclopaedic* entry contains information about the extension and/or denotation of the concept.... The *lexical* entry contains information about the natural language counterpart of the concept: the word or phrase of natural language which expresses it.... information about its syntactic category membership and co-occurrence possibilities, phonological structure and so on. (86, 90)

For Sperber and Wilson the distinction between logical and encyclopaedic entries is crucial. The information in the logical entry of a concept represents the logical properties of that concept. The information in the encyclopaedic entry represents our knowledge of the events, objects and properties which instantiate the concept. The information in logical entries is computational in that it consists of a set of deductive rules, while the information in the encyclopaedic entries is representational, in that it consists of a set of assumptions which may undergo deductive rules. So, the concept AND will have a logical entry which contains the deductive rules in (1):

(1) And-elimination
    (a) Input: (P and Q)
        Output: P
    (b) Input: (P and Q)
        Output: Q (86)

And a concept ORCHID may have an encyclopaedic entry as in (2):

(2) Orchids are rare flowers. (82)

Sperber and Wilson go one step further and propose that not only concepts such as AND and OR have logical entries, but also that concepts such as GIRAFFE, MOTHER and YELLOW have logical properties which are encoded as deductive rules in logical entries. These logical properties are necessary conditions which hold for a concept (as proposed by the classical lexical decomposition view). Sometimes the set of necessary conditions found in a logical entry will be sufficient to define the concept (as in the case of BACHELOR), while in other cases the set of necessary conditions will not amount to a definition. For example, GIRAFFE will have a logical entry as in (3):

(3) Giraffe-elimination rule
    Input: (X – giraffe – Y)
    Output: (X – animal of a certain species – Y) (92)

A further difference between logical and encyclopaedic information is that whenever a conceptual address is accessed, the deductive rules in the logical entry will apply automatically, while encyclopaedic information becomes accessible but need not actually be accessed. Whether encyclopaedic information is actually accessed depends on the context in which the utterance is processed.

In this chapter, I will show that the relevance theory view of concepts is open to different interpretations. Moreover, these different interpretations of what constitutes the content of concepts make different

predictions about what can be taken as part of the proposition expressed
by an utterance (the explicature), and what is implicitly communicated
by an utterance. Within relevance theory, relevance is defined in terms of
cognitive effects derived on the basis of the interaction of the proposition
expressed/ explicature with assumptions in the context. It is therefore
crucial to establish where the explicature-implicature distinction should
be drawn.

2. different views

At first sight, given the view of concepts as labels which perform different
functions, it seems that the meaning of a word, say *horse*, is a simple
unanalyzable concept, say HORSE. However, Sperber and Wilson go on to
treat concepts as triples of entries filed at an address. This means that a
concept is not simply an address, but rather that the address is the form
of a concept while the entries spell out its content:

> ... the distinction between address and entry is a distinction between
> form and content, the address being what actually appears in logical
> forms, and the various entries spelling out its logical, lexical and
> encyclopaedic content. (Sperber and Wilson 1986/1995, 92)

If the different entries represent the content of a concept, and we can
specify the different sorts of information that are stored in these entries,
then it follows that on this view we do not have simple unanalyzable
concepts, but rather that concepts are complexes of information in
different formats (deductive rules, assumptions, representations of
linguistic form).

This seems a bit too strong. If the meaning of a word is a concept, and
the content of a concept is a triple of entries including a lexical entry,
then it seems that part of the meaning of a word consists of its syntactic
properties and phonological form. In other words, the meaning of a
word includes syntactic and phonological information about the word
of which it is the meaning – an undesirable conclusion.

We can retreat from this conclusion by saying that linguistic information
is not conceptual information (although we can conceptualize hypotheses
about what linguistic information is like), so that it cannot be part of
the content of a concept. Instead, we can view the relation between a
conceptual address and a representation of linguistic information as a
mapping relation, so that activation of linguistic information of a word

(e.g. activation of its phonological form) gives access to a conceptual address, and vice versa.

What then is the content of a concept? Following from the above, we could say that the logical and encyclopaedic entries of a concept constitute the content of that concept, while there is a mapping relation between a conceptual address and a linguistic entry. Alternatively, we could say that the claim that the different entries of a concept constitute the content of that concept is too strong, and retreat to the position that conceptual addresses are simple and unanalyzable concepts, i.e. that *horse* means HORSE. This would mean that the concept HORSE has content independent from the different entries stored under it, since otherwise the claim that *horse* means HORSE reduces to the claim that the meaning of the linguistic form *horse* is simply a different form. On one reading of relevance theory, this seems to be the position ultimately endorsed. However, Sperber and Wilson make a further distinction between logical and encyclopaedic entries by postulating that:

> ... the content of an assumption is determined by the logical entries of the concepts it contains, while the context in which it is processed is, at least in part, determined by their encyclopaedic entries. (Sperber and Wilson 1986/1995, 89)

This seems to imply that the content of concepts can be equated with their logical entries, even if not all concepts have logical entries which give a definition of the concept.

What we end up with then is three different possible views of what constitutes the content of concepts:

1. The logical and encyclopaedic entries of a concept constitute the content of the concept.
2. Conceptual addresses are simple, unanalyzable concepts whose entries do not constitute their content.
3. The logical entry of a concept constitutes the content of that concept, while information in the encyclopaedic entry does not contribute to the content of the concept. The role of the encyclopaedic entry is to contribute to the context in which an utterance encoding the concept is interpreted.

These different views of what constitutes the content of concepts make different predictions about what can be taken as part of the proposition expressed by an utterance, and what is implicitly communicated when an utterance is made.

2.1 view 1

If the logical and encyclopaedic entries of a concept constitute the content of a concept, then information in those entries must (in principle) be part of the proposition expressed by an utterance when the concept is part of the proposition expressed by the utterance. To make this a bit more concrete: if I am processing the utterance in (4), and I have as a logical entry for ORCHID a deductive rule which allows me to infer FLOWER OF A CERTAIN SPECIES, then for me part of the proposition expressed by the utterance is (5):

(4) John saw an orchid.

(5) JOHN SAW A FLOWER OF A CERTAIN SPECIES.

Similarly, if I have an encyclopaedic entry ORCHIDS ARE RARE FLOWERS, and I access this assumption, then for me part of the proposition expressed by the utterance is (6):

(6) JOHN SAW A RARE FLOWER.

In other words, 'the proposition expressed by an utterance' turns out to be a complex representation containing a number of different assumptions. This has as a consequence that (6) can't be a contextual implication of the utterance because the encyclopaedic entry contributes to the content rather than the context, even though the context causes me to access the assumption that orchids are rare flowers.

On this view we get an account of word meaning which is dynamic rather than invariant: how we interpret a word in a particular utterance depends on which bits of encyclopaedic information we recover. Proposing the distinction between logical entries (in terms of necessary conditions) and encyclopaedic entries then amounts to the claim that the interpretation of words in utterances is partly context independent and partly context dependent. However, this claim cannot be maintained in view of examples such as the following from Jackendoff (1983, 150):[3]

(7) a. I must have looked at that a dozen times, but I never saw it.
     b. I must have seen that a dozen times, but I never noticed it.

Although we often use the word *see* to communicate a concept which expresses something like *X has a visual experience of Y* and *X's gaze goes to Y*, the examples in (7) show that either of these properties of seeing can be cancelled: we interpret the use of *see* in (7a) as expressing *X has a visual experience of Y*, while we interpret the use of *see* in (7b) as expressing *X's gaze goes to Y*. In view of this it is hard to maintain that what we are dealing with are 'logical implications', in the sense of 'necessary conditions'.

A consequence of this is that we seem to lose the distinction between what determines the content of an assumption and what determines the context, since on this view encyclopaedic information determines content as well as logical information.[4]

2.2 view 2

If conceptual addresses are simple, unanalyzable concepts, whose entries do not constitute their content, then in the above scenario both assumptions (5) and (6) would come out as implicatures: assumptions that I recover on the basis of the proposition expressed by *John saw an orchid*. The question then is what kind of implicatures we are dealing with. Sperber and Wilson propose that there are two kinds of implicatures: implicated premises and implicated conclusions. Implicated premises are recovered from memory or constructed from an assumption schema held in memory, and are used in the derivation of implicated conclusions. Implicated conclusions are deduced on the basis of the explicature(s) of an utterance together with the implicated premise(s). In the above scenario JOHN SAW A RARE FLOWER comes out as an implicated conclusion, which we can deduce on the basis of the explicature JOHN SAW AN ORCHID and the implicated premise ORCHIDS ARE RARE FLOWERS. On the other hand, JOHN SAW A FLOWER OF A CERTAIN SPECIES cannot be an implicated conclusion because it is deduced solely on the basis of the explicature. Nor is it an implicated premise in an obvious way; it is not recovered from memory, nor constructed from an assumption schema. Moreover, although it could operate as a premise in a further deductive process, it is not mandatory that it does so for the utterance to achieve a relevant interpretation. It seems then that on this view we need to distinguish a third kind of implicature, to account for the status of conclusions derived from logical entries. However, this raises a further problem: JOHN SAW A RARE FLOWER comes out as a contextual implication, and therefore contributes to the relevance of the utterance. JOHN SAW A FLOWER OF A CERTAIN SPECIES is not a contextual implication (it is an analytic implication), which raises the question of why we would deduce it at all: in the absence of assumptions about whether or not John has seen some flower, it does not immediately contribute to the relevance of the utterance, because it does not constitute a contextual effect. And although it could operate as the input to a further deductive process it need not do so, so that we may end up with an assumption that does not play a role in the computation of contextual effects.[5]

In fact, Carston (2002a, 138ff) identifies analytic implications such as these as implicatures. She claims that because these implications are derived by deductive inference 'the mechanism involved is essentially the same as that for any implicated conclusion' (141). However, there is a crucial difference. Implicated conclusions are synthetic implications which are deduced from the explicatures of the utterance and the context (Sperber and Wilson 1986/1995, 195) and thereby contribute to the relevance of the utterance. Analytic implications, on the other hand, are deduced by analytic rule only and therefore do not automatically contribute to the relevance of the utterance.

On this view, the contribution a lexical item makes to the proposition expressed by an utterance is invariant. With regard to the distinction between logical and encyclopaedic entries, this view raises the question of what the advantage is in postulating that there are logical entries containing elimination rules representing necessary conditions. Although these rules drive deductive processes, it is not quite clear what these deductive processes are for, unless it can be shown that they always contribute to relevance by yielding contextual effects. If the same information were represented as encyclopaedic information rather than as elimination rules, the resulting implicatures would be contextual implications and therefore contribute to the relevance of the utterance.

2.3 view 3

If the logical entry of a concept constitutes the content of that concept, while information from the encyclopaedic entry is added to the context, then information in the logical entry must be part of the proposition expressed by an utterance when the concept is part of the proposition expressed by the utterance. In the above scenario, this means that (5) comes out as part of the proposition expressed, while (6) is an implicature, which is a contextual implication and therefore contributes to the relevance of the utterance. This means that we do not have to worry about the role of the analytic implication: it is part of the content of the utterance, and may or may not play a role in computing contextual effects. However, this division between content and context has the following consequence: from the assumption JOHN SAW A RARE FLOWER I can conclude JOHN SAW A FLOWER by analytic rule, and because something cannot be a flower without being a flower of some species I can also derive that John saw a flower of some species. On the assumption that logical properties of concepts are deduced automatically, I cannot help but recover these implications. This means that, given the definition of contextual implication, JOHN SAW A FLOWER OF A CERTAIN SPECIES comes out as a contextual implication. But this conclusion also constitutes the content of the assumption that I started out with, so that the same assumption constitutes the content of an assumption and is contextually implicated by that assumption. This then leads to the picture that part of the relevance of an utterance can lie in deducing (or rededucing) its own content. Since this deductive process does not yield a new implication, it seems to go against the rationale of relevance theory.

On this view, as with View 2, the contribution a lexical item makes to the content of the proposition expressed by an utterance is invariant: it consists of the analytic implications deduced via the elimination rules in the logical entry of its associated concept. This raises the question of what is contributed by those lexical items whose meanings are concepts that lack logical entries, or that have entries which do not have necessary conditions which are sufficient to define the concept. One has to assume that these concepts have further content of some sort, because if they didn't, this view would predict that concepts such as ORCHID and ROSE would be synonymous. This further content cannot be supplied by the encyclopaedic entry of the concept, because by hypothesis encyclopaedic entries determine context, not content. This leaves as a possibility that conceptual addresses of those concepts whose logical entries do not exhaust their meaning have independent content. However, this leads to the conclusion that conceptual addresses are forms/labels in the case of defined concepts, while they have content in the case of underdefined concepts. If that is the case, then we can't maintain the claim that logical entries determine content. In order to keep a unitary account of conceptual addresses, we have to postulate that conceptual addresses have independent content (View 2), but that in the case where a logical entry gives us a definition, this logical entry represents that content, rather than determines it.

Alternatively, we could postulate that the (remaining) content of those concepts whose logical entries do not exhaust their content is supplied by a perceptual representation (e.g. by perceptual symbols, as postulated by Barsalou (1994); or the different sorts of perceptual representations as proposed by Jackendoff (1987, 1992)). This seems to make intuitive sense in a case like the concept RED. All we can say about RED is that it is a colour of a certain hue, but we can't describe what that hue is. The best we can do is point at red things and say that their colour is red. On this proposal, then, concepts can get their content from logical entries, from perceptual representations, or from a combination of logical entries and perceptual representations.

However, this runs into difficulties when we look at concepts such as ORCHID and GIRAFFE. As we have seen, the logical entries of these concepts do not exhaust their meaning, so we could appeal to perceptual representations to complement their logical entries. However, unlike the case of RED, we can describe a lot of the properties that would be part of the perceptual representations for these concepts. For example, we can say about a giraffe that it can be up to six metres tall and that at least a third of that height is made up by its neck, that it has four legs, large eyes, a short tail, etc. In other words, a lot of the properties that could be represented by a perceptual representation could also be represented as (more or less precise) conceptual representations, i.e. pieces of encyclopaedic information. Moreover, on the assumption that we draw inferences over conceptual representations, we would have to be able to represent these properties conceptually, for example, to draw the inference that Roddy is an attractive animal from the assumption that Roddy is a giraffe together with the assumption that animals with large eyes are attractive. The proposal that concepts can get their content from perceptual representations, then, entails that encyclopaedic information can contribute to the content of a concept. This brings us to an enriched version of View 1: that logical entries, encyclopaedic entries and perceptual representations constitute the content of a concept (where these different sorts of information are present).

It seems, then, that View 3 reduces either to View 2, or to an enriched version of View 1. These two views of concepts make different predictions about what constitutes the proposition expressed by an utterance (its explicature) and what is implicitly communicated by the utterance. Each of these different possibilities presents us with different problems.

3. the current rt view: view 4

Carston (1996/1997, 2002a, 2002b) develops an alternative view of concepts to the one set out in Sperber and Wilson (1986/1995), which has subsequently become the accepted view of concepts within relevance theory (see for example, Sperber and Wilson (1998), Wilson and Sperber (2000/2002), and Wilson (2003)). On this view a distinction is made between lexically encoded concepts and 'ad hoc' concepts, concepts that are constructed during the process of utterance interpretation by means of pragmatic adjustment of the lexically encoded concept. Carston (2002a, 322) says about this that:

> [t]he idea is that speakers can use a lexically encoded concept to communicate a distinct non-lexicalized (atomic) concept, which resembles the encoded one in that it shares elements of its logical and encyclopaedic entries, and that hearers can pragmatically infer the intended concept on the basis of the encoded one.

The idea here is that concepts can be adjusted. This adjustment takes two forms. Firstly, concepts can be adjusted by a process of narrowing (also called 'strengthening'), which involves selecting a subset of encyclopaedic entries, while the logical entry is retained. Carston (2002a, 324) gives as an example (8):

(8)   I want to meet some bachelors.

When this is uttered by a woman about whom the addressee knows that she would like to get married, this context may lead the addressee to construct the ad hoc concept BACHELORS*,[6] whose extension is a subset of the set of unmarried adult males, namely those with properties such as being youngish, heterosexual and eligible for marriage.

Secondly, concepts can also be adjusted by a process of broadening (also called 'loosening'). This involves selecting a subset of encyclopaedic entries while the logical entry is dropped, as in the case of loose use as in (9) and metaphor as in (10), from Carston (2002b, 84, 85):

(9)   Ken's a (real) *bachelor.*   [where Ken is legally married]
(10) Robert is a bulldozer.

In the interpretation of (9) properties of a certain type of bachelor incompatible with a married lifestyle may be selected, while the logical property UNMARRIED is dropped in the construction of the ad hoc concept. Similarly, in the interpretation of (10) the logical property PIECE OF MACHINERY OF A CERTAIN TYPE will be dropped, while encyclopaedic properties will be selected.

How does this new view of concepts relate to the issues raised in section 2? At first sight, this view seems to have most in common with View 1, in that it gives us an account of word meaning which is dynamic, rather than invariant: how we interpret a word in a particular utterance depends on which bits of information we recover.

Carston (2002a, 339) seems to endorse this view of what makes up the meaning of a word in a particular utterance when she says that an encyclopaedic property such as ELIGIBLE FOR MARRIAGE is given 'content-constitutive status' in the construction of the ad hoc concept BACHELOR*.

Moreover, as Vicente (2005, 190) points out, because ad hoc concept construction involves selecting a subset of logical and/or encyclopaedic entries of a 'linguistically encoded' concept, 'the logical/encyclopaedic distinction is effectively lost…'. As we have seen, this is what View 1 also led us to conclude.

However, Carston's proposals differ from View 1 in that she maintains that concepts are atomic (i.e. simple, unanalyzable concepts), so that although the subset of logical and/or encyclopaedic entries selected for a particular ad hoc concept may function as 'content-constitutive', they should not be viewed as actually being the content of the concept. As a consequence, they are not part of the explicature which the concept occurs in, but rather should be viewed as implicated. This means that we have here a modified version of View 2.

This conception of atomic concepts as ad hoc concepts overcomes the problem faced by View 2 regarding the status of implications derived from logical entries, as set out in section 2: if logical entries do not become available automatically, then we can assume that they will only be recovered as implicatures when they are needed to derive contextual implications. This would make them implicated assumptions.

However, this modified view faces a problem of its own, which becomes apparent when we try to reconcile the assumption that ad hoc concepts are created by narrowing and broadening a lexically encoded concept, with the assumption that concepts are atomic. By definition an atomic concept has no internal structure, so it can't be adjusted by being narrowed or broadened.

According to relevance theory the output of the linguistic system is a non-linguistic logical form, it is a 'structured string of concepts'[7] (Carston 2002a, 57). This logical form needs to be developed in various ways to form a propositional form, or explicature. Let us look at what this would mean in the case of (8), repeated here.

On hearing (8) the addressee will construct a logical form containing the lexically encoded concept BACHELOR:

(8)   I want to meet some bachelors.

BACHELOR will give access to logical and encyclopaedic information, and a subset of this information will be accessed. The particular assumptions that will be accessed will depend on the context of utterance. Since the information in the logical and encyclopaedic entries constitutes knowledge about BACHELOR, the addressee will derive contextual implications on the basis of the logical form containing BACHELOR together with the assumptions made available by the concept BACHELOR. So, if the addressee knows that the speaker of (8) wants to get married, then the logical form containing BACHELOR, together with the assumption that some bachelors are eligible for marriage and assumptions about what is involved in getting married, may well lead the addressee to conclude that the speaker wants to meet some bachelors who are eligible for marriage. However, this will come out as a contextual implication (it is derived on the basis of the logical form containing BACHELOR together with contextual assumptions). Given that the logical form containing BACHELOR gives rise to contextual effects, the addressee can conclude that the completed logical form containing BACHELOR is in fact the explicature.[8]

However, a consequence of this is that it seems that any further contextual effects would be derived on the basis of the implicature that the speaker wants to meet some bachelors who are eligible for marriage, rather than on the basis of the explicature. Since relevance is defined in terms of the inferential interaction of the explicature and assumptions in the context, this would be, as Carston points out, 'a very odd result within relevance theory' (Carston 2002a, 335).

The claim that, during the interpretation of (8), the addressee creates an ad hoc concept amounts to the claim that at some stage during the interpretation process the addressee needs to replace one atomic concept (BACHELOR) in the logical form with another atomic concept (BACHELOR*). It is not clear how this could count as a 'development' of the logical form, nor what would prompt the addressee to perform this exchange, on the assumption that she can derive the appropriate contextual effects on the basis of an explicature containing BACHELOR. All that is said about this process is that explicatures and implicatures are derived in parallel, by a process of 'mutual adjustment' guided by expectations of relevance (Wilson and Sperber 2000/2002, 237). However, no explicit account is given of how this 'mutual adjustment' warrants the exchange of atomic concepts (given that atoms themselves can't be 'adjusted', since they don't have internal structure).

Moreover, given that the assumptions in the logical and encyclopaedic entries for BACHELOR concern BACHELORS and not BACHELORS*, simply selecting a subset of encyclopaedic entries for BACHELOR is not going to give us an ad hoc concept. Whereas SOME BACHELORS ARE ELIGIBLE FOR MARRIAGE may be an assumption we have about bachelors, SOME BACHELORS* ARE ELIGIBLE FOR MARRIAGE is a tautology. The information would therefore have to be restated in terms of a logical entry for BACHELOR*, so that it can be derived as an analytic implication, which can then function as an implicated premise.[9]

Note that this has a further consequence: even if we can give an explicit account of how an addressee develops a logical form of 'I want to meet some BACHELORS' into an explicature containing BACHELORS*, this would not be enough to explain how the relevance of the utterance is established. Given that encyclopaedic entries for BACHELOR have to be restated as logical entries for BACHELOR*, we won't have any other assumptions about BACHELORS* with which the explicature could interact to give us contextual implications.[10] This means that all contextual implications would derive from the implicatures (i.e. the analytic implications), and not from the explicature, contrary to what is claimed by Carston, and Wilson and Sperber. Since relevance is defined in terms of contextual effects derived on the basis of the interaction of the proposition expressed/explicature with assumptions in the context, this is not an outcome which is consistent with the central thesis of relevance theory.

After considering a number of issues arising out of the view of the derivation of concepts, as sketched above, Carston (2002a, 360) suggests that maybe we should view what is linguistically encoded not as atomic concepts, but 'rather [as] concept-schemas or pointers to a conceptual space, on the basis of which, on *every* occasion of their use, an actual concept is pragmatically inferred'. This conception of what is linguistically encoded would overcome the problem of accounting for how the addressee develops a logical form by constructing an ad hoc concept, since no atomic concept would be inserted in the initial logical form. However, Carston's insistence that the ad hoc concept created is atomic would still leave the problem of how we can derive contextual effects on the basis of explicatures containing them, given that by definition we don't have assumptions concerning the ad hoc concept with which the explicature could interact.

On the contrary, if encyclopaedic entries constitute the content of a concept in an explicature (View 1), the above problem does not arise, regardless of whether the concept is created as an ad hoc concept or whether it is retrieved as a chunk from memory.

We end up, then, with two different possible views of concepts within relevance theory, View 1 and View 4, which is a modified version of View 2, the view that concepts are atomic, even if they are created on-line, rather than stored in memory. The question, then, is how we can decide between the different views.

4. decision criteria

To make the distinction between explicit and implicit communication, Sperber and Wilson propose the following definition of explicitness:

> An assumption communicated by an utterance U is explicit if and only if it is a development of a logical form encoded by U. (Sperber and Wilson 1986/1995, 182)

Any assumption which is communicated but not a development of a logical form encoded by the utterance, then, is an implicature. However, this definition does not help us in deciding whether some assumption counts as an explicature or an implicature, without having a notion of what an explicature looks like, which is the question at stake. That is, we need to know in what ways a logical form can be developed. Unfortunately, as Burton-Roberts (2005, 397) points out, '"[d]evelopment" is a black hole at the centre of the theory', in that no definition of what counts as 'development' is given by Sperber and Wilson or Carston.[11, 12]

Alternatively, we can look for independent criteria on which to base a decision. Grice (1975) proposes a number of properties of implicatures, the most important being that implicatures are cancellable without causing a contradiction in 'what is said'. This property predicts that (5) would come out as part of the proposition expressed by (4) – its explicature – because cancelling it does cause a contradiction, as in (11):

(4)   John saw an orchid.
(5)   JOHN SAW A FLOWER OF A CERTAIN SPECIES.
(11) ? John saw an orchid, but he didn't see a flower of a certain species.

Furthermore, (6) would also come out as part of the proposition expressed (the explicature), because if I believe that orchids are rare flowers, then I can't believe that John has seen an orchid without believing that he has seen a rare flower. On these terms, (12) would be contradictory:

(6)   JOHN SAW A RARE FLOWER.
(12) ? John saw an orchid, but he didn't see a rare flower.

Of course, someone might argue that (12) in fact does not constitute a contradiction, by uttering something like (13), which I may accept if I trust her/him enough:

(13) John saw an orchid, but he didn't see a rare flower, because orchids aren't rare.

However, that doesn't mean that (12) does not constitute a contradiction *for me* as long as I believe that orchids are rare flowers. Rather, accepting (13) would cause me to change the content of my concept ORCHID.

Wilson and Sperber (1981) and Carston (2002a) argue that this property of cancellability without causing a contradiction can't be a sufficient criterion for distinguishing implicatures from explicatures, because some explicit content is cancellable without causing a contradiction.[13] However, one way of rescuing cancellability as a criterion of the explicature/implicature distinction is by proposing that it is necessary, although not sufficient: if an assumption is not cancellable without causing a contradiction, then it must be part of the explicature, but if it is cancellable without causing a contradiction that does not provide sufficient evidence that it is an implicature. Vicente (1998, 254) points out that this version of the criterion gives us a contrast between cases such as (14) and (15) on the one hand, and (16) on the other hand, in that (14e) and (15e) give us contradictions, while (16d) does not:

(14) a. A: Does John drink whisky?
b. B: He doesn't drink alcohol.
c. John does not drink whisky. (implicature?)
d. Whisky is alcohol. (implicature?) (Sperber and Wilson 1986/1995)
e. John does not drink alcohol and he drinks whisky (which is alcohol).

(15) a. A: Have you read Susan's book?
b. B: I don't read autobiographies.
c. B has not read Susan's book. (implicature?)
d. Susan's book is an autobiography. (implicature?) (Carston 1988)
e. I do not read autobiographies and I have read Susan's book (which is an autobiography).

(16) a. A: Would you like a coffee?

b. B: I have just had one.

c. B does not want a coffee. (implicature)

d. I've just had a coffee and I want another one.

Vicente writes:

> The reason it has seemed so natural to speak of conversational implicature in [14–15] is that the contextual assumptions in [14d–15d] are needed for their derivation. But notice that before we can decide that [14c–15c] constitute implicated conclusions we must have made a decision concerning the explicit contents of [14b–15b] and the generic terms they include, and that just as bridging reference requires the construction or retrieval of contextual assumptions that are 'incorporated into a representation of the proposition expressed by the utterance' (Wilson 1993, 177) so too, deciding on the extension class of the generic noun phrases may well require a similar process. And so the automatic assignment of the assumptions in [15c–16c] to the domain of implicatures must be reconsidered. (Vicente 1998, 254)

Carston (2002a, 139) posits that [15c–16c] can't be explicatures because 'there is no logical form (or sentential subpart of a logical form) from which they could be developed'. However, it is conceivable that propositional forms are representations with constituents that contain propositions themselves. For example, one way of looking at the enrichment of *Susan's book* in *Susan's book is an autobiography* to *the book written by Susan* could be envisaged in the spirit of (17):

$$(17) \left[\left[\begin{array}{c} \text{BOOK22} \\ \left[\begin{array}{c} \text{BOOK22} \\ \text{is written by SUSAN} \end{array} \right] \end{array} \right] \quad [\text{IS}] \; [\text{INSTANCE OF AUTOBIOGRAPHY}] \right]$$

Furthermore, it is conceivable that (17) in turn is inserted in the constituent [(ANY INSTANCE OF) AUTOBIOGRAPHY], when the propositional form of (15b) is computed, and that the inference to B HAS NOT READ SUSAN'S BOOK is drawn directly from this representation, to form a further part of the representation.

A second property of implicatures that Grice proposes is that implicatures should be calculable, i.e. that they are derived by an inferential process. However, Sperber and Wilson (1986/1995) argue that this is not a valid way of distinguishing between explicit and implicit content:

On a more traditional view, the explicit content of an utterance is a set of decoded assumptions, and the implicit content a set of inferred assumptions. Since we are claiming that no assumption is simply decoded, and that the recovery of any assumption requires an element of inference, we deny that the distinction between the explicit and the implicit can be drawn this way. (Sperber and Wilson 1986/1995, 182)

Recanati (1989) proposes that we should take our intuitions as speakers seriously in deciding what is said, which he formulates as the Availability Principle:

Availability Principle: In deciding whether a pragmatically determined aspect of utterance meaning is part of what is said, that is, in making a decision concerning what is said, we should always try to preserve our pre-theoretic intuitions on the matter. (Recanati 1989, 310)

On this proposal many assumptions that previously have been analyzed as implicatures come out as being part of the proposition expressed, including assumptions whose status have been more uncertain (i.e. in RT terms, assumptions recovered from the logical entry of a concept). An example of an assumption recovered from a logical entry coming out as part of what is said is the assumption *I bought some fruit* in the following exchange:

(18) a. John: Did you buy any fruit?
      b. Mary: I bought some apples.
      c. John: Yes, but did you buy any fruit?
      d. Mary: Well, I said I bought some apples, didn't I?

By uttering (d) Mary communicates that she considers *I bought some fruit* to be part of what she said in (b). The conversation seems rather strange to me precisely because my intuitions agree with hers.

     An example of the same effect involving an assumption recovered from encyclopaedic information, and a conclusion based on this assumption (normally analyzed as an implicated premise and an implicated conclusion) is (15), given below as (19). Here Mary could reply with either (d) or (e) to John's second question. It depends on the strength of her belief that Susan's book is an autobiography:

(19) a. John: Have you read Susan's book?

b. Mary: I don't read autobiographies.
c. John: Yes, but have you read Susan's book?
d. Mary: Well, I said I don't read autobiographies, didn't I?
e. Mary: What do you mean? Susan's book is an autobiography, isn't it?

A problem with the Availability Principle, then, is that not everybody's intuitions agree when confronted with examples such as the one in (19).

Carston (1988) proposes that the distinction between explicatures and implicatures lies in the fact that implicatures function independently of the explicature as the premises and conclusions of arguments. However, as Recanati (1989, 316) points out, it is not perfectly clear what is meant by 'functional independence':[14] although JOHN SAW A FLOWER OF A CERTAIN SPECIES ((5) above) and JOHN SAW A RARE FLOWER ((6) above) represent assumptions, they do not function independently from the (rest of) the explicature during the interpretation process: both (5) and (6) are derived from JOHN SAW AN ORCHID ((4) above), and whatever conclusions we can derive on the basis of (5) and (6), we can only derive by virtue of (5) and (6) first being derived from (4).

Carston (2002a, 190) posits functional independence in terms of distinguishing the explicature from the implicature: 'the proposition expressed [...] should have a role to play, distinct from and independent of its implicatures, ... it should function independently as a premise in arguments'. This means that for Carston JOHN SAW AN ORCHID is the explicature of (4), because it is used as a premise together with the assumption ORCHIDS ARE RARE FLOWERS to derive the contextual implication in (6) JOHN SAW A RARE FLOWER.

However, consider the following exchange, between a rather officious religious official and a girl who has arrived at a religious establishment together with her father:

(20) Official: Girls may only enter the temple accompanied by their *female* parent.
     Girl: But my mother is ill!

Here we see that contextual implications can only be derived on the basis of recovering that the girl's female parent is ill. Since this entails that the girl's mother is ill, there is no independent role for the assumption that Carston would want to come out as the explicature, so that the functional independence principle predicts that 'female parent' is part of the explicature in this case.[15]

Recanati (1989) proposes a further principle, the Scope Principle, which he envisages operating in tandem with the Availability Principle to give us a clear distinction between what is said and what is implicated:

> Scope Principle: A pragmatically determined aspect of meaning is part of what is said (and, therefore, not a conversational implicature) if – and, perhaps, only if – it falls within the scope of logical operators such as negation and conditionals. (Recanati 1989, 325)

On this proposal, both (5) and (6) come out as implicatures, because if John didn't see an orchid, that doesn't mean that he didn't see a (rare) flower. He could have seen a different (rare) flower. The problem with this proposal is that it would make different predictions in the case of ORCHID, and in the case of BACHELOR. This is because if John didn't see a bachelor, he also didn't see an unmarried human adult male, so that the information in the logical entry for BACHELOR falls within the scope of the negation. This is no wonder, since *unmarried human adult male* is a bundle of properties which may represent the whole content of the concept BACHELOR. By contrast, *(rare) flower* does not give us a bundle of properties which constitute the whole content of the concept ORCHID. Hence we are not comparing like with like. Similarly, in the case of an ad hoc concept such as BACHELOR*, the Scope Principle predicts that properties such as ELIGIBLE FOR MARRIAGE are part of the explicature, because if the speaker does not want to meet any BACHELORS*, she also does not want to meet any UNMARRIED HUMAN ADULT MALES WHO ARE ELIGIBLE FOR MARRIAGE. In fact, the Scope Principle predicts that only those assumptions which entail what is said will come out as part of the proposition expressed. Assumptions which are derived in the same way, but do not entail what is said, come out as implicatures.

What we see, then, is that the calculabilty principle is ruled out on the assumption that inference is involved in deriving explicatures as well as implicatures. Both the Scope Principle and the functional independence principle are ruled out, because they make contradictory predictions depending on whether the assumptions derived from the logical entry of a concept (or from encyclopaedic entries, where these are 'content-constitutive') constitute a definition of the concept or not. This means that, of all the different properties proposed to distinguish implicatures from explicatures, a case could be made for Grice's proposal of cancellability, which may be taken as necessary, although it is not sufficient.

Similarly for Recanati's Availability Principle, although its usefulness depends on everyone having the same intuitions. As we have seen above, these criteria favour View 1, the view that encyclopaedic entries constitute the content of a concept, over View 4, the view that concepts are atomic, even if they are created on-line, rather than stored in memory. What the addressee takes as explicated on this view, then, is the complex of assumptions that an addressee is justified in concluding the speaker to be committing herself to.

notes

1. With thanks to Begoña Vicente for many fruitful discussions about meaning and concepts.
2. An earlier version of this chapter was presented at the University of Hertfordshire Relevance Theory Workshop and published as 'Concepts and word meaning'. In M. Groefsema (ed.). (1997). *Proceedings of the University of Hertfordshire Relevance Theory Workshop.*
3. See also Groefsema (1995a).
4. There may in fact be a solution to this problem but it is beyond the scope of this chapter to present it.
5. Sperber and Wilson (1986/1995, 107) say that : '[a]nalytic implications [...] are only worth recovering as a means to an end, the end being the recovery of further synthetic implications', which seems to reflect this point.
6. The * indicates that we are dealing with an ad hoc concept rather than the lexically encoded one.
7. As pointed out by Burton-Roberts (2005, 394), it is not clear 'that structures are – or concepts form – strings'.
8. This would, of course, have been the 'classic' relevance theory account.
9. This seems to be what is in fact envisaged by Carston (2002a, 339), who says that 'an *ad hoc* concept formed by strengthening a lexical concept seems to involve elevating an encyclopaedic property of the latter to a logical (or content-constitutive) status, as is the case of ELIGIBILITY FOR MARRIAGE in the concept BACHELOR*'.
10. If we had, then BACHELOR* would not be an ad hoc concept, but would already be stored in memory, and the word 'bachelor' would be polysemous. Deriving BACHELOR* would then be a case of disambiguation.
11. However, see Groefsema (1992, 1995a, 1995b, 1998) for an account of the development of a logical form into an explicature.
12. A similar point is made by Recanati (1989) with regard to the Minimalist Principle, which he gives as: 'Minimalist Principle: A pragmatically determined aspect of meaning is part of what is said if and only if its determination is necessary for the utterance to express a complete proposition' (Recanati 1989, 302).

    Recanati argues that in order for this principle to be of help in deciding between what is said and what is implicated, we already need to have a notion of what it means for a proposition to be complete.
13. But see Burton-Roberts (2005) for arguments against this position.

14. Recanati gives a counter-example to Carston's proposal. However, Carston (2002a) argues that the way in which he states it differs from what she intended.
15. Burton-Roberts (2005, 397, fn. 8) gives a further counter-example to this principle.

references

Barsalou, L.W. (1994). 'Flexibility, structure, and linguistic vagary in concepts: manifestations of a compositional system of perceptual symbols'. In A. Collins, S.E. Gathercole, M.A. Conway and P.E. Morris (eds). *Theories of Memory*. Hillsdale, NJ: Erlbaum.

Burton-Roberts, N. (2005). 'Robyn Carston on semantics, pragmatics and "encoding"'. *Journal of Linguistics* 41.2: 389–409.

Carston, R. (1988). 'Implicature, explicature and truth-theoretic semantics'. In R.M. Kempson (ed.). *Mental Representations: The interface between language and reality*. Cambridge: Cambridge University Press.

— (1996). 'Enrichment and loosening: complementary processes in deriving the propostion empressed.' *UCL Working Papers in Linguistics* 8: 205–32. Reprinted 1997 in *Linguistische Berichte*, Special Issue on Pragmatics 8: 103–27.

— (2002a). *Thoughts and Utterances: The Pragmatics of Explicit Communication*. Oxford: Blackwell.

— (2002b). 'Metaphor, ad hoc concepts and word meaning – more questions than answers'. *UCL Working Papers in Linguistics* 14.

Grice, H.P. (1975). 'Logic and conversation'. In P. Cole and J. Morgan (eds). *Speech Acts*. New York: Academic Press. 41–58.

Groefsema, M. (1992). 'Processing for relevance: a pragmatically driven account of how we process natural language'. University of London PhD thesis.

— (1995a). 'Understood arguments: a semantic/ pragmatic approach'. *Lingua* 96: 139–61.

— (1995b). 'Anticipating the interpretation: a dynamic view of human sentence input processing'. *Proceedings of the 4th international conference on the cognitive science of natural language processing*. Dublin: Dublin City University.

— (1997). 'Concepts and word meaning'. In M. Groefsema (ed.). *Proceedings of the University of Hertfordshire Relevance Theory Workshop*. Chelmsford: Peter Thomas and Associates.

— (1998). 'Processing for Relevance'. *Revista Alicanta de Estudios Ingleses* (special issue on relevance theory) 11: 95–116.

Jackendoff, R. (1983). *Semantics and Cognition*. Cambridge, Mass.: MIT Press.

— (1987). 'On beyond zebra: the relation of linguistic and visual information'. *Cognition* 26: 89–114.

— (1992). *Languages of the Mind*. Cambridge, Mass.: MIT Press.

Recanati, F. (1989). 'The pragmatics of what is said'. *Mind and language* 4: 295–329.

Sperber, D. and D. Wilson (1986/1995). *Relevance: Communication and Cognition*. Oxford: Blackwell.

— (1998). 'The mapping between the mental and the public lexicon'. In P. Carruthers and J. Boucher (eds). *Language and Thought*. Cambridge: Cambridge University Press. 184–200.

Vicente, B. (1998). 'Against blurring the explicit-implicit distinction'. *Revista Alicanta de Estudios Ingleses* (special issue on relevance theory) 11: 241–58.

— (2005). 'Meaning in relevance theory and the semantics/pragmatics distinction'. In S. Coulson and B. Lewandowska-Tomaszczyk (eds). *The Literal and Non-Literal in Language and Thought.* Frankfurt am Main: Petr Lang.

Wilson, D. (1993). 'Reference and relevance'. *UCL Working Papers in Linguistics* 4: 167–91.

— (2003). 'Relevance theory and lexical pragmatics'. *Italian Journal of Linguistics/ Rivista di Linguistica* 15.2: 273–91. Special Issue on Pragmatics and the Lexicon. Rep. 2004. *UCL Working Papers in Linguistics* 16.

Wilson, D. and D. Sperber (1981). 'On Grice's theory of conversation'. In P. Werth (ed.). *Conversation and Discourse.* London: Croom Helm.

— (2000/2002). 'Truthfulness and relevance'. *UCL Working Papers in Linguistics* 12: 215–54. Rev. version 2002 in *Mind* 111 (443): 583–632.

9

neo-gricean pragmatics: a manichaean manifesto

Dualists proudly trace their lineage back to the Manichaeans, who detected a decidedly moral dimension in the universal dichotomies of nature and society:

> The Manicheans account for the mixture of good and evil in the universe, by the opposite agencies of two co-eternal and independent principles.
> [1793 D. STEWART *Outl. Moral Philos.* II. ii. §293, cited in *OED*, s.v. Manichaean]

For Confucianists and Taoists, these principles map into an overarching opposition of *yin* and *yang:*

(1) | YANG | YIN |
|---|---|
| male | female |
| positive | negative |
| light | dark |
| heaven | earth |
| high | low |
| creative/active | receptive/passive |
| gods | ghosts |
| large | small |
| hard | soft |

But these opposed principles are less 'independent' than co-dependent, each containing and defined by the other, as we are reminded by the familiar symbol:

Figure 9.1   Great Ultimate T'ai Chi

Having received my graduate training in California in the 1960s, I lean towards a no-fault version of Manichaeanism, beyond good and evil. After all, one woman's yin is another man's yang.

1. manichaeanism in pragmatics

The heirs of Manichaeus are legion, but within the pragmatics of communication two emerge from the pack under the entry of ([H. Paul] Grice). While the philosopher Herbert Paul Grice was not named for the philologist Hermann Paul, Grice's (1989) framework for implicature can be seen as one of several milestones on the journey initiated by Paul towards an understanding of the role of pragmatics in lexical acquisition, lexical choice, and semantic change.

In his *Prinzipien der Sprachgeschichte* – whose English translation appeared in 1889, precisely a century before Grice's posthumous collection – Paul surveys a range of phenomena whose form and distribution reflect the interplay of two functional principles, the tendency to reduce expression (later formulated by G.K. Zipf as the linguistic correlate of the more general Principle of Least Effort) and the communicative requirements on sufficiency of information:

> The more economical or more abundant use of linguistic means of expressing a thought is determined by the *need*. It cannot be denied that these means are often employed in luxurious superfluity. But, on the whole, our linguistic activity is characterised by a certain trait of parsimony. Everywhere we find modes of expression forced into existence which contain only just so much as is requisite to their being understood. The amount of linguistic material employed varies

in each case with the situation, with the previous conversation, with the relative approximation of the speakers to a common state of mind. (Paul 1889, 351)

The lineal descendants of Paul's dualism include the speaker's vs hearer's economies of Zipf and Martinet and the two halves of Grice's Maxim of Quantity.

While known primarily for his least effort principle, Zipf (1935; 1949, 20ff) in fact distinguished the SPEAKER'S ECONOMY, tending towards 'a vocabulary of one word which will refer to all the m distinct meanings', from the AUDITOR'S ECONOMY, tending towards 'a vocabulary of m different words with one distinct meaning for each word'. The former places an upper bound on the form of the message, while the latter places a lower bound on its informational content. By Zipf's LAW OF ABBREVIATION, the relative frequency of a word is inversely related to its length; the more frequent its tokens, the shorter its form. But relative frequency, and the concomitant effect on length and phonological reduction, is partly a matter of the speaker's assumptions about the hearer and their shared common ground:

> High frequency is the cause of small magnitude... A longer word may be truncated if it enjoys a high relative frequency [either] throughout the entire speech community [or] if its use is frequent within any special group. (Zipf 1935, 31–2)

Zipf's two mutually constraining mirror-image forces are periodically invoked (or rediscovered) in the diachronic and psycholinguistic literature:

> The linguist must keep in mind two ever-present and antinomic factors: first, the requirements of communication, the need for the speaker to convey his message, and second, the principle of least effort, which makes him restrict his output of energy, both mental and physical, to the minimum compatible with achieving his ends. (Martinet 1962, 139)

> The speaker always tries to optimally minimize the surface complexity of his utterances while maximizing the amount of information he effectively communicates to the listener. (Carroll and Tanenhaus 1975, 51, the MINIMAX PRINCIPLE)

This minimax of effort and information is directly reflected in phonetic form, given that motor economy in phonetics 'occurs only insofar as communicative listener-oriented goals permit' (Lindblom 1983, 232). More recently, Hayes (1997, 14) observes that 'virtually all of segmental phonology is driven by considerations of articulatory ease and perceptual distinctness', while Flemming (2001, 2004) and Kirchner (2001) insightfully explore the functional dialectic of perceptual salience vs articulatory cost.

The Zipfian parameter of familiarity is part of the phonological picture as well: vowel reduction and palatalization are characteristic of familiar or frequent items, while unfamiliar or unpredictable words get extra stress or pitch. This is seen in the minimal pairs adduced by Fidelholtz (1975, 205–6), where stress reduction on a lax vowel in an initial strong pretonic syllable correlates with the frequency or (global or local) predictability of the item:

(2) astronomy   gàstronomy
    mistake   mìstook
    mosquito   Mùskegon

Residents of that last-named Michigan city predictably destress its first syllable, and more generally least effort reductions will occur in local (and hence frequent) pronunciations of place names (*Loo-uh-ville*, *T'ronno*, *Clumps* [= Columbus], *Amerst*, *'Sconsin*), while outlanders retain unreduced pronunciations. (See papers in Bybee and Hopper 2001 for much more on frequency effects.)

More apposite is the recognition of the trade-off between brevity and clarity within classical rhetoric, as captured in Horace's apothegm *Brevis esse laboro; obscurus fio* ('I strive to be brief; I become obscure': *Ars Poetica* l. 25). Similar sentiments appear elsewhere, as in the Golden Mean (or Goldilocks?) Principle:

If it is prolix, it will not be clear, nor if it is too brief. It is plain that the middle way is appropriate..., saying just enough to make the facts plain. (Aristotle, *Rhetoric* 3.12–3.16)

Personally, when I use the term brevity *[brevitas]*, I mean not saying less, but not saying more than the occasion demands. (Quintilian, Institutio Oratio IV.ii. 41–3)

The speaker aims for ease and brevity, correlates of least effort; the hearer requires sufficiency of content and discriminability of form. Speaker and hearer are aware of their own and each other's desiderata, a mutual awareness generating a variety of effects based on what was said and what wasn't. It is this Manichaean interaction that led me to fold the maxims (Grice 1989, 26ff) into two general principles, dubbed Q and R in deference to Grice's (first) Quantity maxim and Relation maxim respectively.

In the dualistic model I have been urging (Horn 1984, 1989, 1993, 2004), implicatures may be generated by either the Q Principle (essentially 'Say enough', a generalization of Grice's first maxim of Quantity) or the R Principle ('Don't say too much', subsuming the second Quantity maxim, Relation, and Brevity). The hearer-oriented Q Principle is a lower-bounding guarantee of the sufficiency of content. It collects the first Quantity maxim along with the first two 'clarity' submaxims of Manner and is systematically exploited to generate upper-bounding (typically scalar) implicata. The R Principle, by contrast, is an upper-bounding correlate of Zipf's principle of least effort dictating minimization of form. It collects the Relation maxim, the second Quantity maxim, and the last two submaxims of Manner, and is exploited to induce strengthening implicata.

The functioning of Q-based scalar implicature allows for a systematic (and Occamistic) treatment of both logical operators and ordinary non-proposition embedding predicates that can be arrayed on a quantity scale (Horn 1972, 1989):

(3) Q-scales: logical operators: Q-scales: 'ordinary' values:
     <all, most, many, some>   <hot, warm>
     <always, usually, often, sometimes>   <cold, cool, lukewarm>
     <and, or>   <excellent, good, OK>
     <certain, likely, possible>   <adore, love, like>
     <the, a>   <thumb, finger>

In each case, given a stronger value S and a weaker value W plotted on the same (positive or negative) scale <S, W>, as determined canonically by unilateral entailment, in asserting [...W...] I implicate, ceteris paribus, that I was not in an epistemic position to have asserted [...S...] salva veritate, i.e. that I don't know that S holds, and hence, all things being equal, that I know that ~[...S...] holds. We thus predict that scalar predications will be ascribed a one-sided (lower-bounded) linguistic meaning pragmatically enrichable to a two-sided (lower- and upper-bounded) communication:

(4) SCALAR PREDICATION   1-SIDED MEANING   →   2-SIDED UNDERSTANDING
     a. You ate *some* of the cake. '...some if not all...'   '...some but not all...'
     b. It's *possible* she'll win.   '...at least possible...' '...possible but not certain...'
     c. He's a knave *or* a fool.   '...and perhaps both'   '...but not both'
     d. It's *warm*.   '...at least warm...'   '...but not hot'

(Contra Horn 1972, however, I do not see cardinals as working in the same way, for reasons noted in Horn 1992, 2004.)

This model allows us to provide a satisfactory ending to the story of *O, i.e. to predict the non-occurrence of values corresponding to the O (south-east) vertex of the Square of Opposition:

(5)

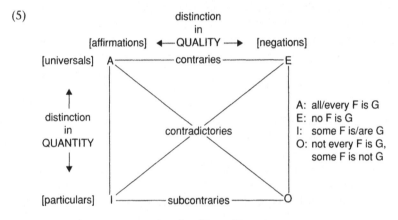

Figure 9.2 Traditional Square of Opposition

Table 9.1 The Asymmetries of Lexicalization

	DETERMINERS/ QUANTIFIERS	QUANTIF. ADVERBS	BINARY QUANTIFIERS	CORRELATIVE CONJUNCTIONS	BINARY CONNECTIVES
A:	all α, everyone	always	both (of them)	both...and	and
I:	some α, someone	sometimes	one (of them)	either...or	or
E:	no α, no one	never	neither (of them)	neither...nor	nor
	(=all~/~some)	(=always~)	(=both~/~either)	(=[both...and]~)	(=and~)
O:	*nall α, *neveryone	*nalways	*noth (of them)	*noth...nand	*nand
	(=some~/~all)	(=~always)	(=either~/~both)	(=[either...or]~)	(=and~/~or)

This cross-linguistic asymmetry extends to modal operators and other values that can be plotted on the Square (Horn 1972, ch. 4), as well to 'O→E drift', the tendency for sequences that might be expected to express

O values to take on strengthened, E meanings, as when French *Il ne faut pas que tu meures* (lit., 'it is not necessary that you die') is understood as 'you must [not die]' (cf. Tobler 1882; Horn 1989, section 4.5). The systematic restriction of values mapping onto the O vertex in their potential for lexicalization or direct expression can be attributed to the Q-based implicature relation obtaining between the two subcontraries. (cf. Horn 2006, section 5 on competing but less general explanations).

2. R-based effects in lexical and semantic change

Unlike the upper-bounding associated with Q-based implicature, R-based effects may involve either formal reduction or informational strengthening: the speaker makes her contribution relatively brief or uninformative and counts on the hearer to recognize the operation of least effort and fill in the missing material. Within the lexicon, the hand of R can be detected in processes like acronymy, blending, and clipping, abbreviating relatively long or complex labels for frequently invoked referents:

(6)   Parole-based reductions:
      a. Acronyms
      radar, sonar, laser, CAT/PET [scans], NATO, NASA
      Initialisms: *U.S., G.I., U.N., M.I.T., UCLA, MSU, T.N.T., DDT, OK, TV*
      b. Blends
      moTor hoTel > *motel*; smoke + fog > *smog*, CREMated + REMains > *cremains*
      televangelist, chunnel, metrosexual, flexitarian ('flexible vegetarian')
      sexile ('student temporarily exiled from dormitory room due to roommate's privacy requirements'; also verb and abstract nominal corresponding to this practice)
      c. Clipping (truncation)
      bus, van, bike, cab (or *taxi*), *plane*   *piano* (< *pianoforte*)
      gas, exam, poli sci, math(s), doc, prof   *cello* (< *violoncello*)
      phone, fax (< *facsimile*), *telly* (cf. *TV*)
      'Clipronyms': *Pakistan, Gestapo, hazmat*
      Reduction of compounds/phrases to one member:
      express [train] (cf. *espresso* [coffee]), [motor] *car*
      private [soldier], *general* [officer]
      chemical [substance], *vegetable, criminal, mortal*
      substance-free [floors/dorms] (those on which drugs, alcohol, and tobacco are banned)
      zoo[logical gardens], *narc*[otics agent], *mob, movies,...*

These are straightforward applications of Zipf's Law of Abbreviation, but the processes in question cannot operate unchecked. As Stern (1931, 257) puts it, 'The demands of the speech functions must set a limit to the economic tendency.' That is to say, the freedom of R is curtailed by the demands of Q.

R-based effects are a robust factor in semantic change, where it is primarily information rather than articulatory complexity that is economized. In broadening, a term denoting a culturally salient member of a given category comes to denote the superordinate category itself, typically through the loss of a specifying feature:

(7) dog   (originally a particular breed of dog)
    uncle   (originally = mother's brother)
    oil   (originally = olive oil)
    guy(s) (broadening to include female referents)

This process is especially productive in the genericization (aka 'genericide') of trade names (cf. Shuy 2002 and much other work):

(7') xerox   'a copy' (n.); 'to copy' (v.)   jello   'gelatin dessert'
     scotch-tape 'cellophane tape'   thermos   'insulating
                                                           bottle'
     band-aid   'adhesive bandage'   kleenex   'facial tissue'

In the complementary process of sense narrowing, we can distinguish Q-BASED NARROWING, which is hearer-based and linguistically motivated, from R-BASED NARROWING, the socially motivated restriction of a set-denoting term to its culturally salient subset or member. Instances of Q-based narrowing, where the existence of a specific hyponym H of a general term licenses the use of the general term for the complement of the extension of H, are given in (8).

(8) lion   (including or excluding lionesses)
    cat   (including or excluding kittens)
    rectangle (including or excluding squares)
    finger   (including or excluding thumbs)
    animal   (including or excluding humans)

In R-based narrowing, a general term denoting a set S narrows to pick out a culturally or socially salient subset of S, allowing the speaker to avoid overtly specifying the (often taboo) subdomain via the assumption

that the hearer will fill in the intended meaning. Unlike the cases in
(8), this process does not depend on an inference from what wasn't
said, but counts on the hearer's knowledge of what needn't be said.
This may result in a referential shift as in (9) or in the development of
autohyponymy (where the original broader sense persists alongside the
narrowed meaning) as in (10):

(9) hound   (originally 'dog', as in Ger. *Hund*)
     deer   (originally '(wild) animal', as in Ger. *Tier*)
     poison   (originally 'potion, drink')
     corn   ('wheat' [England], 'oats' [Scotland], 'maize' [US])
     liquor   (originally 'liquid substance')
     wife   (originally 'woman')

(10) drink   (in particular [+alcoholic])
     colour   (in particular 'hue', excluding black, white, grey)
     temperature (in particular, one in the 'fever' range)
     friend   (in the sense of 'friend-plus')
     Ger. *Frau*,   ('woman' or, in particular, 'wife')
     Fr. *femme*   ('woman' or, in particular, 'wife')
     Sp. *mujer*   ('woman' or, in particular, 'wife')
     number   (in particular 'integer')
     man   (orig. 'human', now chiefly 'male adult human')

If genericide represents the most productive class of R-based broadening,
the locus classicus of socially motivated R-based narrowing is EUPHEMISM,
ranging from the sexual and excretory domains (*sleep with, make love,
boyfriend, lover; toilet, go to the bathroom*) to the realm of death and illness
(*disease, accident, undertaker, pass*).

Related to lexical narrowing, and again motivated by social considerations – in particular, those relating to what Erving Goffman describes as
respect for negative face (cf. Brown and Levinson 1987) – is the R-based
strengthening of negative force. As Bosanquet (1911, 281) puts it, 'The
essence of formal negation is to invest the contrary with the character
of the contradictory.' Across a wide range of languages we can attest the
tendency for the speaker to weaken the force of her intended negative
judgements, counting on the hearer to fill in the intended stronger
negative. In English contrary negatives in contradictory clothing include
affixal negation, so-called 'neg-raising', and simple litotes, as illustrated
in (11a–c) respectively; cf. Horn (1989, ch. 5) for details.

(11) R-based negative strengthening

a. contrary readings for affixal negation (conventionalized/ lexicalized strengthening)

He is unhappy	(> ~[He is happy])
She was unfriendly	(> ~[She was friendly])
I disliked the movie	(> ~[I liked the movie])

b. 'neg-raising' effects (strengthened understanding as a convention of usage)

I don't believe it'll snow	(= I believe it won't)
I don't want you to go	(= I want you not to go)
It's not likely they'll win	(= It's likely they won't)

c. litotes (understatement) in simple denials ('on-line' non-conventionalized strengthening)

He's not happy with it	(> ~[He's happy with it])
I don't like ouzo	(> ~[I like ouzo])
I'm not optimistic that ϕ	(> ~[I'm optimistic that ϕ])

In each case a general, formally contradictory negation is strengthened to a specific, contrary understanding, but the constructions differ in the degree of conventionalization, as indicated above. I say *I don't like ouzo* or *I'm not exactly thrilled with your advice* precisely to avoid acknowledging my antipathy directly, while counting on you to fill in my intended R-strengthened (contrary) interpretation rather than simply taking me at my (contradictory) word. In an embedding environment, this same practice is responsible for the 'neg-raising' effect seen in (11b), resulting in the understanding of a negation outside the scope of certain predicates of opinion, desire, or likelihood as if it had lower-clause scope. Here again, the contrary meaning *(x disbelieves that p, x believes that not-p)* is sufficient but not logically necessary to establish the truth of the contradictory *(x does not believe that p)*, yet it is treated as if it were necessary – not surprisingly, since it represents the inductively salient case that makes the contradictory true and since there may be social constraints against direct expression of the stronger contrary. (See Horn 2000a for a general account of the R-strengthening of sufficient to necessary-and-sufficient conditions.)

This process was recognized a millennium ago, when St Anselm observed that we say *non debet peccare* ['he NEG-should sin'] when we mean *debet non peccare*. But for which values of *V* does α *doesn't V that* ϕ convey 'α Vs that not-ϕ'? Which predicates license a lower-clause understanding of higher-clause negation? The pattern is indicated in (12) (cf. Horn 1989, ch. 5):

(12)   *believe, suppose* but not *know, doubt, disbelieve*
       want, suggest but not *insist, forbid, prohibit*
       advisable, desirable but not *obligatory, forbidden*
       should, ought to, better but not *have to, must, can*
       likely, probable but not *certain, impossible*
       most but not *all, many, some, few*
       usually but not *always, often, sometimes, rarely*

What counts here is the scalar position of the relevant value and the euphemistic motivation (downtoning the expression of negative judgement) for strengthening. Note also that the values that induce the strengthening process cross-cut the distinction between 'lexical' and 'functional' operators.

A subtle illustration of negative strengthening is provided in a passage from Kingsley Amis. Our hero is telling a friend about a certain problem he's been having with his wife in that pre-Viagra era, and the therapy prescribed for it:

> 'I'm supposed to be working out what I feel about her. I don't dislike her, which is a start of a kind... I like chatting to her, but I don't find myself wanting to tell her things – I remember in the old days whenever I read or heard or thought of anything funny or striking or whatever it might be, my first thought was always, I must tell Brenda about that. Not any more. I suppose I ought to tell her just the same – my "therapist" works on the principle that the way of getting to want to do something you don't want to do is to keep doing it. Which seems to me a handy route *from not...pause...wanting* to do it *to not-wanting, wanting not*, to do it. But I am paying him to know best. Brenda wants affection, physical affection... My chap is always on at me to go through the motions of it on the principle I've described. I'm a bit scared of being shifted *from not-pause-wanting* to do that *to not-wanting* to do it.' (Kingsley Amis, *Jake's Thing* (1979): 217–18, emphasis added)

3. two kinds of pragmatic strengthening

Having surveyed the effects of the R Principle in lexical narrowing and negative strengthening, we can now address Carston's critique (1995;

2002, ch. 3) of the Manichaean position. She argues that Q-based and R-based implicature can be collapsed, since 'there is a strengthening of communicated content from "at least some" to "just some"' (Carston 2005, 314–15) that is entirely parallel to, say, Jake's strengthening of 'not wanting' to 'not-wanting' or 'wanting-not'. But does the upper-bounding effect of Q-based, and in particular scalar, implicature amount to strengthening, as Carston argues? Additional support for this view comes from Chierchia (2004), who correlates the blocking of scalar implicatures in downward entailing contexts with the licensing of Negative Polarity Items (NPIs) in the same contexts, a correlation he seeks to account for via the parallel strengthening effect yielded by NPIs and scalar implicatures. I have argued elsewhere (Horn 2006, section 2) that scalar implicatures are not in fact blocked by negation and other scale-reversing operators but rather computed in terms of the inverted scale (see also Levinson 2000, 254–5) and that in any case NPIs do not necessarily yield a strengthening of negative force (cf. Israel 1996 on attenuating NPIs). Our concern here, however, is more specifically with the question of whether a scalar implicature, by upper-bounding an assertion, does in fact strengthen it. What do we mean by strength?

In fact, while R-based implicature increases both the informative and rhetorical strength (positive or negative) of the assertion, what is communicated as a result of Q-based upper-bounding, while more specific and hence INFORMATIVELY stronger than the unbounded utterance, is not RHETORICALLY stronger than the utterance *sans* implicature. Thus, while *some* is consistent with *all*, *some but not all* (let's call it *some*l) is inconsistent with *all*. Thus *some*l *F are G*, while unilaterally entailing *some F are G*, yields a more SPECIFIC but not a STRONGER positive assertion.

Further, as Michael Israel (personal communication) points out, a statement with *some* is clearly stronger than one with *some*l in the terms of Ducrot's theory of argumentation (cf. e.g. Anscombre and Ducrot 1983). Thus, a sentence like (13a) represents a stronger argument for the (emphasized) conclusion than does the more specific but rhetorically weaker (13b).

(13) a. I've graded some of the exams, *so it's time for a break*.
      b. ?I've graded some, but not all, of the exams, *so it's time for a break*.

As Israel also notes, *already* is possible in (13a) but not in (13b), because rendering the Q-implicature explicit is incompatible with the suggestion that things are ahead of schedule.

(14) a. I've already graded some of the exams (so let's go out for a
         beer).
     b. #I've already graded some, but not all, of the exams (so let's go
         out for a beer).

Another argument for separating the two notions of strength comes
from the distribution of rank orders (Horn 2000b), such as those in
(15):

(15) <<general, colonel, lieutenant, sergeant, corporal, private>>
      <<full house, flush>>
      <<full professor, associate professor, assistant professor>>

In a scale <S, W>, ...S... unilaterally entails ...W...: if it's hot, it's warm;
in a RANK order <<S, W>>, on the other hand, ...S... unilaterally entails
...~W...: if they're married, they're NOT engaged; if he's a colonel, he's
NOT a lieutenant. Similarly, if she's a full professor, it's false that she's
an assistant professor – although it's true that she's AT LEAST an assistant
professor. Similarly, compare these exchanges between players in (non-
wild card) poker:

(16) A: Do you have a flush?
      B: {No/#Yes} (in fact) I have a full house.

(17) A: Do you have at least a flush?
      B: {Yes/#No} (in fact) I have a full house.

Rank-ordered items essentially semanticize the upper bound: *Chris has
a full house* and *Chris has a flush* are equally informative in that neither
entails the other. Similarly for *Jones is a full professor* vs *Jones is an associate
professor*. Yet the first member of each pair is rhetorically or assertorically
stronger in asserting that the higher rank holds. Once again, rhetorical
strength proves distinct from informative strength.

4. Q and R in (inter)action:
the division of pragmatic labour

Modern lexical pragmatics originated with McCawley's study of the
penetration of Gricean implicature into word-formation and word use;
it was the goal of extending this work (along with related morphological
studies by Aronoff 1976 and Kiparsky 1983 on synonymy avoidance that

bypass pragmatic modes of explanation) that prompted my own dialectic model (Horn 1984) in which an R-based correlate of least effort squares off against a Q-based principle of sufficiency of information. McCawley notes that a speaker who opts for a marked communication like *John ceased to be in the kitchen and came to be in the living room*, forgoing its default counterpart *John went from the kitchen to the living room*, would be understood as implicating teleportation, magic, or some other unusual circumstances, given that the unmarked communication would evoke the unmarked context:

> Reference to one of the more marked situations requires comment, and if the speaker does not provide the addressee with warning that the marked situation is intended, the addressee is justified in assuming that one of the less marked situations is intended. (McCawley 1978, 255)

But this additional layer of conveyed meaning follows directly from Gricean reasoning:

> [T]he lack of interchangeability between the lexical item and its periphrastic equivalent are due not to idiosyncratic restrictions that must be incorporated into the relevant dictionary entries, but rather are consequences of general principles of cooperative behavior. (McCawley 1978, 257–8)

To capture and extend this insight, generalizing it to a range of examples beyond those involving simple periphrasis, I proposed a Division of Pragmatic Labour (Horn 1984, 1993; cf. also Levinson 2000, section 2.4). The idea is that while the inevitable clash, or dialectic, between Q and R in simple cases results in an indeterminacy of what is implicated that is typically resolvable through various contextual factors (see Levinson 2000 for insightful discussion within a related framework), in the theoretically more interesting cases the interaction of the two functional drives is dynamically resolved into an equilibrium. Given a pair of a priori co-extensive linguistic expressions, the relatively unmarked (briefer and/or more lexicalized) expression will tend to become R-associated (pragmatically or conventionally) with a particular unmarked, stereo-typical meaning, use, or situation, while its less lexicalized counterpart (typically more complex or prolix) will tend to be Q-restricted to those situations outside the stereotype, where the unmarked expression could not have been used appropriately. Thus consider:

(18) a. He got the car to stop.
      b. He stopped the car.

(19) a. Her blouse was pale red.
      b. Her blouse was pink.

(20) a. She wants her to win.
      b. She wants PRO to win.

(21) a. I am going to marry you.
      b. I will marry you.

(22) a. My brother went to {the church/the jail/the school}.
      b. My brother went to {church/jail/school}.

(23) a. It's not impossible that the Sox will win.
      b. It's possible that the Sox will win.

(24) a. That's my father's wife.
      b. That's my mother.

S is aware that H knows that S will be attempting to reduce her effort. Given this knowledge, H recognizes that S's choice of a relatively complex or marked utterance in (a) implicates that she was not in a position to use the simpler or less marked alternative in (b). The crucial assumption is that if S has expended what may appear to be unnecessary effort in her utterance, there must have been a sufficient reason to have done so – although just WHICH reason may be indeterminate; see Horn (1991) for detailed elaboration with respect to the double negation case in (23).

When the speaker appears to have gone out of her way to provide additional material (as in the form of modification), the hearer will assume – given the R Principle – that (*ceteris paribus*) the extra material is relevant. This is not a new observation. Ducrot, for example, recognizes that positing any restriction will tend to suggest that the general predication holds not just when, but ONLY when, this restriction is satisfied:

> Le locuteur observe, dans le choix de son énoncé, *une espèce de loi d'économie*. Si on dit d'une personne qu'elle aime les romans policiers, l'auditeur est tenté de conclure, pour s'expliquer la précision apportée par le mot 'policiers', qu'elle aime peu, ou moins, les autres romans. Car,

si elle aimait tous les romans, *à quoi bon* ajouter cette détermination[?]
(Ducrot 1969, 22, emphasis added)

Similar considerations yield the tendency to pragmatically 'perfect' a
conditional of the form *if p then q* into a biconditional with the force of
if and only if p, q; cf. Horn (2000a). The same pragmatic effect is strikingly
illustrated in Cecil Adams' revised take on the dictum 'The exception
proves the rule' in his 'Straight Dope' column posted at <http://www.
straightdope.com/classics/a3_201.html>. The original Latin form of the
adage, adapted into English through legal commentaries, is *Exceptio
probat/confirmat regulam in casibus non exceptis*: The exception proves (or
confirms the existence of) the rule in cases not excepted. (In Cicero's
alternative statement of the principle, to prohibit something in specified
cases implies that it's otherwise permitted.) One modern corollary is
the warning 'NO PARKING EXCEPT SUNDAYS AND HOLIDAYS', implicating that
parking is permitted on those days. If an exception is not relevant – if
Ducrot's reader liked all novels, not just detective novels – why would a
cooperative speaker or writer make the effort to specify it?

As Carston and others have observed, the relevant notion of effort
does not always correlate directly with articulatory expense but is often
a function of other considerations. Thus, the tendency exemplified
in (18a,b) for a lexicalized causative like *kill* to restrict the domain of
application of the corresponding periphrastic form *cause to die* (McCawley
1978) does not generalize straightforwardly to causatives of adjectives:
while *Chris caused Pat to die* implicates indirect causation, *Chris angered
Pat* does not partially block *Chris made Pat angry* in the same way. (See
Horn 1978 and especially Matsumoto 1995 for discussion.) The notion
of markedness involved in triggering the Division of Pragmatic Labour is
a complex one, and as Carston (2005, 315–16) observes, frequency plays
a major role in determining the outcome.

In this connection, though, it is worth noting that the 'speaker's
economy' employed in my framework, and its predecessors in the work
of Zipf, Martinet et al, is itself internally dialectic in its operation. This
can best be seen in Martinet's distinction (Martinet 1962, 139) between
mental and physical inertia, as explicated elsewhere through his
opposition (Martinet 1964, section 6.6) between PARADIGMATIC economy
(*économie mémorielle* or mental inertia), which involves the reduction in
the inventory of entries in the mental lexicon, and SYNTAGMATIC economy
(*économie discursive* or articulatory inertia), which involves the reduction
in the number of linguistic units per utterance:

What one may call the economy of language is this permanent search
for equilibrium between the contradictory needs which it must satisfy:
communicative needs on the one hand and articulatory and mental
inertia on the other, the two latter in permanent conflict. (Martinet
1964, 169)

Pidgins and early-stage creoles emphasize paradigmatic constraint at
the cost of syntagmatic overabundance: few morphemes, longer sentences
(Haiman 1985, 167). The process of creolization can be seen as the pursuit
of an equilibrium of economy guided by Zipf's law of abbreviation and
our correlated principle of Familiarity Breeds CNTNT.

The opposite extreme is best illustrated by Borges' legendary nineteenth-
century Uruguayan Ireneo Funes. In the face of Locke's observation that
it is both unnecessary and impossible for every particular object to have a
distinct name (Locke 1690, Book III, ch. 3), Funes – after being thrown by
a blue-tinted horse – reawakens into a consciousness in which particulars
are all, *l'économie mémorielle* nothing. He invents an idiom in which every
object, every number has its own unanalyzable proper name: 7013 is
Máximo Perez, 7014 *The Train*.

It was not only difficult for him to understand that the generic term
dog embraced so many unlike specimens of differing sizes and different
forms; he was disturbed by the fact that a dog at 3:14 (seen in profile)
should have the same name as the dog at 3:15 (seen from the front).
(Borges 1963, 114)

The narrator/author's point is, of course, precisely Locke's: 'I suspect ... that
he was not very capable of thought. To think is to forget a difference.'

5. synonymy and homonymy avoidance

Our final arena for the Manichaean conflict of Q and R is the avoidance
of synonymy and homonymy in the lexicon and, in particular, lexical
acquisition. Sweet (1874) and Passy (1890) expatiate on the role of a
'principle of economy' in the avoidance of synonymy as well as in sound
change, and Sayce (1880, 192) cites the role of the principle of least effort
or 'laziness' in word meaning, syntax, and phonology, while conceding
that 'Laziness will not explain everything in speech any more than it will
in the ordinary dealings of mankind'. Paul, remarking that 'Language
abhors superfluity' (Paul 1889, ch. 14), explores the resolution of potential
synonymy by the disappearance of one of the two synonymous forms

or their gradual differentiation in meaning (cf. Bréal 1900 for a similar account). Typically, the older form becomes restricted to a specialized or secondary meaning: *brethren* (vs *brothers*), *deer* (vs *animal*), *fowl* (vs *bird*). Paul attributes children's overgeneralization of word meaning to the same underlying principle.

Paul's observations appear elsewhere in a variety of incarnations, including the ELSEWHERE CONDITION, which some have traced back to Pāṇini (cf. Anderson 1992; Giegerich 2001), BLOCKING (Aronoff 1976), PRE-EMPTION BY SYNONYMY ('If a potential innovative word-form would be precisely synonymous with a well-established word, the innovative word is pre-empted by the well-established word and is therefore considered unacceptable' – Clark and Clark 1979), the AVOID SYNONYMY Condition (Kiparsky 1983), and within language acquisition the principles of CONTRAST and MUTUAL EXCLUSIVITY. Contrast (E. Clark 1987) stipulates that any two distinct forms contrast in meaning and that innovative forms fill lexical gaps but don't displace established lexicalizations. Mutual Exclusivity (cf. Markman and Wachtel 1988 and much subsequent work), to which we return below, addresses children's predisposition to reject lexical overlap, in which an unfamiliar label is applied to a familiar object with a known name.

If synonymy avoidance is a reflex of the R Principle, as suggested by its characterization in terms of least effort, laziness, or paradigmatic economy, why do we not find analogous principles correlated with the Q Principle, Zipf's hearer's economy? Or do we? Note first the functional parallel between the two tendencies:

AVOID SYNONYMY:	AVOID HOMONYMY:
2 forms → 1 meaning	2 meanings → 1 form
R-based (Costly for Speaker)	*Q-based* (Hard for Hearer)
Result: 1 form grows a new meaning	Result: 1 meaning grows a new form

Whence then the asymmetry? In fact, earlier sources do find a symmetry between the two principles, with the proviso (e.g. in Paul 1889) that apparent homonymy is tolerated because the context determines the intended or salient meaning, as in the differential interpretations of *sheet* at a clothing store, on a yacht, or at a printer's shop. Pernicious homonymy arises only when H is generally unable to recover S's intended meaning because of an overlap not just in the phonology but in the grammatical category, subcategory, sense-domain, and register of each homophone:

Only when the words are alike in sound, when they are in common use in the same social and intellectual circles, when they perform the same syntactical functions in the language, within the same sphere of ideas, do they become subject to mutual confusion and conflict. (Williams 1944, 5)

Thus no problem is posed by pairs like *fly* (N/V), *red/read, limp* (A/V), *cape, pound* (weight/currency); but homonymy destroys the weaker member of pairs like *gat* (*<gallus*) 'rooster' vs *gat (<gattus)* 'cat' within the area of their merger in south-western France (Gilliéron 1921; Bloomfield 1933). Relevant cases of homonymic obsolescence in English include *let* 'allow' vs *let* 'hinder' (the latter surviving in the *let ball* of tennis), *queen* 'sovereign' vs *quean* 'harlot', *straight* vs *strait, pail* 'bucket' vs *pale* 'shovel', *an ear* vs. *a neer* 'kidney', etc. (Useful discussions are provided in Bloomfield 1933, 396–9; Menner 1936; Williams 1944; and Bolinger 1961.)

The effects of pernicious homonymy extend to the phenomenon of taboo avoidance, in which (as the linguistic analogue of Gresham's law of currency) the 'bad' meaning drives out the 'good'. To the stock examples *cock, ass, coney*, we can now add *niggardly*, despite the not-quite-homophony between the slur and its lexically unrelated victim. In such cases the interference is more psychological than referential; as Bloomfield (1933, 396) remarks, there is little danger of true confusion here in a given context but the 'powerful stimulus' of the taboo doppelgänger makes life difficult for 'the innocent homonym'.

As with the parallel cases of synonymy avoidance, the resolutions of Avoid Homonymy are various: one of the homonymous forms may disappear (to be replaced via borrowing, transfer, or other means), one of the items may change in form (e.g. through adoption of a diminutive affix), or one homonym may be limited to non-contrastive contexts or extended by artificial contrast *('funny strange or funny ha-ha?' 'lightweight or light-coloured?')*; the sources mentioned above are rich in illustrations of each of these outcomes. Indeed, the tendency to avoid homonymy is strong enough to overcome the usual linguistic antipathy to redundancy: especially when the loss of semantic transparency results in potential unclarity, superficially redundant derivational or inflectional morphology (double or triple marking) is often tolerated, as with *unravel, unloosen, unthaw, debone,* or *irregardless*, despite the seeming violation of both paradigmatic and syntagmatic economy. In such cases, Q supersedes R. (See Horn 1991, 1993 for elaboration.)

Recent empirical findings suggest that children tend to reject homonymy in tandem with their rejection of synonymy. Thus, for example, children are predisposed to reject pseudo-homonyms, as in the experimental application of a familiar word to an unfamiliar object, although their resistance is decreased when the known word is assigned to a frame inappropriate for the original sense (Mazzocco 1997; Doherty 2004; Casenhiser 2005). Bontly (2005) has even argued that the strongest support for a generalized notion of parsimony in the theory of meaning along the lines of the Modified Occam's Razor principle ('Senses are not to be multiplied beyond necessity' – Grice 1989, 47) can be provided by findings on the role of homonymy avoidance in the acquisition of language.

Just as Q-based homonymy avoidance is overridden when the context rules out an implausible reading, so too on the R side of the coin mutual exclusivity is relaxed when the child can infer that multiple labels are associated with different perspectives. One particularly interesting result emerging from work on Contrast and mutual exclusivity (Clark 1997; Bloom 2000; Diesendruck and Markson 2001) is that these principles appear not to be domain-specific; that is, they are not restricted to word learning. Further, there is a strong correlation with what psychologists call THEORY OF MIND, in that the child, in computing whether to reason from the prior establishment of a given label for an object, must be assumed to formulate assumptions about the knowledge state of the hearer. Given that the avoidance of lexical overlap is based on expectations about communicative or rational behaviour of others, there is an essentially pragmatic basis for synonymy avoidance, as Paul Bloom and others have observed.

There also appears to be some interesting evidence that non-human primates apply mutual exclusivity (Bloom 2000). And even the implicit no-nonprimates-need-apply signage may need to come down, now that one particular border collie, Rico, who has a working vocabulary of 200 words, has been claimed to be governed by mutual exclusivity in his lexical learning, as evidenced by the consistency of his association of unfamiliar words with unknown objects (Bower 2004). Such results, while initially surprising, can be understood if we step back from the standard Gricean formulation of the maxims in terms of cooperation. The R Principle, as a correlate of the Principle of Least Effort, is not in itself subsumable under a Gricean Cooperative Principle (as noted by Carston 2005, 313). It is for this reason that I have argued (Horn 2004, 2006) for an essentially RATIONALITY-based pragmatics.

Grice himself regarded linguistic exchange as 'a special case of purposive, indeed rational behavior', observing that 'the specific expectations or presumptions connected with at least some of the ... maxims have their analogues in the sphere of transactions that are not talk exchanges' (Grice

1989, 28). Asa Kasher has emphasized the role of rationality in pragmatics; his PRINCIPLE OF EFFECTIVE MEANS (Kasher 1982, 32) stipulates 'Given a desired end, one is to choose that action which most effectively, and at least cost, attains that end, ceteris paribus.' Kasher's maxim incorporates the same minimax give-and-take of effort and cost that underlies the unitarian account of the relevance theorists, the dualistic Q- and R-based approach considered here, and the trinitarian account of Levinson.

The speaker's and hearer's joint (though tacit) recognition of the rational tendency to avoid unnecessary effort, and the inferences S expects H to draw from S's efficient observance of this tendency, are more explicable directly from rationality than from cooperation as such. While Grice (1989, 28) recognizes that the maxims apply to cooperative ventures outside of language (baking a cake, fixing a car), cooperation is not a necessary condition, much less communication. In particular, the generalized forms of both Q and R Principles – 'Do enough; Don't do too much' – can plausibly be taken to govern ANY goal-oriented rational activity: a person brushing her hair, a dog digging a hole to bury a bone. In this way, the maxim of quantity, in both its opposed (Q and R) subforms, is a linguistic instantiation of these rationality-based constraints on the expenditure of effort. Of course, as Grice recognized, the shared tacit awareness of such principles to generate conversational implicatures is a central property of speaker meaning within the communicative enterprise.

6. the manichaean mandate: in defence of the magic number 2

This brings us to the question of whether our two principles might be either too many or too few. Levinson (2000) trifurcates the dualistic framework into an opposition of Q, I (=R), and M heuristics. M here stands for Manner: 'What's said in an abnormal way isn't normal; or Marked message indicates marked situation' (Levinson 2000, 33ff, essentially capturing the generalization expressed in the Division of Pragmatic Labour; in earlier work Levinson annotates this as Q/M). Even if the complexity adduced by Levinson proves ultimately warranted, his system can be seen as a refinement of the two-pronged one in Horn (1984) (which in turn draws on Atlas and Levinson 1981). But what of the apparently simpler model advanced within RT?

My response is (perhaps unsurprisingly) twofold. First, I find an appeal to two oppositely-oriented principles both descriptively and explanatorily more insightful, allowing for the treatment of clash effects reviewed here (and in greater detail in the full Gricean and neo-Gricean *oeuvre*), the dialectic equilibrium depicted in the division of pragmatic labour, and the role of pragmatics in lexical choice and lexical change; see especially the work presented and reviewed in Traugott and Dasher (2002) and Traugott (2004a) (cf. also Traugott 2004b for an argument that a binary system is both adequate and more explanatory than Levinson's tri-heuristic alternative as a motivated account of meaning shift). Second, I question whether the notion of Relevance, as defined by Sperber and Wilson (1986) and refined and applied in various works by them, Carston, and many others since, is fundamentally monist. In many ways, the RT programme is in fact covertly dualistic in that Relevance, too, is understood in terms of a minimax of effort and effect. As Carston (1995, 231) puts it, 'Human cognitive activity is driven by the goal of maximizing relevance: that is ... to derive as great a range of contextual effects as possible for the least expenditure of effort.'

As we have seen, the paper trail of this minimax antedates both neo-Gricean and RT models by a matter of millennia and – like the principles of least effort and sufficiency of effort – is not limited to linguistic interaction. Within more recent pragmatic theory, as I have argued here, nothing crucial hinges on the centrality of Grice's conversation-specific Cooperative Principle for the account of speaker-based implicature and hearer-based pragmatic inference.

But if this is so, there is no point in seeking to reduce the stock of active ingredients in the pragmatic medicine bottle from two to one. Indeed, the elaboration of central issues in the theory of implicature and lexical pragmatics, including diachronic questions on how word meaning changes over time, involves the dialectic between the two opposed principles and (as in all dialectical systems) the means of resolving these oppositions, as seen in particular from the parallel structure of the twin Q and R correlates, Avoid Pernicious Homonymy and Avoid Pernicious Synonymy. If RT were truly monist rather than dualist, it would find such phenomena difficult to capture. As it is, the interplay of effort and effect does allow many of the relevant phenomena to be insightfully discussed in diverse frameworks, although – as argued by Saul (2002) – the discrepancy between a (neo-)Gricean model of speaker meaning (including implicature) and a relevance-theoretic model of utterance interpretation will tend to yield descriptions of different parts of the communicative elephant.

acknowledgements

Earlier versions of some of this material were presented at the 2003 LSA summer Linguistic Institute (Michigan State University), the 2004 LSA annual meeting (Boston), the 9th National Conference on Pragmatics (Shanghai, July 2005), and the Workshop on Word Meaning, Concepts and Communication (Windsor, UK, September 2005). I am grateful to the participants at those venues and to Barbara Abbott, Mira Ariel, Kent Bach, Robyn Carston, Michael Israel, and Noel Burton-Roberts for comments and suggestions, which it's not their fault if I misused. Some of this material appeared previously in a different form in *Intercultural Pragmatics* as Horn 2005; thanks to the editor Istvan Kekcses and the publisher Mouton de Gruyter for granting permission to reuse it here.

references

Anderson, Stephen (1992). *A-Morphous Morphology*. Cambridge: Cambridge University Press.

Anscombre, Jean-Claude and Oswald Ducrot (1983). *L'argumentation dans la langue*. Brussels: Pierre Mardaga.

Aronoff, Mark (1976). *Word-Formation in Generative Grammar*. Cambridge Mass.: MIT Press.

Atlas, Jay David and Stephen C. Levinson (1981). 'It-clefts, informativeness, and logical form'. In P. Cole (ed.). *Radical Pragmatics*. New York: Academic Press. 1–51.

Bloom, Paul (2000). *How Children Learn the Meanings of Words*. Cambridge, Mass.: MIT Press.

Bloomfield, Leonard (1933). *Language*. New York: H. Holt.

Bolinger, Dwight (1961). 'Contrastive accent and contrastive stress'. *Language* 37: 83–96.

Bontly, Thomas (2005). 'Modified Occam's Razor: Parsimony arguments and pragmatic explanations'. *Mind and Language* 20: 288–312.

Borges, Jorge Luis (1963). 'Funes the Memorious'. *ficciones*. New York: Grove Press. 107–15.

Bosanquet, Bernard (1911). *Logic*. Vol. 1. 2nd edn. Oxford: Clarendon Press.

Bower, Bruce (2004). 'A fetching lexicon'. *Science News* 165: 371–72.

Bréal, Michel (1900). *Semantics*. Trans. Mrs Henry Cust. New York: Henry Holt.

Brown, Penelope and Stephen Levinson (1987). *Politeness*. Cambridge: Cambridge University Press.

Bybee, Joan and Paul Hopper (eds). (2001). *Frequency and the Emergence of Linguistic Structure*. Amsterdam/Philadelphia: John Benjamins.

Carroll, John and Michael Tanenhaus (1975). 'Prolegomena to a functional theory of word formation'. *Papers from the Parasession on Functionalism*. Chicago: CLS. 47–62.

Carston, Robyn (1995). 'Quantity maxims and generalized implicature'. *Lingua* 96: 213–44.

— (2002). *Thoughts and Utterances: The Pragmatics of Explicit Communication*. Oxford: Blackwell.

— (2005). 'Relevance theory, Grice, and the neo-Griceans: A response to Laurence Horn's "Current issues in neo-Gricean pragmatics"'. *Intercultural Pragmatics* 2: 303–20.

Casenhiser, Devin (2005). 'Children's resistance to homonymy: an experimental study of pseudohomonyms'. *Journal of Child Language* 32: 319–43.

Chierchia, Gennaro (2004). 'Scalar implicatures, polarity phenomena, and the syntax/pragmatics interface'. In A. Belletti (ed.). *Structures and Beyond.* Oxford: Oxford University Press. 39–103.

Clark, Eve (1987). 'The principle of Contrast'. In B. MacWhinney (ed.). *Mechanisms of Language Acquisition.* New York: Academic Press. 1–33.

— (1997). 'Conceptual perspective and lexical choice in acquisition'. *Cognition* 64: 1–37.

Clark, Eve and Herbert Clark (1979). 'When nouns surface as verbs'. *Language* 55: 547–90.

Diesendruck, Gil and Lori Markson (2001). 'Children's avoidance of lexical overlap: A pragmatic account'. *Developmental Psychology* 37: 630–41.

Doherty, Martin (2004). 'Children's difficulty in learning homonyms'. *Journal of Child Language* 31: 203–14.

Ducrot, Oswald (1969). 'Présupposés et sous-entendus'. Rep. in O. Ducrot. *Le dire et le dit.* (1984). Paris: Les éditions de Minuit 13–31.

Fidelholtz, James (1975). 'Word-frequency and vowel reduction in English'. *CLS* 11: 200–13.

Flemming, Edward (2001). *Auditory Representations in Phonology.* New York: Routledge.

— (2004). 'Contrast and perceptual distinctiveness'. In B. Hayes, R. Kirchner and D. Steriade (eds). *Phonetically Based Phonology.* Cambridge: Cambridge University Press.

Giegerich, Heinz (2001). 'Synonymy blocking and the elsewhere condition: Lexical morphology and the speaker'. *Transactions of the Philological Society* 99: 65–98.

Gilliéron, Jules (1921). *Pathologie et thérapeutique verbales.* Paris: E. Champion.

Grice, H.P. (1989). *Studies in the Way of Words.* Cambridge Mass.: Harvard University Press.

Haiman, John (1985). *Natural Syntax.* Cambridge: Cambridge University Press.

Hayes, Bruce (1997). 'Phonetically-driven phonology', ms, UCLA. Later version published in M. Darnell et al (eds), *Functionalism and Formalism in Linguistics.* Vol. 1. Amsterdam: John Benjamins. 243–85.

Horn, Laurence (1972). 'On the Semantic Properties of Logical Operators in English'. UCLA dissertation. Distributed by Indiana University Linguistics Club, 1976.

— (1978). 'Lexical incorporation, implicature, and the least effort hypothesis'. *Papers from the Parasession on the Lexicon.* Chicago: Chicago Linguistic Society. 196–209.

— (1984). 'Toward a new taxonomy for pragmatic inference: Q-based and R-based implicature'. In D. Schiffrin (ed.). *Meaning, Form, and Use in Context (GURT '84).* Washington, DC: Georgetown University Press. 11–42.

— (1989). *A Natural History of Negation.* Chicago, IL: University of Chicago Press. Reissued Stanford: CSLI, 2001.

— (1991). 'Duplex negatio affirmat...: The Economy of Double Negation'. In *Papers from the Parasession on Negation. CLS* 27/2, 80–106.

— (1992). 'The said and the unsaid'. *SALT II: Proceedings of the Second Conference on Semantics and Linguistic Theory.* Columbus: Ohio State University Department of Linguistics. 163–92.

— (1993). 'Economy and redundancy in a dualistic model of natural language'. In S. Shore and M. Vilkuna (eds). *SKY 1993: 1993 Yearbook of the Linguistic Association of Finland*. 33–72.

— (2000a). 'From *if* to *iff*: Conditional perfection as pragmatic strengthening'. *Journal of Pragmatics* 32: 289–326.

— (2000b). 'Pick a theory (not just *any* theory): Indiscriminatives and the free-choice indefinite'. In L. Horn and Y. Kato (eds). *Negation and Polarity*. Oxford: Oxford University Press. 147–92.

— (2004). 'Implicature'. In Laurence Horn and Gregory Ward (eds). *The Handbook of Pragmatics*. 3–28.

— (2005). 'Current issues in Gricean pragmatics'. *Intercultural Pragmatics* 2: 191–204.

— (2006). 'The Border Wars: A neo-Gricean perspective'. In K. Turner and K. von Heusiger (eds). *Where Semantics Meets Pragmatics*. Amsterdam: Elsevier. 21–48.

Horn, Laurence and Gregory Ward (eds). (2004). *The Handbook of Pragmatics*. Oxford: Blackwell.

Israel, Michael (1996). 'Polarity sensitivity as lexical semantics'. *Linguistics and Philosophy* 19: 619–66.

Kasher, Asa (1982). 'Gricean inference revisited'. *Philosophica* 29: 25–44.

Kiparsky, Paul (1983). 'Word-formation and the lexicon'. *Proceedings of the 1982 Mid-America Linguistics Conference*. Lawrence: University of Kansas Department of Linguistics. 47–78.

Kirchner, Robert (2001). *An Effort Based Approach to Consonant Lenition*. New York: Routledge.

Levinson, Stephen (2000). *Presumptive Meanings: The Theory of Generalized Conversational Implicature*. Cambridge, Mass.: MIT Press.

Lindblom, Bjorn (1983). 'Economy of speech gestures'. In P. MacNeilage (ed.). *The Production of Speech*. New York: Springer-Verlag. 217–45.

Locke, John (1690). *An Essay Concerning Human Understanding*. Repr. 1975, Oxford: Clarendon Press.

Markman, Ellen and G.F. Wachtel (1988). 'Children's use of mutual exclusivity to constrain the meanings of words'. *Cognitive Psychology* 20: 121–57.

Martinet, Andre (1962). *A Functional View of Language*. Oxford: Clarendon Press.

— (1964). *Elements of General Linguistics*. Trans. E. Palmer. London: Faber and Faber.

Matsumoto, Yo (1995). 'The conversational constraint on Horn scales'. *Linguistics and Philosophy* 18: 21–60.

Mazzocco, Michele (1997). 'Children's interpretations of homonyms: a developmental study'. *Journal of Child Language* 24: 441–67.

McCawley, James (1978). 'Conversational implicature and the lexicon'. In P. Cole (ed.). *Syntax and Semantics 9: Implicature*. New York: Academic Press. 245–59.

Menner, Robert (1936). 'The conflict of homonyms in English'. *Language* 12: 229–44.

Passy, Paul (1890). *Étude sur les changements phonétiques et leurs caractères généraux*. Paris: Firmin-Didot.

Paul, Hermann (1889). *Principles of the History of Language*. Trans. H.A. Strong. London: Macmillan.

Saul, Jennifer (2002). 'What is said and psychological reality: Grice's project and relevance theorists' criticisms'. *Linguistics and Philosophy* 25: 347–72.

Sayce, A.H. (1880). *Introduction to the Science of Language*. London: C.K. Paul & Co.

Shuy, Roger (2002). *Linguistic Battles in Trademark Disputes*. New York: Palgrave.

Sperber, Dan and Deirdre Wilson (1986). *Relevance: Communication and Cognition*. Cambridge, Mass.: Harvard University Press.

Stern, Gustaf (1931). *Meaning and Change of Meaning*. Bloomington, IN: Indiana University Press.

Sweet, Henry (1874). *History of English Sounds from the Earliest Period*. London: English Dialect Society.

Tobler, Adolf. (1882). 'Il ne faut pas que tu meures "du darfst nicht sterben"'. *Vermischte Beiträge zur französischen Grammatik 1*. 3rd edn., Oxford: Blackwell. Leipzig: S. Hirzel. 201–5.

Traugott, Elizabeth C. (2004a). 'Historical pragmatics'. In Laurence Horn and Gregory Ward (eds). *The Handbook of Pragmatics*. 538–61.

— (2004b). 'A critique of Levinson's view of Q- and M-inferences in historical pragmatics'. *Journal of Historical Pragmatics* 5: 1–25.

Traugott, Elizabeth C. and Richard Dasher (2002). *Regularity in Semantic Change*. Cambridge: Cambridge University Press.

Williams, Edna Rees (1944). *The Conflict of Homonyms in English*. New Haven: Yale University Press.

Zipf, George Kingsley (1935). *The Psycho-Biology of Language*. New York: Houghton Mifflin.

— (1949). *Human Behavior and the Principle of Least Effort*. Cambridge, Mass.: Addison-Wesley.

10
the why and how of experimental pragmatics: the case of 'scalar inferences'

ira noveck and dan sperber

Although a few pioneers in psycholinguistics had, for more than twenty years, approached various pragmatic issues experimentally, it is only in recent years that investigators have begun employing experimental methods in order to test pragmatic hypotheses (see Noveck and Sperber 2004). We see this emergence of a proper experimental pragmatics as an important advance with a great potential for further development. In this chapter we want to illustrate what can be done with experimental approaches to pragmatic issues by presenting one case, that of so-called 'scalar inferences', where the experimental method has helped sharpen a theoretical debate and has provided uniquely relevant evidence. We will focus on work done by the first author and his collaborators or work closely related to theirs, but other authors have also made important contributions to the topic (e.g. Papafragou and Musolino 2003; Guasti et al 2005; De Neys and Schaeken in press).

1. methodological background: the limits of pragmatic intuitions as evidence

Theoretical work in pragmatics relies heavily – often exclusively – on pragmatic intuitions. These are rarely complemented with observational data of a kind more common in sociologically oriented pragmatics. The use of statistical data from corpuses and from experiments is even less common. This situation results partly from the fact that most theoretical pragmatists have been trained in departments of linguistics where, quite often, linguistic intuitions are the only kind of data considered. Optimally, of course, one would want pragmatists to use whatever kind of data might significantly confirm or disconfirm hypotheses. Moreover, a sensible methodological pluralism is not the only reason to diversify the types of evidence used in pragmatics. There are also principled limits to the use of pragmatic intuitions.

It makes sense (even if it is not uncontroversial) to judge a semantic description by its ability to account for semantic intuitions. Of course, the use of semantic intuitions and of linguistic intuitions generally, raises methodological problems and calls for methodological caution. For instance, a linguist's intuitions may be biased by prior theoretical commitments. Also, one may mistake what are in fact pragmatic intuitions for semantic ones (as, Grice argued, ordinary language philosophers systematically did). Still, there are good reasons why semantic intuitions are so central to semantics. Semantic intuitions are not just *about* semantic facts; they are semantic facts themselves. For instance, the intuition that sentence (1) entails (2) is not *about* some semantic property that this sentence would have anyhow, regardless of its accessibility to speakers' intuitions.

(1) John knows that it is raining.
(2) It is raining.

Rather, for (1) to have the meaning it has *is*, among other aspects, to be intuitively understood as entailing (2). A semantic analysis of linguistic expressions that accounts for all the speaker-hearer's semantic intuitions about these expressions may not be the best possible analysis, but it is descriptively adequate (in Chomsky's sense – an explanatory adequate description of the semantics of a given language, on the other hand, involves hypotheses about the capacities that make the acquisition of this semantics possible, and here observational and experimental evidence should be of relevance).

The use of pragmatic intuitions raises the same methodological problems as does the use of semantic intuitions and then some. It is a mistake to believe that pragmatic intuitions of the kind used in pragmatics are data of the same kind as semantic intuitions used in semantics. Genuine pragmatic intuitions are those that addressees have about the intended meaning of an utterance addressed to them. Quite generally, pragmatic intuitions invoked in theoretical pragmatics are not about actual utterances addressed to the reader of a pragmatic article, but about hypothetical cases involving imaginary or generic interlocutors. Pragmatic intuitions on hypothetical utterances have proved useful in a variety of ways, but it is important to keep in mind that these are not about how an utterance is interpreted, but about how an utterance *would be* interpreted if it were produced in a specific situation by a speaker addressing a listener, with referring expressions having actual referents, and so on. These intuitions are educated guesses – and, no doubt, generally good ones – about hypothetical pragmatic facts, but are not themselves pragmatic facts and they may well be in error. That is, we may be wrong about how, in fact, we would interpret a given utterance in a given context.

Besides helping compensate for the inherent limits of pragmatic intuitions, an experimental approach can provide crucial evidence when deciding between alternative theories that may agree on the content of the interpretations of utterances, but that have different implications regarding the cognitive mechanisms through which these interpretations are arrived at. Of course, for their contribution to be of value, experimentalists must conform to fairly strict methodological criteria and measure just what they are intent on measuring – typically the effect of one 'independent' variable on another 'dependent' variable without other uncontrolled variables affecting the results. We will show how this plays out in the study of 'scalar inferences'.

2. theoretical background: scalar implicatures as generalized conversational implicatures

The experiments we will present are relevant to the study of so-called 'scalar implicatures'. Here we just remind readers of the main features of the Gricean and neo-Gricean account of scalar implicatures, and focus on the claim that scalar implicatures are Generalized Conversational Implicatures, or GCIs. Scalar implicatures are illustrated by cases such as (3a) which is said to implicate (3c), or (4a) said to implicate (4c):

(3) a.   It is possible that Hillary will win.
    b.   It is certain that Hillary will win.
    c.   It is not certain that Hillary will win.
(4) a.   Some of the guests have arrived.
    b.   All of the guests have arrived.
    c.   Not all of the guests have arrived.

Proposition (3b) is more informative than (3a), which it entails. If the more informative proposition would make a greater contribution to the common purpose of the conversation, then, a speaker obeying Grice's first Maxim of Quantity ('Make your contribution as informative as is required') would be expected to express it unless she could not do so without violating the Supermaxim of Quality ('Try to make your contribution one that is true'). Hence, on a Gricean account, a speaker stating (3a) typically implicates (3c) (i.e. the negation of (3b)). For the same reasons, a speaker stating (4a) typically implicates (4c) (i.e. the negation of (4b)).

Such implicatures are described as 'scalar' because, according to an account developed by neo-Griceans and in particular Laurence Horn (1972), the derivation of these implicatures draws on pre-existing linguistic scales consisting in a set of alternate terms or expressions ranked by order of informativeness; <possible, certain> and <some, all> are examples of such scales. When a less informative term is used in an utterance in a way that does not satisfy the first maxim of quantity, the speaker can be taken to implicate that the proposition that would have been expressed by the use of a stronger term in the scale is false. This account of implicatures such as those carried by (3a) or (4a) extends to a wide variety of cases and has some intuitive appeal. It should not be seen however as obviously correct or without alternatives. In particular, its implications for processing are less attractive. According to such an account, the inference from the utterance to its scalar implicature goes through a consideration not just of what the speaker said and the context but also of what the speaker might have said but did not. It is this type of onerous inference that makes the Gricean account of implicature derivation seem implausible from a cognitive and developmental point of view.

Levinson draws on another idea of Grice, that of Generalized Conversational Implicatures, to offer an account that might provide a solution to the problem posed by the derivational complexity of scalar implicatures. Grice noted that some implicatures are generally valid (from a pragmatic rather than logical point of view, of course) and therefore could be inferred without consideration of the context, except in cases where the context happens to make them invalid. Grice contrasted these GCIs with Particular Conversational Implicatures, which are valid only in specific contexts. In his book *Presumptive Meanings: The Theory of Generalized Conversational Implicatures* (Levinson 2000), Levinson elaborates Grice's original and somewhat vague notion. For Levinson, GCIs are *default inferences*, that is, inferences that are automatically generated and that can be cancelled if there are contextual reasons to do so. Levinson treats scalar implicatures as paradigmatic cases of GCIs (whereas Grice's own examples of GCIs do not include scalar implicatures). This has the advantage of making the inference of these implicatures a relatively light one-step process, which needs to access neither contextual premises nor the full Gricean rationale for their derivation.

Levinson's own rationale for GCIs so conceived has to do with the optimization of processing. The existence of GCIs speeds up the process of communication that is slowed down, Levinson argues, by the need for phonetic articulation: some unencoded aspects of the speaker's meaning can be inferred from metalinguistic properties of the utterance such as the choice of a given word from among a set of closely related alternatives. For instance, the speaker's choice of 'some' rather than the stronger 'all' in (4a) ('Some of the guests have arrived') justifies inferring that (4c) is part of her meaning. These are non-demonstrative inferences, of course. There are cases where these inferences are invalid. For instance, if it were contextually established that the speaker of (4a) has only partial information about the arrival of the guests, then (4c) would not be part of her meaning. Still, given that GCIs are valid in most contexts (or so it is assumed), the overall speeding up of communication made possible by the automaticity of GCIs is not compromised by the rare cases where contextual considerations force the hearer to countermand them.

The theory of scalar implicatures as default GCIs combines four claims:

(a) These inferences are made by default, irrespective of the context, and cancelled when the context demands.
(b) The fact that these inferences are made by default adds to the speed and efficiency of communication.
(c) These inferences contribute implicatures to the interpretation of the utterance, as opposed to contributing enrichments of its explicit content ('what is said' in Grice's terms or 'explicatures' in relevance theory's terms).
(d) These inferences are scalar: they exploit pre-existing scales such as <some, all>, <or, and>, <possible, necessary>.

We doubt all four claims. The bulk of this chapter will be devoted to explaining how experimental evidence has cast strong doubts on claim (a). First, however, we briefly present an argument that also casts doubt on (b), and we outline the relevance-theoretic approach, which is in contradiction with all four claims.

This idea that default implicatures or GCIs would permit more efficient and speedier communication may seem sensible and capable of lending support to the whole theory. It raises however the following empirical issue. If the frequency of GCI cancellations were too high, their cost would offset the benefit of deriving GCIs by default. Suppose for instance that a given type of GCI had to be cancelled a third of the time. The cost of the use of such a GCI would be that of deriving it by default in all cases plus the cost of cancelling it in one third of the cases. This would have to be compared with the cost of deriving the implicature as a 'particularized conversational implicature', that is, in a contextually sensitive and therefore more costly way, in two-thirds of the cases, but without any cost of default derivation followed by cancellation in the other third of the cases. It is not clear that, with such frequencies, the rationale given for GCIs in terms of economy would make much sense.

To show that this kind of calculus is not unrealistic, consider the example of 'P or Q' and its alleged GCI *not (P and Q)*. We are not aware of any statistical data regarding the frequency of exclusive uses of 'or' and we share the common intuition that quite often, when people utter a sentence of the form 'P or Q' they can be taken to consider that *P and Q* is excluded. This exclusion however need not be part of their meaning. In most cases this exclusion follows from real world knowledge and not from the interpretation of 'or', as illustrated in (5)–(7):

(5) He is a bachelor or he is divorced.
(6) Jane is in Paris or in Madrid.
(7) Bill will arrive Monday or Tuesday.

If 'P or Q' implicates by default that *not (P and Q)*, then, in all cases such as (5)–(7) where the two disjuncts cannot both be true for common sense reasons, people automatically compute a GCI that causes the speaker's meaning to redundantly implicate what is already part of the common ground, and surely, this is a cost without associated benefit. Moreover, if one carefully excludes cases where mutual exclusivity of the disjuncts is self-evident and need not be communicated, and looks at cases such as (8)–(10) where neither the inclusive nor the exclusive interpretation is a priori ruled out, it is not at all obvious that the exclusive interpretation of 'or' is dominant:

(8)   She wears sunglasses or a cap.
(9)   Our employees speak French or Spanish.
(10) Bill will sing or play the piano.

We have no hard statistical data to present, but it seems less than obvious that a disposition to understand by default utterances of the form 'P or Q' as implicating *not (P and Q)* would render communication speedier or more efficient. More generally, the effect that GCIs would have on the efficiency of communication should be investigated rather than assumed.

3. relevance theory's approach

We will assume that the basic tenets of relevance theory are familiar (Sperber and Wilson 1995; see also Wilson and Sperber 2004 for a recent restatement), and focus on how it applies to what neo-Griceans describe as 'scalar implicatures'. Two basic ideas play a crucial role here:

(a) Linguistic expressions serve not to *encode* the speaker's meaning but to *indicate* it. The speaker's meaning is inferred from the linguistic meaning of the words and expressions used taken together with the context.

(b) Inferring the speaker's explicit and implicit meaning (her explicatures and implicatures) is not done sequentially but in parallel. The final overall interpretation of an utterance results from a mutual adjustment of implicatures and explicatures guided by expectations of relevance.

Here is a simple illustration of these two points:

(11) *Henry*: Do you want to go on working, or shall we go to the cinema?
Jane: I am tired. Let's go to the cinema.

Jane's describing herself as 'tired' achieves relevance as an explanation of her acceptance of Henry's suggestion. For this it must be understood that she is not just tired, but too tired to go on working, and at the same time not too tired to go to the cinema. Her use of 'tired' serves to indicate an ad hoc concept TIRED* with an extension narrower than that of the linguistically encoded concept TIRED. Whereas TIRED extends from a minimal level of tiredness to complete exhaustion, TIRED* extends just over those levels of tiredness that explain why Jane would rather go to the cinema than work. Henry correctly understands Jane's explicature to be (12) and her implicature to be (13), yielding an optimally relevant interpretation:

(12) I am TIRED*.
(13) The reason why I would rather go to the cinema than work is that I am TIRED*.

Note that explicature (12), and in particular the interpretation of 'tired' as indicating TIRED*, is calibrated so as to justify implicature (13). The explicature therefore could only be inferred once the implicature had been tentatively assumed to be part of Jane's meaning. The overall interpretation results from a process of mutual adjustment between explicature and implicature.

Consider now an expression typically supposed to give rise to 'scalar implicatures' such as 'some of the Xs'. From a semantic point of view, 'some of the Xs' has as its extension the set of subsets of n Xs where n is at least 2 and at most the total number of the Xs. From a relevance-theoretic pragmatic point of view, the use of an expression of the form 'some of the Xs', just as that of any linguistic expression, serves not to encode the speaker's meaning, but to indicate it. In particular the denotation of the concept indicated by a given use of 'some of the Xs' may be an ad hoc concept SOME OF THE XS* with a denotation different from that of the literal SOME OF THE XS. Rather than ranging over all subsets of Xs between 2 and the total number of the Xs, the extension of SOME OF THE XS* may be narrowed down at either end, or it may be extended so as to include subsets of one.

Imagine (14) uttered in a discussion of the spread of scientific knowledge in America:

(14) Most Americans are creationists and some even believe that the Earth is flat.

Clearly, the speaker is understood as meaning that a number of Americans much greater than two believe that the Earth is flat. Two Americans with such a belief – say two inmates in a psychiatric hospital – would be enough to make her utterance literally true, but not, and by a wide margin, to make it relevant. Given that the speaker can be assumed to know that it is common knowledge that not all Americans believe that the Earth is flat, there is no ground to assume that this is a part of her meaning (inferring it would not add any cognitive effect and it would involve a processing cost, hence it would detract from relevance). On the other hand, the speaker's contrastive use of 'most' and 'some' and her use of 'even' make it part of her meaning that the Americans who believe the Earth to be flat are fewer than those who believe in creationism (this, of course, entails that not all Americans believe that the Earth is flat, but not every entailment of a speaker's meaning is part of that meaning). So the denotation indicated by 'some' in (14) is narrower than its literal denotation at both ends: the subsets of Americans in the denotation of this occurrence of 'some' are large enough to be relevant and hence much larger than sets of two Americans, and are smaller than the set of American creationists.

Let us now go back to a version of example (4). Jane and Henry have invited a few friends to a dinner party. Suppose first that it was agreed that Henry would go and get the dessert from the pastry shop as soon as the guests started arriving. Henry is in the garage, he hears the bell ring and then Jane shouting (15) to him:

(15) *Jane to Henry*: Some of the guests have arrived.

Henry does not know whether one, many, or all the guests have arrived, or, for that matter, whether Jane has already opened the door and seen how many of them there are, and the question need not even come to his mind. What makes Jane's utterance relevant is that it implies that he should go now and this does not depend on the number of guests at the door. Henry's construal of 'some' is compatible with any number of guests having arrived, even just one, and hence is an extended construal of 'some'.

Consider now a different scenario. Henry is alone in the kitchen cooking. Jane comes in and tells him (15). The consequences that Henry considers are that he should come and greet the guests and bring the finger food he has prepared as an appetizer. The value of 'some' is taken to be a value for which these are the main consequences. If all the guests had come, what he should do would be not just to greet the guest and bring the finger food, but also and even more importantly, to put the fish in the oven and make the ultimate preparations for the meal itself. The fact that Jane's utterance achieves relevance without bringing to mind consequences more typical of the arrival of all the guests causes Henry to construe 'some' with some vague cardinality above one and below all. Henry need not actively exclude *all*, he may just not even consider it. If however Henry is wondering whether all the guests have arrived, then he will take Jane's utterance to license the inference that not all of them have. If, moreover, Henry had asked Jane whether all the guests had arrived, or if he knew that she knew that it was particularly relevant to him at this point in time, he would take that inference to be intended. He would also do so if she had put a contrastive stress on 'some', causing an extra effort and suggesting an extra effect. In other words, if there is some mutually manifest, actively represented reason to wonder whether all the guests have arrived, then (15) can be taken to implicate that not all of them have.

From a relevance theory point of view, (11), (14), and (15) are just ordinary illustrations of the fact that linguistic expressions serve to indicate rather than encode the speaker's meaning and that the speaker's meanings are quite often a narrowing down or broadening of the linguistic meaning. Taking 'some' to indicate not *at least two and possibly all* but *at least two and fewer than all* is a common narrowing down of the literal meaning of 'some' at the level of the explicature of the utterance. It is not automatic but takes place when the consequences that render the utterance relevant as expected are characteristically carried by this narrowed down meaning.

We are not denying that a statement of the form '...some...' may, in some cases carry an implicature of the form *...not all...* (or, in other cases we will not discuss here, an implicature of the form *...some...not...*). This occurs when the '...some...' utterance achieves relevance by answering a tacit or explicit question as to whether *all* items satisfy the predicate. The fact that it does not answer it positively *implicates* a negative answer and therefore a narrowed down construal of 'some' as excluding all. Standard accounts of 'scalar implicatures' fail to distinguish the cases where the explicature merely entails *...not all...* and the much less frequent cases where, moreover, the utterance implicates *...not all....*

In all the cases where the meaning of 'some' in an utterance is narrowed down so as to exclude *all*, this is the result of an inferential process that looks at consequences that might make the utterance relevant as expected, and that adjusts the meaning indicated by 'some' to these consequences. In particular, if what may make the utterance relevant is an implication that is true of some Xs but not of all Xs, then the meaning of 'some' is adjusted so as to exclude *all*. These inferential processes result from the automatic attempt by the hearer to find an interpretation of the utterance that meets his expectation of relevance and they all follow the same heuristics. There is nothing distinctive in the way 'scalar' inferences are drawn. Moreover, the class of cases described in the literature as scalar inferences is characterized by an enrichment at the level of the explicature (where, for instance, 'some' is reinterpreted in a way that excludes *all*) and only in a small sub-class of these is the exclusion of the more informative concept not just entailed but also implicated.

According to relevance theory, then, so called 'scalar implicatures' are not scalar, nor necessarily implicatures. Of course, the notion of 'scalar implicature' could be redefined to fit just cases where there is an explicit or implicit question as to whether the use of a more informative expression than the one employed by the speaker (e.g. 'all' instead of 'some') would have been warranted, and in such cases, a denial of a more informative claim can indeed be implicated by the use of the less informative expression. However, 'scalar implicatures' in this restricted sense depend on contextual premises (linked to the fact that the stronger claim was being entertained as a relevant possibility) rather than on a context-independent scale, and are not candidates therefore for the status of GCI.

From the point of view of relevance theory, then, the classical neo-Gricean theory of scalar implicatures can be seen as a mistaken generalization of the relatively rare case where a weaker claim genuinely *implicates* the denial of a stronger claim that is contextually under consideration to the much more common case where the denotation of an expression is narrowed down so as to exclude marginal or limiting instances carrying untypical implications. For instance, 'possible' as in (3a) ('It is possible that Hillary will win') is often construed as excluding, on one side, mere metaphysical possibility with very low empirical probability, and, on the other side, certainty and quasi-certainty. The trimming of 'possible' at both ends results in an enriched and generally more relevant meaning. Since the trimming at the very high probability end is not different from that at the very low probability end, both should be explained in the same way, ruling out the scalar aspect of the 'scalar implicature' account, which works, if at all, only at the upper end. On the other hand, if (3a) ('It is possible that Hillary will win') were uttered, then it would indeed implicate (3c) ('It is not certain that Hillary will win') because it would achieve relevance by implicitly answering in the negative a question that had been asked. From a relevance theory point of view, the two cases should be distinguished.

This is not the place to compare in detail the GCI and the relevance-theoretic approaches. We focus rather on a testable difference in prediction between them. Levinson writes: 'GCI theory clearly ought to make predictions about process. But here the predictions have not yet been worked out in any detail' (Levinson 2000, 370). There is however one prediction about process that follows quite directly from GCI theory since it is hardly more than a restatement of some of the tenets of the theory. According to the theory, GCIs are computed by default and are contextually cancelled when needed. Both the computation of GCIs and their cancellation are processes and therefore should each take some time and effort (even if the default character of GCI should make their computation quite easy and rapid). Everything else being equal, less effort should be expended and less time taken in the normal case where a GCI is computed and not cancelled than in the exceptional case where a GCI is first computed and then cancelled. Relevance theory predicts just the opposite pattern.

From a relevance-theoretic perspective, the speaker's meaning is always inferred, even when it consists in a literal interpretation of the linguistic expressions used. The inferences involved, however, differ in the time and effort they require. Both the sentence meaning and the context contribute to making some interpretations more easily derived than others. If only sentence meaning were involved, one should predict that the smaller the distance between it and the speaker's meaning it serves to indicate, the lesser would be the time and effort required to infer the speaker's meaning. Contextual factors, however, must be taken into account. For instance, an enriched interpretation may be primed by the context and, as a result, may be easier to infer than a literal interpretation. Consider a variation of example (11):

(16) *Henry*: You look tired, let's go to the cinema.
      Jane: I am tired, but not too tired to go on working.

A natural interpretation of Henry's utterance involves the ad hoc concept TIRED* such that being TIRED* is a sufficient reason to stop working and not a sufficient reason to stay at home. Jane could have answered, 'No, I am not tired, I'll go on working', meaning that she was not TIRED*. When Jane, rather, asserts that she *is* tired, Henry is primed to interpret 'tired' as TIRED*. A relevant interpretation of Jane's whole utterance, however, imposes a broader, more literal and, in this situation, more effortful construal of the term.

Even when an enriched interpretation of an utterance is not primed, it may require less processing effort than would the literal interpretation because the contextual implications that render relevant the enriched interpretation are more easily arrived at than those that would render relevant the literal interpretation. This typically occurs with metaphorical utterances: a relevant literal interpretation is often hard or even impossible to construct.

In the absence of contextual factors that make an enriched interpreta-tion of an utterance easier to arrive at, relevance theory predicts that a literal interpretation – which involves just the attribution to the speaker of a meaning already provided by linguistic decoding – should involve shallower processing and take less time than an enriched one – which involves a process of meaning construction. Such is the case in particular in the experiments we describe below.

The difference in prediction between GCI theory and relevance theory can be presented in table form:

Table 10.1: Contrasting predictions of GCI Theory and relevance theory regarding the speed of interpretation of scalar term (when an enriched construal is not contextually primed)

Interpretation of the scalar term	GCI theory	relevance theory
literal	default enrichment + context-sensitive cancellation, hence slower	no enrichment, hence faster
enriched	default enrichment, hence faster	context-sensitive enrichment, hence slower

Moreover, this difference in prediction between the two theories is of a type that lends itself to experimental investigation.

4. methodological considerations in experimental approaches to 'scalar inferences'

In the experimental study of scalar inferences,[1] one has to keep in mind four methodological considerations. To begin with, one wants to be sure that a given result (whether it be the rate of responses that indicate a pragmatic enrichment or the mean reaction time associated with an enrichment) is a consequence of the experiment's intended target and not of other contextual variables. For example, one would want to be sure that the understanding of a disjunctive statement of the form *P or Q* as excluding *P and Q* is due to the pragmatic enrichment of the term 'or' (from an inclusive to an exclusive interpretation) and not to some other feature. Thus, one would avoid investigating utterances that invite an exclusive understanding of the situation described rather than of the description itself. In example (6) ('Jane is in Paris or in Madrid') above, the exclusive understanding is based on our knowledge that a person cannot be in two places at the same time and need not involve any pragmatic enrichment of the meaning of the word 'or'. In devising experimental material, it thus becomes important to invent examples where an enriched interpretation is not imposed by extra-pragmatic considerations. One can do this by using either examples where participants' knowledge is equally compatible with a literal or an enriched interpretation of a scalar term, or examples where knowledge considerations might bias participants in favour of a literal interpretation: in both cases, if one finds evidence of enrichment, one will be confident that it comes from a pragmatic inference about what the utterance meant, rather than from a mere understanding of how the world is.

Second, one would want a paradigm that allows for two identifiable outcomes so that the presence of an enrichment can be indicated by a unique sort of response while a non-enrichment can be indicated by a different response. This is why most of the experiments on scalars described here involve a scenario that could be described by means of a more informative utterance than the test utterance (uttered by a puppet or some other interlocutor). Imagine, for example, being shown five boxes each containing a token and then being told, 'Some boxes contain a token'. If one interprets 'some' literally (i.e. as compatible with *all*), one would agree with the statement; if one enriches 'some' so as to make it incompatible with *all*, one would have to disagree. In such conditions, a participant's response (agrees or disagrees) is revealing of a particular interpretation.

Third, one wants every assurance that an effect is robust. That is, one wants to see the same result over and over again and across a variety of comparable tasks. When two similar studies (for instance, two studies investigating different scalar terms but in an equivalent manner) present comparable outcomes, each strengthens the findings of the other. On the other hand, if two very similar experiments fail to produce the same general effects, something is wrong. This does not mean that negative results are necessarily fatal for an experimental paradigm. If one carefully modifies an experiment and it prompts a different sort of outcome than previous ones (and in a predictable manner), it helps determine the factors that underlie an effect. This occurs with the developmental findings to be described below, which have generally shown that children are more likely than adults to *agree* with a weak statement (for instance, the statement 'Some horses jumped over a fence') when a stronger one would be pragmatically justified (because, in fact, all the horses jumped over a fence). All sorts of follow-up studies have aimed to put this effect to the test. In general, the effect has been resilient; a few studies, however, show that one can get children to appear more adult-like through specific sorts of modifications. For example, experimenters have aimed to verify the effect under conditions where participants are given training or where scenarios are modified to highlight the contrast between the weak utterance and the stronger scenario. The net result is that the outcomes of these tests collectively help identify the factors that can encourage scalar inference-making.

Fourth, it is important for any experiment to include as many reasonable controls as possible. These are test questions that are similar to the main items of interest, but aim basically to confirm that there is nothing bizarre in the task. For example, if one finds that participants' responses indicate that they enrich 'some' but also that the same participants endorse the use of the word 'some' to describe a scene where 'none' would be appropriate, then there is something questionable about the experiment. This rarely happens (the above example is presented for illustrative purposes only), but one needs to provide assurances to oneself and to readers that such bizarreness can be ruled out. Any decent task will include several controls that lead to uncontroversial responses in order to, in effect, contextualize the critical findings. The studies we will discuss exemplify the four methodological considerations we have just described.

5. developmental studies

The experimental study of scalar inferences started within the framework of developmental studies on reasoning. Noveck (2001) investigated the way children responded to (by agreeing or disagreeing with) a puppet who presented several statements, including one that could ultimately lead to a pragmatic enrichment. All statements, even those that served as controls to confirm that the participants understood the task, were about the contents of a covered box and were presented by a puppet (handled by the experimenter). Participants were told that the contents of the covered box resembled those of one or the other of two boxes, both of which were open and with their contents in full view. One open box contained a parrot and the other contained a parrot and a bear. The participants then heard the puppet say:[2]

(17) A friend of mine gave me this (covered) box and said, 'All I know is that whatever is inside this box (the covered one) looks like what is inside this box (the one with a parrot and bear) or what is inside this box (the one with just a parrot).'

The participant's task was to say whether or not he agreed with further statements of the puppet. The key item was ultimately the puppet's 'underinformative' statement:

(18) There might be a parrot in the box.

Given that the covered box *necessarily* contained a parrot, the statement in (18) can be answered in one of two ways. The participant can 'agree' if she interprets 'might' literally (so that ...*might*... is compatible with ...*must*...) or she can 'disagree' if she interprets *might* in an enriched way (where ...*might*... is incompatible with ...*must*...). Adults tended to be equivocal with respect to these two interpretations (35 per cent agreed with the statement) while children (five-, seven- and nine-year-olds) tended to interpret this statement in a minimal way, i.e. literally. Collectively, 74 per cent of the children responded by agreeing with the statement in (18). However, not all children were alike.

The five-year-olds agreed with (18) at a rate of 72 per cent (a percentage that is unlikely to occur by chance, which would yield 50 per cent in such agree/disagree contexts). Nevertheless, they failed to answer many control questions at such convincing rates. For example, when asked to agree or disagree with statements about the bear ('There has to be a bear', 'There might be a bear', 'There does not have to be a bear', 'There cannot be a bear') they answered at levels that were comparable to those predicted by chance (55 per cent correct across the four questions). Seven-year-olds, on the other hand, did manage to answer practically all seven control problems at rates that indicated they understood the task overall (77 per cent). This is why Noveck (2001) reported that seven-year-olds were the youngest to demonstrate competence with this task while at the same time revealing that they preferred the literal interpretation of 'might' (at a rate, 80 per cent, that is statistically distinguishable from expectations based on chance). The seven-year-olds thus provided the strongest evidence showing that linguistically competent children who perform well on the task overall still interpret 'might' in an unenriched way. As one might expect, the nine-year-olds also answered control problems satisfactorily. Response rates indicating unenriched interpretations of 'might' were high (69 per cent) and much higher than the adults' but they were nevertheless statistically indistinguishable from predictions based on chance suggesting that these children were *beginning* to appear adult-like with respect to (18). Overall, these results were rather surprising for a reasoning study because they indicated that children were more likely than adults to produce a logically correct evaluation of the under-informative modal statement. This sort of response is surprising and rare, but thanks to a pragmatic analysis – where pragmatic enriched interpretations are viewed as likely to result from a richer inferential process than minimal interpretations that add nothing to semantic decoding – these results had a ready interpretation.

Despite taking every precaution (having numerous control items and sampling many children), one can never exclude that such effects might be the result of some subtle factor beyond the experimenter's intention or control. That is why – especially when encountering counter-intuitive results like these – it pays to do follow-ups. There have been essentially two sorts.

The first sort aims to verify the effect. In one follow-up (Noveck 2001, Experiment 2), the same task as the one above was given to five-year-olds and seven-year-olds as well as adults, but all participants were given more thorough training to ensure that they understood the parameters of the task. This was done through training on an identical scenario (one box containing a horse and a fish and another just a horse) where pointed questions were asked about the covered box (e.g. *Could there be a fish by itself in the box?*). Overall, the training increased rates of minimal interpretations of 'might' across all three ages when it came to the task of Experiment 1. Agreement with a statement like the one in (18) was now 81 per cent for five-year-olds, 94 per cent for seven-year-olds, and 75 per cent for adults. Although rates of such minimal interpretations were statistically comparable across ages, one finds the same trends as in the first experiment. Seven-year-olds again demonstrated (through performance with the control problems) that they were the youngest to demonstrate overall competence with the task while *tending* to be more likely than adults in retaining a literal interpretation of the weak scalar term. The data also revealed that the extra training encourages adults to behave more 'logically' (to stick to the literal meaning of 'might'), like the children.

In an effort to establish the developmental effect's reliability and robustness, Noveck (2001, Experiment 3) took advantage of an older study that (a) unintentionally investigated weak scalar expressions among four-to seven-year-old children and that (b) also failed to show evidence of pragmatic enrichment. Smith (1980) presented statements such as 'Some giraffes have long necks' to children and reported that it was surprising to find the children accepting these as true. In a third experiment, therefore, Noveck (2001) essentially continued from where Smith left off. The experiment adopted the same technique as Smith (which included pragmatically felicitous statements such as 'Some birds live in cages' as well as statements with 'all') in order to verify that the developmental findings of the first two experiments were not flukes. The only differences in this third experiment were that the children were slightly older (eight and ten years old) than in the first two studies and that the experimenter was as 'blind' to the intention of the study as the participants (the student who served as experimenter thought that unusual control items such as 'Some crows have radios' or 'All birds have telephones' were the items of interest). The results showed that roughly 87 per cent of children accepted statements like 'Some giraffes have long necks' whereas only 41 per cent of adults did. Again, adults were more likely than children to enrich the interpretation of the underinformative statements (understanding

...*some*... as excluding ...*all*...) and thus tended to reject them (since all giraffes have long necks). All participants answered the five sorts of control items (25 items altogether) as one would expect.

These data prompted Noveck (2001) to revisit other classic studies that serendipitously contained similar scenarios (ones where a stronger statement would be appropriate but a weaker one is made) to determine whether they tell the same story as 'might' and 'some'. In fact, three studies concerning 'or' (Paris 1973; Braine and Rumain 1981; Sternberg 1979), where a conjunctive situation is described with a weaker disjunction, provide further confirming evidence. The authors of these studies also reported counter-intuitive findings showing younger children being, in effect, more logical than adults (children tend to treat 'or' inclusively more often than adults). None of these authors, lacking a proper pragmatic perspective, knew how to make sense of these data at the time. All told, this effect appeared robust.

Other follow-up studies have actually taken issue with Noveck's *interpretation* of the findings. In fact, Noveck (2001, 184) insisted that his data show that children are ultimately less likely than adults to pragmatically enrich underinformative items across tasks; this did not amount to a claim that children lacked pragmatic competence. Still, much work has been aimed at showing that young children are more competent than it might appear. These studies usually take issue with Noveck's Experiment 3 (the one borrowed from Smith 1980) because it concerns the quantifier 'some' (which is of more general interest than 'might') and because the items used in that task are admittedly unusual (see Papafragou and Musolino 2003; Chierchia et al 2004; Guasti et al 2005; Feeney et al 2004).

We highlight here the main advances of these studies. In two sets of studies, Papafragou and colleagues (Papafragou and Musolino 2003; Papafragou and Tantalou 2004) aimed to show that children as young as five are generally able to pragmatically enrich if the circumstances are right. Actually, Papafragou and Musolino (2003, Experiment 1) first confirmed the developmental effect summarized above by showing that five-year-olds are less likely than adults to produce enrichments with 'some', 'start', and 'three', in cases where a stronger term was called for (namely, 'all', 'finished', and a 'larger number', respectively). They then modified the experimental set-up in two ways in order to prepare their second experiment. First, before they were tested, participants received training aimed at enhancing their awareness to pragmatic anomalies. Specifically, children were told that the puppet would say 'silly things' and that the point of the game was to help the puppet say it better (e.g. they would be asked whether a puppet described a dog appropriately by saying 'this is a little animal with four legs'). In the event that the child did not correct the puppet, the experimenter did. Second, the paradigm put the focal point on a protagonist's performance. Unlike in their Experiment 1, where participants were asked to evaluate a quantified statement like 'Some horses jumped over the fence' (when in fact all the horses did), the paradigm in Experiment 2 raises the expectation that the stronger statement (with 'all') might be true. Participants would hear a test statement like, 'Mickey put some of the hoops around the pole' (after having been shown to succeed with all of the hoops), and they were also told how Mickey claims to be especially good at this game and that this is why another character challenges him to get all three around the pole. With these changes, five-year-olds were more likely to produce enrichments than they were in the first experiment. Nevertheless, the five-year-olds, even in the second experiment, still produced enrichments less often than did adults. This indicates that – even with training and with a focus on a stronger contrast – pragmatic enrichments require effortful processing among children.[3]

Guasti et al (2005) argue that pragmatic enrichments ought to be as common among five-year-olds as they are among adults and further investigated the findings of Noveck (2001) and Papafragou and Musolino (2003). In their first experiment, they replicated the finding of Noveck (2001, Experiment 3) concerning 'some' with seven-year-olds and used this as a baseline to study independently the role of the two factors manipulated by Papafragou and Musolino (2003). One factor was the role of training and how it affects children's proficiency at computing implicatures (Experiments 2 and 3) and the other was the role of placing emphasis on the outcome of a scalar implicature (Experiment 4). Their Experiments 1 through 3 showed that training young participants to give the most specific description of a given situation can indeed have a major effect on performance. While their initial experiment showed that seven-year-olds accept statements such as 'Some giraffes have long necks' 88 per cent of the time (against 50 per cent for adults), when trained in this manner their acceptance rate drops to 52 per cent, becoming adult-like. Nonetheless, this effect is short lasting, i.e. it does not persist when the same participants are tested a week later (Experiment 3). In the last experiment, the authors rendered the *all* alternative more salient in context. This was achieved, for instance, by presenting participants with a story where several characters have to decide whether the best way to go collect a treasure was to drive a motorbike or ride a horse. After some discussion, all of them choose to ride a horse. In this way it is made clearer that the statement subjects have to judge, 'some of the characters chose to ride horse', is underinformative. The results indicated that children are more likely to infer an enriched interpretation in an adult-like manner when the context makes this enrichment highly relevant.

This last finding shows that one can create situations that encourage children to pragmatically enrich weak-sounding statements and to do so in an adult-like manner. It does not alter the fact that in less elaborate scenarios where cues to enrichment are less abundant, seven-year-olds do not behave in this manner and it does not tell us what younger children do. Overall, the developmental effect shows that pragmatic enrichments are somewhat effortful. In experimental settings, the required effort can be somewhat lowered or the motivation to perform it may be heightened, but in the absence of such contextual encouragements, younger children faced with a weak scalar term are more likely to stick with its linguistically encoded meaning.

If children had been found to perform scalar inferences by default, this would have been strong evidence in favour of the GCI theory approach. However, taken together, developmental data suggest that, for children, enriched interpretations of scalar terms are not default interpretations. This sort of data is not knock down evidence against GCI theory, because it is compatible with two hypotheses: (1) scalar inferences are not default interpretations for adults either (even if adults are more likely to derive them because they can do so with relatively less effort and because they are more inclined to invest effort in the interpretation of an utterance given their greater ability to derive from it cognitive effects); or (2) in the course of development, children become capable and disposed to perform scalar inferences by default. The first hypothesis is consistent with the relevance theory approach while the second is consistent with the GCI approach. To find out which approach has more support, further work had to be done with adults.

6. time course of comprehension among adults

As we mentioned before, GCI theory implies that a literal interpretation of a scalar, resulting from the cancellation of default enrichment, should take longer than an enriched interpretation, whereas relevance theory, denying that enrichment takes place by default, implies that an enriched interpretation, being computed when needed to meet contextual expectations of relevance, should take longer than a literal one. What is needed to test these contrasting predictions are experiments manipulating and measuring the time course of the interpretation of statements with weak scalar terms.

As in the developmental tasks, one wants to make sure that enriched interpretations are clearly identifiable through specific responses, that the tasks used include a variety of controls, and that the effect is reliable and robust. One way to identify enriched vs literal interpretations is provided by earlier studies where participants were asked to judge true or false statements (such as 'some elephants are mammals') that could either be construed as literally true but underinformative, or in an enriched manner (as implying ...*not all*...) and false. Hence participants' truth-value judgements reflect their literal or enriched interpretation.

As we indicated, prior work is often critical to developing the appropriate measures. In fact, Rips (1975) unintentionally included the right sort of cases when looking at other issues of categorization and with materials such as 'some congressmen are politicians'. He examined the effect of the interpretation of the quantifier by running two studies, one in which participants were asked to treat 'some' as meaning *some and possibly all* and another where they were asked to treat 'some' as meaning *some but not all*. This comparison demonstrated that participants given the *some but not all* instructions in one experiment responded more slowly than those given the *some and possibly all* instructions in another. Despite these indications, Rips modestly hedged when he concluded that 'of the two meanings of *Some*, the informal meaning *may* be the more difficult to compute' (emphasis added). To make sure that Rips' data were indeed indicative of a slowdown related to *Some but not all* readings, Bott and Noveck (2004) ran a series of four experiments that followed up on Rips (1975) and essentially verified that enriched interpretations take longer than literal ones.

Bott and Noveck's categorization task involved the use of underinformative items (e.g. 'Some cows are mammals') and five controls that varied the quantifier (*Some* and *All*), the category-subcategory order, as well as proper membership. The six types of statements are illustrated with the six possible ways one can employ the subcategory *elephants* below, but it should be pointed out that the paradigm was set up so that the computer randomly paired a given subcategory with a given category while verifying that, for each experimental session, there were nine instances of each type:

(19) a.   Some elephants are mammals (Underinformative).
      b.   Some mammals are elephants.
      c.   Some elephants are insects.
      d.   All elephants are mammals.
      e.   All mammals are elephants.
      f.   All elephants are insects.

In the first experiment, a sample of 22 participants was presented with the same task twice, once with instructions to treat 'some' as meaning *Some and possibly all* and once with instructions to treat 'some' as meaning *Some but not all* (and, of course, the order of presentation was varied). When participants were under instruction, in effect, to engage the scalar inference, they were shown to be less accurate and take significantly longer to respond to the underinformative items (like those in (19a)). Specifically, when instructions called for a *Some but not all* interpretation, rates of correct responses to the underinformative item (i.e. judging the statement 'false') were roughly 60 per cent; when instructions called for a *Some and possibly all* interpretation, rates of correct responses to the underinformative item (i.e. judging the statement 'true') were roughly 90 per cent. For the control items, rates of correct responses were always above 80 per cent and sometimes above 90 per cent. One can see that the underinformative case in the *Some but not all* condition provides exceptional data.

The reaction time data showed that the correct responses to the underinformative item in the *Some but not all* condition were exceptionally slow. It took roughly 1.4 seconds to correctly evaluate the underinformative statements in the *Some but not all* condition and around 0.8 seconds in the *Some and possibly all* conditions. To answer the control items – across both sorts of instructions – took at most 1.1 seconds but more often around 0.8 to 0.9 seconds. Thus, the underinformative statement in the *Some but not all* condition is the one most affected by the instructions. All this confirms Rips' initial findings. More importantly, there is not a single indication that interpreting 'some' to mean *Some but not all* is an effortless or quasi effortless step. Again, a default view of scalar inference would predict that under *Some but not all* instructions, responses to underinformative statements would require less time than responses under *Some and possibly all* instructions. According to an account based on relevance theory, one should find the opposite. The data more readily support the relevance-theoretic account.

A potential criticism of this experiment is that the lower accuracy and the slowdown might be due to a response bias in favour of positive rather than negative response, given that the correct response to the underinformative statement with the *Some and possibly all* instructions is to say 'True' while the correct response to the underinformative statement with the *Some but not all* instructions is to say 'False'. To allay concerns regarding such a potential response bias, Bott and Noveck demonstrated experimentally that the effects linked to pragmatic effort are not simply due to hitting the 'False' key.

In a second experiment, the paradigm was modified so that the same overt response could be compared across both sorts of instructions; this way, participants' response choice (True vs False) could not explain the observed effects. In order to arrive at this comparison, participants were not asked to agree or disagree with first-order statements such as those in (19), but with second-order statements made about these first-order statements. For example, participants were presented with the two statements: 'Mary says the following sentence is false' / 'Some elephants are mammals'. They were then asked to agree or disagree with Mary's second-order statement. In such a case, participants instructed to treat 'some' as meaning *Some but not all* should agree, whereas participants instructed to treat 'some' as meaning *Some and possibly all* should disagree, reversing the pattern of positive and negative response of the previous experiment.

The results from this second experiment were nevertheless remarkably similar to those of the first one. Here, when participants were under instruction to, in effect, draw the scalar inference, they were less accurate and took significantly longer to respond correctly to the underinformative item. When 'agree' was linked with instructions for a *Some but not all* interpretation, rates of correct responses were roughly 70 per cent; when 'agree' was linked with instructions for a *Some and possibly all* interpretation, rates of correct responses were roughly 90 per cent. For all control items, rates of correct responses were always above 85 per cent and often above 90 per cent. One can see that, once again, the underinformative case in the *Some but not all* condition provides exceptional data. The reaction time data also showed that the correct 'agree' responses to the underinformative item in the *Some but not all* condition were exceptionally slow. It took nearly 6 seconds to evaluate the underinformative statements correctly when 'agree' was linked with instructions for a *Some but not all* interpretation and around 4 seconds when 'agree' was linked with instructions in the *Some and possibly all* condition (all reaction times were longer than in the previous experiment due to the *Mary says* statement). The control items across both sorts of instructions took on average around 4.5 seconds and never more than 5 seconds. Again, the experiment demonstrated that any response that requires a pragmatic enrichment implies extra effort.

Both of these experiments, though inspired by previous work, are arguably unnatural. It is unusual to instruct participants in a conversation, as was done in Experiment 1, as to how they should interpret the word 'some'; the second experiment doubles the complexity by compelling participants to make metalinguistic judgements from statements like *Mary says the following is false.* Bott and Noveck's third experiment simplified matters by asking participants to make true/false judgements about the categorical statements themselves and without prior instruction. With this sort of presentation, there is no useful sense in which a response is 'correct' or not. Rather, responses reveal the participant's literal or enriched interpretation and can be compared in terms of reaction time.

Roughly 40 per cent of participants responded 'true' to underinformative items and 60 per cent 'false'. This corresponds to the rates found among adults in Noveck's developmental studies (also see Noveck and Posada 2003; Guasti et al 2005). The main finding was that mean reaction times were longer when participants responded 'false' to the underinformative statements than when they responded 'true' (3.3 seconds versus 2.7, respectively). Furthermore, 'false' responses to the underinformative statements appear to be slower than responses to all of the control statements (including three, (18c), (18e), and (18f), that require a 'false' response). The 'true' response was made at a speed that was comparable to all of the control items.

In their last experiment, Bott and Noveck varied the time available to participants to respond to the statements. The rationale for this design was that, if as implied by GCI theory, literal interpretations of weak scalar terms take longer than the default enriched interpretations, then limiting the time available should decrease the rate of literal interpretations and increase the rate of enriched ones. On the other hand, if as implied by relevance theory, enriched interpretations take longer, then limiting the time should have the opposite effect (i.e. shorter lags should be associated with higher rates of literal interpretations). While following the same general procedure as the prior experiments (asking participants to judge the veracity of categorical statements), the paradigm manipulated the time available for the response. In one condition, participants had a relatively short time to respond (0.9 seconds), while in the other they had a relatively long time to respond (3 seconds). Only the time to *respond* was manipulated. To control for uptake, participants were presented with the text one word at a time and at the same rate in both conditions, thus there is no possibility that participants in the Short-lag condition spend less time reading the statements than those in the Long-lag condition.

Bott and Noveck reported that when a shorter period of time was available for participants to respond, they were more likely to respond 'True' to underinformative statements (indicating a literal interpretation). 72 per cent of participants responded true in the 'Short-lag' condition and 56 per cent did so in the 'Long-lag' condition. This strongly implies that they were less likely to derive the scalar inference when they were under time pressure than when they were relatively pressure-free. As in all the prior experiments, control statements provide a context in which to appreciate the differences found among underinformative statements. These showed that performance among control statements in the Short-lag condition was quite good overall (rates of correct responses ranged from 75 to 88 per cent) and that, as one would expect, rates of correct performance among the control items *increased* with added time (by 5 per cent on average). The contrast between a percentage that drops with extra time (as is the case for the underinformative statements) and percentages that increase provide a unique sort of interaction confirming that time is necessary to provoke scalar inferences.

The experiments we have described so far take into account the four methodological considerations we discussed earlier and allow well-controlled dependent variables: the rate or the speed of literal vs enriched interpretations of weak scalar terms. Together, they provide strong evidence that an enriched interpretation of a weak scalar term requires more processing time than an unenriched, literal interpretation, as predicted by relevance theory and contrary to the prediction implied by GCI theory.

Still, one might argue that the categorization tasks used, even if methodologically sound from an experimental psychology point of view, are too artificial to test pragmatic hypotheses. If the argument were that laboratory tasks are somehow irrelevant to pragmatics, we would argue that the onus of the proof is on the critics: after all, participants bring to bear on experimental verbal tasks their ordinary pragmatic abilities, just as they do in any uncommon form of verbal exchange. In particular, if it is part of adult pragmatic competence to make scalar inferences by default, it would take some arguing to make it plausible that an experimental setting somehow inhibits this basic disposition. On the other hand, if the argument is that fairly artificial laboratory experiments are not enough and that they should be complemented with more ecologically valid designs, we agree. Happily, Breheny, Katsos and Williams (2006) have provided just this kind of welcome complement.

Following up on a procedure from Bezuidenhout and Cutting (2002), Breheny et al presented disjunctive phrases (such as 'the class notes or the summary') in two kinds of contexts: Lower-bound contexts (where the literal reading of a scalar term is more appropriate as in (20) below), and Upper-bound contexts (where the enriched reading of the scalar is more appropriate as in (21) below). These were presented as part of short vignettes (along with many 'filler' items to conceal the purpose of the study) and participants' reading times were measured. More specifically, participants were asked to read on a computer screen short texts that were presented one fragment at a time, and to advance in their reading by hitting the space bar (the slashes in (20) and (21) delimit fragments).

(20)   *Lower-bound context*
       John heard that / the textbook for Geophysics / was very advanced. / Nobody understood it properly./ He heard that / if he wanted to pass the course / he should read / *the class notes or the summary.*

(21)   *Upper-bound context*
       John was taking a university course / and working at the same time. / For the exams / he had to study / from short and comprehensive sources. / Depending on the course, / he decided to read / *the class notes or the summary.*

If, in such a task, one found shorter reading times in the Upper-bound contexts that call for scalar inferences than in the Lower-bound contexts where the literal interpretation is more appropriate, this would support the GCI claim that scalar inferences are made by default. Findings in the opposite direction would support the relevance theory account. What Breheny et al found is that phrases like the *class notes* or *the summary* took significantly longer to process in Upper-bound contexts than in Lower-bound contexts, a result consistent with findings reported above.

7. conclusions

The experimental work we have summarized here verifies predictions derived from relevance theory, and falsifies predictions derived from GCI theory. Does this mean that relevance theory is true and GCI theory is false? Of course not. Nevertheless, these results should present a serious problem for GCI theorists. It is quite possible however that they will find a creative solution to the problem. They might for instance show that, in spite of the methodological precautions we have outlined, the studies reported failed to eliminate some uncontrolled factor, and that better studies provide evidence pointing in the opposite direction. They might, more plausibly, revise their theory so as to accommodate these results. One line of revision would be to reconsider the idea that GCIs are default inferences (or to water down the notion of default to the point where it does not anymore have implications for processing time). After all, not all neo-Griceans agree with Levinson's account of GCI (see in particular Horn 2004, 2006). Still, it is worth noting that, if scalar inferences are not truly default inferences and involve each and every time paying attention to what the speaker chose not to say, then we are back to the worry that such inferences are excessively cumbersome. Generally speaking, experimental findings such as those we have summarized here should encourage neo-Griceans to work out precise and plausible implications of their approach at the level of cognitive processing.

Relevance theorists are not challenged in the same way by the work we have described – after all, their prediction is confirmed – but they should be aware that this prediction could be made from quite different theoretical points of view: it follows from relevance theory, but relevance theory does not follow from it. They might then try to develop aspects of these experiments that could give positive support to more specific aspects of the theory. For instance, according to the theory, hearers aim at an interpretation that satisfies their expectations of relevance and the relevance of an interpretation varies inversely with the effort needed to derive it. It should then be possible to cause participants to choose a more or a less parsimonious interpretation by increasing or decreasing the cognitive resources available to participants for the process of interpretation. The fourth experiment of Bott and Noveck (2004) can be seen as a first suggestive step in this direction.[4]

As we have just explained, we do not expect readers to form a final judgement on the respective merits of GCI theory and relevance theory on the basis of the experimental evidence presented. What we do hope is to have convinced you that, alongside other kinds of data, properly devised experimental evidence can be highly pertinent to the discussion of pragmatic issues, and that pragmatists – and in particular students of pragmatics – might greatly benefit from becoming familiar with relevant experimental work and from contributing to it (possibly in interdisciplinary ventures).

notes

1. From now on, for ease of exposition, we will use the term 'scalar' without quotes to refer to the phenomena so described in the neo-Gricean approach. This use, of course, implies no theoretical commitment on our part.
2. The contents of parentheses were not said, but indicated.
3. Papafragou and Tantalou (2004) aim to show that five-year-olds can be encouraged to produce scalar inferences and at adult levels. However, we do not discuss their results here because their data are based on a non-standard paradigm in which participants are given no justifiable reason to accept the 'minimal' interpretation of a term such as 'some'. In other words, the paradigm does not provide participants with two clear options. Moreover, much of the study's claims are based on children's self-reports and even these lead to the

conclusion that at most 56 per cent of Papafragou and Tantalou's participants derived scalar inferences.
4. For other experimental explorations based on relevance theory, see Van der Henst and Sperber (2004).

references

Bezuidenhout, A. and J.C. Cutting (2002). 'Literal meaning, minimal propositions, and pragmatic processing'. *Journal of Pragmatics* 34: 433–56.

Bott, L. and I.A. Noveck (2004). 'Some utterances are underinformative: The onset and time course of scalar inferences'. *Journal of Memory and Language* 51: 437–57.

Braine, M. and B. Rumain (1981). 'Children's comprehension of "or": Evidence for a sequence of competencies'. *Journal of Experimental Child Psychology* 31: 46–70.

Breheny, R., N. Katsos and J. Williams (2006). 'Are generalized scalar implicatures generated by default? An on-line investigation into the role of context in generating pragmatic inferences'. *Cognition* 100.3: 434–63.

Chierchia, G., T. Guasti, A. Gualmini, L. Meroni, S. Crain and F. Foppolo (2004). 'Adults and children's semantic and pragmatic competence in interaction'. In I.A. Noveck and D. Sperber (eds). *Experimental Pragmatics*. Basingstoke: Palgrave Macmillan.

Feeney, A., S. Scrafton, A. Duckworth and S.J. Handley (2004). 'The Story of *Some*: Everyday Pragmatic Inference by Children and Adults'. *Canadian Journal of Experimental Psychology* 58.2: 121–32.

Guasti, M.T., G. Chierchia, S. Crain, F. Foppolo, A. Gualmini and L. Meroni (2005). 'Why children and adults sometimes (but not always) compute implicatures'. *Language and Cognitive Processes* 20.5: 667–96.

Horn, L.R. (1972). 'On the Semantic Properties of Logical Operators in English'. PhD dissertation, UCLA.

— (2004). 'Implicature'. In G. Ward and L. Horn (eds). *Handbook of Pragmatics*. Oxford: Blackwell. 3–28.

— (2006). 'The Border Wars: A neo-Gricean perspective'. In K. von Heusinger and K. Turner (eds). *Where Semantics meets Pragmatics*. Oxford: Elsevier.

Levinson, S. (2000). *Presumptive Meanings: The Theory of Generalized Conversational Implications*. Cambridge, Mass.: MIT Press.

Noveck, I.A. (2001). 'When children are more logical than adults: Experimental investigations of scalar implicature'. *Cognition* 78.2: 165–88.

Noveck, I.A. and A. Posada (2003). 'Characterizing the time course of an implicature: An evoked potentials study'. *Brain and Language* 85: 203–10.

Noveck, I.A. and D. Sperber (2004). *Experimental Pragmatics*. Basingstoke: Palgrave Macmillan.

Papafragou, A. and J. Musolino (2003). 'Scalar implicatures: Experiments at the semantics-pragmatics interface'. *Cognition* 86.3: 253–82.

Papafragou, A. and N. Tantalou (2004). 'Children's computation of implicatures'. *Language Acquisition* 12.1: 71–82.

Paris, S.G. (1973). 'Comprehension of language connectives and propositional logical relationships'. *Journal of Experimental Child Psychology* 16.2: 278–91.

Rips, L.J. (1975). 'Quantification and semantic memory'. *Cognitive Psychology* 7.3: 307–40.

Smith, C.L. (1980). 'Quantifiers and question answering in young children'. *Journal of Experimental Child Psychology* 30.2: 191–205.

Sperber, D. and D. Wilson (1995). *Relevance: Communication and Cognition.* Oxford: Blackwell.

Sternberg, R.J. (1979). 'Developmental patterns in the encoding and combination of logical connectives'. *Journal of Experimental Child Psychology* 28.3: 469–98.

Van der Henst, J.B. and D. Sperber (2004). 'Some experimentally testable implications of relevance theory'. In I.A. Noveck and D. Sperber (eds). *Experimental Pragmatics.* Basingstoke: Palgrave Macmillan.

Wilson, D. and D. Sperber (2004). 'Relevance Theory'. In G. Ward and L. Horn (eds). *Handbook of Pragmatics.* Oxford: Blackwell.

11

indexicality, context and pretence: a speech-act theoretic account

françois recanati

Indexicals – words like 'I', 'here', 'now', etc. – are expressions whose semantic value systematically depends upon the context of the speech act: 'I' refers to the agent of the speech act (the speaker), 'here' to the place of the speech act, etc. There is, however, something misleading in the definite description '*the* speech act', which implies unicity. We know, since Austin, that a number of *distinct* acts are jointly performed in speaking: the phonetic act, the phatic act, the rhetic act, the locutionary act which includes them all, and the illocutionary act one additionally performs *in* performing the locutionary act. It is true that Austin also speaks of 'the total speech act', but if that is what we mean by 'the speech act', then it is misleading to talk of '*the* context of the speech act', for there may be distinct contexts corresponding to the 'ancillary acts' one can distinguish within the total speech act.

In this chapter, I will investigate the phenomenon of *context-shift* and argue, on that basis, that the notion of 'context' that has to be used in the study of indexicals is far from univocal. A first distinction has to be made between the real context of speech and the context in which the speech act is supposed to take place – only the latter notion being relevant when it comes to determining the semantic values of indexicals. Second, we need to draw a distinction between the context of the locutionary act and the context of the illocutionary act: contrary to a standard assumption of speech act theory, they can diverge, and their possible divergence explains a number of puzzling phenomena involving indexicals.

I. indexicality, context, and speaker's intentions

Indexicals, I said, are expressions whose semantic value systematically depends upon the context of the speech act. Before raising issues regarding what counts as the context, we must enrich this preliminary characterization of indexicals and make it more specific. Indexicals are expressions whose semantic value systematically depends upon the context *and whose linguistic meaning somehow encodes this dependency upon the context of speech.* Thus one should not count as *indexical in the strict sense* expressions whose semantic value depends upon the context merely because they are semantically under-specified and function as 'free variables' to which a value must be contextually assigned. A good example of under-specification is the genitive construction, as in 'John's car': this phrase refers to a car bearing a certain relation R to John, which relation is determined in context, without being linguistically specified. (It may be the car John bought, or the car he dreamt of last night, or anything.) This is not indexicality strictly speaking. Whenever an expression is indexical in the strict sense, its linguistic meaning encodes a *token-reflexive rule* which tells us how, for each particular token of the expression, we can determine the content carried by that token as a function of the circumstances of utterance. Thus the meaning of 'I' is the rule that a token of that word refers to the producer of that token, the meaning of 'today' is the rule that a token of that word refers to the day on which the token is produced, the meaning of 'we' is a rule that a token of that word refers to a group that contains the speaker, and so on.

Whether a context-sensitive expression is indexical in the strict sense or merely semantically under-specified, its content depends upon some feature of the context of utterance. Semantically under-specified expressions are such that their content uniformly depends upon *the speaker's intention* (or at least, the intention which it is reasonable, in context, to ascribe to the speaker). Thus when I use a genitive as in 'John's car', the relation R between John and the car is determined in context as a function of the speaker's intentions. In contrast, indexical expressions are such that *their content in each case depends upon a designated feature of the context of utterance.* That feature which, following Nunberg, I call the 'index', is specified by the token-reflexive rule associated with the indexical. For the first person pronouns 'I' and 'we' the index is the person producing the utterance. For 'you' it is the addressee. For the tenses and temporal adverbs like 'today', 'tomorrow', etc. it is the time of utterance. In each case, the reference of the indexical is determined as a function of the contextual index.

Note that its being indexical in the strict sense does not prevent an expression from *also* being semantically under-specified. 'We' is a case in point. As we have seen, the semantic value of 'we' is a group containing *the speaker* among its members. Here the speaker is the index (so 'we' has the same index as 'I') but we also need the speaker's intentions to fix the relevant group which is not fully determined, but merely constrained, by the linguistic meaning of 'we'. In this type of case, the contextual value of the expression depends both upon the designated index *and* the speaker's intentions. In contrast, the meaning of 'I' or 'tomorrow' fully determines the content of the word as a function of the index: once the index is contextually identified, the referent is *eo ipso* identified.

Another tricky case is that of demonstratives like 'this' or 'this car'. If we treat them as indexical expressions, as one typically does, what will be the contextual index? The index for demonstratives is standardly taken to be the *demonstratum*, i.e. the entity to which the speaker using the demonstrative draws the hearer's attention by means of a pointing gesture or by any other means.[1] Now there is an ongoing debate regarding the determination of the *demonstratum* itself: is it determined by the speaker's intentions, or is it determined by objective factors such as which entity of the relevant sort first intersects the straight line emanating from the speaker's pointing finger? I side with the 'intentionists' in this debate: I take the index to be what *the speaker* demonstrates, i.e. the entity such that the speaker makes manifest to the hearer his or her intention to bring it to the hearer's attention by means of the hearer's recognition of this intention (where 'this' reflexively refers to the whole, complex intention, as in standard Gricean analyses). On this view, even though a demonstrative is taken to be an indexical (in the strict sense), still the speaker's demonstrative intention *is* the crucial aspect of the context on which the reference of a demonstrative depends. An indexical is an expression whose semantic value is a function of some contextual index, but in this case the contextual index itself is determined by the speaker's intentions.

2. circumstance-shift vs context-shift

According to David Lewis, it is often the case that 'the truth of a sentence in a context depends upon the truth of some related sentence when some feature of the original context is shifted' (Lewis 1998, 27). This happens, according to Lewis, whenever we can isolate a sentential operator O such that the truth of any complex sentence consisting of that operator O applied to some sentence p is systematically related to the truth of p when some feature of the original context (the context of the complex sentence) has been shifted. The contextual features which may be shifted in this sense are few in number, Lewis says: he mentions the time, the place, and the world of the context, plus the standards of precision in force in the context. The first three features can be shifted because temporal, spatial and modal operators are such that the truth of any complex sentence Op consisting of one such operator O applied to some sentence p is systematically related to the truth of p when the time, place or world of the original context (the context in which Op is uttered) has been shifted. Thus 'There have been dogs' is true now if 'there are dogs' is true at some time before now; 'somewhere the sun is shining' is true here if 'the sun is shining' is true somewhere; and so on.

Before considering the standards of precision, which Lewis takes to be the fourth (and ultimate) shiftable feature of the context in what he admits is a 'short list', let me say why I think it would be misleading to talk of *context-shift* in connection with the phenomenon discussed by Lewis. Lewis describes a feature-shifting process that takes place in the course of evaluating the complex sentence Op: starting from the initial situation s in which the complex sentence itself is being evaluated, we shift some feature of s and evaluate the embedded sentence p with respect to the distinct situation s' resulting from the shift induced by O. I have two reasons for denying that the shift here is a *context* shift. First, I am not certain that the initial situation s – that in which the complex sentence Op itself is evaluated – has to or can be equated with the 'context' of Op; so I am not certain that the situation that serves as input to the shift qualifies as context. Second, and more importantly, I am certain that the output situation s' – that which results from the shift – does not, or not necessarily, qualify as context. So I agree that a shift takes place in the course of evaluating the complex sentence Op, but I take the shift in question to affect what Kaplan (1989) calls the circumstance of evaluation (and what Lewis himself calls the 'index') rather than the context of utterance.

Let me start with my doubts regarding the input situation. For a situation to count as a context, an utterance must take place in that situation. That means that there must be an agent a and a language L such that a utters an expression e of L, thereby performing, or attempting to perform, what Austin calls a 'locutionary act'; an act which requires on the part of the agent certain beliefs and intentions.[2] I grant that a context, in that sense, always includes a time, a place and a world feature (simply because any utterance is bound to take place somewhere, at a particular time, and in a particular world). I also grant that a temporal, spatial or modal operator O shifts the time, place or world of the initial situation s in which the complex sentence Op is being evaluated, and thereby determines the (distinct) situation s' in which the sentence p it operates on has to be evaluated in the course of evaluating Op. What I deny is that the initial situation *s* in which the complex sentence is evaluated has to be identified with *the context in which that complex sentence is uttered and interpreted*. Or, to put it another way: I deny that the time, place and world with respect to which the complex sentence is evaluated – the time, place and world which the operator systematically shifts – is the time, place and world of the context of utterance. It need not be: there is a principled difference between, say, the place of the context of utterance, and the place with respect to which the uttered sentence is evaluated. Take 'it's raining'. To evaluate that sentence we need a place; but that need not be the place of the context (i.e. the place where 'it's raining' is uttered). It may be any place which the speaker is currently considering and talking about. Similarly, the time and world with respect to which we evaluate a sentence need not be the time and world of the context in which that sentence is uttered. This is undoubtedly the most common and the simplest case, but this is only a particular case nevertheless. The place, time and world with respect to which we evaluate a sentence are features of *the situation talked about in uttering that sentence*; and the situation talked about need not be identical to the situation of utterance.

The situation *resulting from* the shift is not a context either; or at least, it need not be one (nor does Lewis claim that it does). It need not contain a speaker, an utterance, nor a language. Of course, it *may* possess such features: nothing prevents the sentence *p* in the scope of the circumstance-shifting operator from describing a situation in which someone says something. Thus in the sentence 'Someday, someone will stand up and say something' the operator 'someday it will be the case that' takes us to a shifted situation *s'* that is located in the future, and which (if the sentence is true) happens to be a situation of utterance: a situation in which someone says something. Even in that sort of case, however, the output situation cannot serve to fix the value of the indexicals that occur in the sentence *p* which is to be evaluated with respect to that situation. The values of the indexicals that occur in the embedded sentence *p* are fixed by the context in which the complex sentence O*p* is uttered. Thus if the complex sentence is 'Someday, someone will stand up and say something about the clothes I am wearing today', the values of the indexicals 'I' and 'today' (as well as that of the present progressive) will not be determined by the features of the future situation in which someone stands up and says something. 'I' will not refer to the person who speaks in that situation, and 'today' will not refer to the day of that situation; nor will the present progressive refer to the time of that situation (even though the time of the original situation has been shifted). Rather, 'I' will refer to the speaker in the original context of utterance (that in which the complex sentence is uttered), and 'today' and the present tense will have their values determined as a function of the time of that same context.

The only case in which it seems that something like a context-shift occurs is the last one mentioned by Lewis: the 'standards of precision'. Let's assume that we start with a context in which certain standards of precision are in force – say, loose standards, as, for example, in 'France is hexagonal'. In such a context 'hexagonal' has a certain content, in virtue of which it truly applies to France. This is distinct from the content the same word has in a context in which stricter standards of precision are in force (as is shown by the fact that, under those stricter standards, 'hexagonal' does *not* apply to France). We may construe the standards of precision as an aspect of the *language* spoken in the context: in the first context the language spoken is loose, in the second context it is strict. Now, as Lewis points out, an expression like 'strictly speaking' works by turning a context in which a loose language is spoken into a context in which a strict language is spoken. As a result, '"Strictly speaking, France is not hexagonal" is true even under low standards of precision if "France is not hexagonal" is true under stricter standards' (Lewis 1998, 27). We start with a context in which a loose language is spoken, and wind up in a context in which a strict language is spoken. The words that are uttered after 'strictly speaking' are interpreted according to the rules of the strict language, in force in the shifted context. This is analogous to what happens in the following example:

(1) As the French say, *on n'est pas sortis de l'auberge.*

Here we start with a context in which English is spoken, but, after the phrase 'as the French say', the language feature of the context shifts from English to French.

Lewis says the context-shift effected by 'strictly speaking' is a matter of rules: the operator 'strictly speaking' has a certain context-shift potential determined by the semantic rules of the language. This is similar, he says, to what happens with temporal or modal operators, which shift the circumstance of evaluation according to rules. I disagree. As against Lewis, I favour a pragmatic (rather than semantic) account of the shift in this type of case.

The pragmatic account I have in mind relies on a distinction I have already alluded to between two sorts of contextual feature. Some features of the context essentially depend upon the speaker's intentions. Thus whom the speaker is addressing, or to what he is referring when he uses a demonstrative, or how his words are to be taken (strictly or loosely, say), all this to a large extent depends upon the speaker's intentions. When an aspect of the context depends upon the speaker's intention in this way, it is possible to shift that feature of the context by making one's intention to do so sufficiently explicit. This, I claim, is what happens with 'strictly speaking'. By using that expression one indicates one's intention to speak strictly in the bit of discourse that follows. Expressing that intention is enough to actually determine how one's words ought to be taken, for the following reason: how the speaker's words are to be taken is an aspect of what the speaker means, and speaker's meaning works by getting itself to be recognized, i.e. by letting the hearer know what the speaker's communicative intentions are. The speaker's communicative intentions have the distinctive property that their recognition leads to, or possibly constitutes, their fulfilment, as many authors in the Gricean tradition have suggested. So, to make John my addressee, I have simply to make clear that it is him I intend to address. Thus I may say, 'You, John...', or I may look at him while speaking, or use whatever means are available for making my intention sufficiently manifest. In this way I may easily shift the addressee feature of the context. (Imagine I start by addressing a crowd. At some point in my discourse I may shift the addressee feature of the context by making sufficiently explicit that, from now on, I am addressing John.) This is similar to the shift in standards of precision described by Lewis, and in both cases what makes it possible to shift the context is not a semantic rule assigning a specific context-shift potential to some expression, but simply the fact that one is making one's intention manifest, in an area where the speaker's intentions are the crucial factor.

When an aspect of the context does *not* depend upon the speaker's intention, but is fixed by some objective fact, one simply cannot shift that feature of the context by making explicit one's intention to do so. Who the speaker is or when the utterance takes place is an objective fact independent of the speaker's intentions. Such features of the context of utterance cannot be shifted at will. Thus the word 'I', in the mouth of S, will of necessity refer to S, who happens to be the speaker, even if the speaker intends to refer to Napoleon, and makes manifest his intention to do so (Barwise and Perry 1983, 148). This is different from a demonstrative like 'that country' whose reference depends upon what the speaker intends to refer to. Here the relevant aspect of context – the speaker's reference – is up to the speaker and can be fixed by him at will ('that country, I mean France...'). The speaker can *stipulate* what his words 'that country' refer to; but the speaker cannot stipulate that *x* is the speaker, or that *t* is the time of utterance. This is simply not in his power.

3. shifting the context through pretence

I have just said that only features of the context which are 'up to the speaker' can be shifted by expressing one's intention to do so. The other features of the context are given as a matter of objective fact and cannot be shifted. Thus the speaker has no way, in speaking, to shift the reference of 'I', or of 'today'.

This conclusion must be qualified, however. The objective features of the context of utterance are indeed 'given' and, to that extent, they cannot be shifted. But what the speaker can do is *pretend that the context is different from what it is*. If the pretence is mutually manifest, it will be part of what the speaker means that the sentence is uttered in a context different from the actual context c. In such a situation a context-shift does occur: there are two contexts, the actual context c in which the sentence is produced, and the pretend context c' in which the utterance presents itself as being produced.

Such a dual context situation, based on pretence, is very common in the literary realm. Thus a novelist can write:

> It's been three years since we left the Earth. A couple of weeks after the Last Day, we lost track of the other spaceships. I still don't know what happened to my twin brother Henry. If he is alive, he probably thinks I died in the collision.

Let's imagine that this is the first paragraph of a novel. What is the context for those sentences? Clearly, two sorts of 'context' are relevant here. First, there is the actual context of utterance: the novelist writes those sentences at the beginning of her novel. But that is not the 'context' in the ordinary sense, that is, what determines the reference of indexicals. The word 'I', in the third sentence, does not denote the person who, in the actual context, issues the sentence (the novelist); rather, it purports to denote a character *in* the novel: the narrator, distinguished from the actual author. In a perfectly good sense, then, the context for those sentences is not the actual context, but an imaginary context. In that imaginary context, the speaker is on board a spaceship, he or she has a twin brother called 'Henry', there has been a collision, etc.[3]

As Ducrot pointed out many years ago, we need something like the author/narrator distinction to deal with a number of cases of language use in which the actual utterer is not the person whom the utterance itself presents as the speaker; and we need similar distinctions for the other features of the context (Ducrot 1980, 35–6; 1984, 193–203). A simple case of that sort involves a spokesperson reading a speech for someone else, say the president of the company. The word 'I' in the speech will refer to the president, even if the utterer is the spokesperson. Don't object that the president has written the speech, for that need not be the case. The speech may well have been written by the president's aide, and the president need not even have seen and endorsed it. What counts is only that the utterance, as part of its meaning, presents itself as issued by the president. The president is the speaker (hence the referent of 'I'), not because he is the utterer in the actual world, but because he is the utterer in all the worlds compatible with the ongoing pretence.

What must be qualified, then, is the idea that the context is 'given' when it comes to the objective, non-intentional features listed above, such as who the speaker is or when the utterance is made. It turns out that those features themselves are determined by the meaning of the utterance (or of the discourse), which meaning to a large extent depends upon the speaker's intentions. Since they depend upon the speaker's intentions (insofar as the latter are made manifest in the overt manner characteristic of Gricean communication) those features can be shifted through pretence. What the author does in her novel, any language user can do in ordinary discourse.

The most significant area in which the utterer/speaker distinction can be fruitfully applied is that of direct speech reports. According to the traditional analysis, in an utterance like

(2) ... and then John said, 'I'm fed up with all this!' And he walked away.

the sentence 'I'm fed up with all this' is not used, but mentioned. As a result, the words do not carry their normal semantic values, and in particular 'I' does not refer to the speaker (Bill, say). What is being referred to is the sentence 'I'm fed up with all this', which contains the word 'I'; but the word itself does not refer, nor does the sentence in which it occurs say anything in this context. Only the complex, embedding sentence says something: it identifies what John said and states a relation between John and the sentence 'I'm fed up with this'.

Like Ducrot (1984, 197–99), I take this view to be deeply misguided. The sentence 'I'm fed up with all this' is actually used (which is not to say that it is not 'mentioned' as well). As for the word 'I', it keeps its normal semantic function, that of referring to the speaker. But the speaker is not Bill. To be sure, it is Bill who utters 'I'm fed up with all this' in the course of reporting John's speech. But in uttering this sentence Bill is overtly *playing John's part*: he temporarily pretends that he is John at the time of the reported speech, and utters the sentence 'I'm fed up with all this' accordingly (Clark and Gerrig 1990). The pretence is constitutive of the meaning of the utterance, which presents itself as uttered by John at that time. This is enough to confer to John the status of 'speaker', and to the time of the reported speech the status of 'time of utterance'. In this framework we can maintain that, in the quoted sentence, 'I' refers to the speaker, namely John, and the present tense refers to the time of utterance. (2) therefore displays a context-shift: the complex sentence is interpreted against a context in which Bill, the utterer, is the speaker and t^* is the actual time of utterance, but the quoted material within the complex sentence is interpreted with respect to a shifted context in which John is the speaker and the time of utterance is some time t such that $t < t^*$, namely the time of the reported speech act.[4]

Another type of example possibly amenable to treatment in terms of context-shift are examples involving delayed communication, such as:

(3) I am dead, my dear children, and you are rich.

Imagine that a billionnaire recorded that message in order for it to be listened to after his death. The billionnaire arguably pretends to be speaking from the grave; it is with respect to that imaginary context that the utterance is meant to be interpreted. Or consider the following example, analyzed in Recanati (1995):

(4) I have your letter in front of me, and what you're reading is my point-by-point response.

Once again, this is a situation of delayed communication: the speaker is writing his response to the letter in front of him much before the addressee can read the response in question. Still, the two conjuncts are in the present tense, and if we take seriously the idea that the present tense refers to the time of utterance, this suggests that the utterance is meant to be interpreted with respect to an imaginary context in which the act of communication is instantaneous rather than delayed. In other words, the writer speaks as if he was talking to the addressee in a normal, face-to-face communication situation.

A third type of example for which the notion of context-shift seems appropriate involves the so-called historical present and related phenomena. The historical present is a narrative device by means of which we 'presentify' the scene we are reporting, as in this passage:

(5) I had no resource but to request to be shown into a private room: and *here I am waiting, while all sorts of doubts and fears are troubling my mind.* (C. Brontë)

By using the present tense in reporting a past scene, the speaker or writer gives the reader or hearer the impression that the scene described is presently happening before them. Arguably, that effect is achieved by shifting the context, i.e. by speaking as if the act of speech was simultaneous with the scene described (Schlenker 2004). Similarly, there are 'presentifying' uses of the spatial indexical 'here', characterized by the fact that one speaks as if the speech was occurring at the very place one is talking about. The following passage, quoted by Predelli from a guidebook (Predelli 1998, 407), is an example:

(6) If an entire neighborhood could qualify as an outdoor museum, the Mount Washington district would probably charge admission. *Here,* just northwest of downtown, are several picture-book expressions of desert culture within a few blocks.

4. two types of context and two types of pretence

The notion of context-shifting pretence itself is not univocal. Consider examples like the following:

(7) *John to Bill:* Okay, I am stupid and I don't understand the matter. Why do you ask me for advice, then?

Here, presumably, John is echoing Bill's remarks – perhaps exaggerating them – in the first part of the utterance. The sentence 'I am stupid and I don't understand the matter' is not asserted by John, not even in a concessive manner. What the sentence expresses is something that John puts in the mouth of his addressee, Bill. It is Bill who is supposed to think or say that John is stupid and does not understand the matter; and his so saying or thinking provides John with a reason for asking the question in the second part of the utterance: 'Why do you ask me for advice, then?'

In a nutshell, the first part of the utterance *displays Bill's assertion*, in an echoic manner. In saying what he says, John is playing Bill's part.

We may describe that sort of case by saying that the speaker engages in a form of pretence and assumes Bill's point of view – puts himself in Bill's shoes. But note how different this sort of pretence is from that illustrated by direct speech reports such as (2). In (7) the indexical 'I' refers to John, not to the person whose view is being expressed or assumed (Bill). Bill himself, if he were to express the view in question, would not say 'I am stupid and I don't understand the matter', but 'You are stupid and do not understand the matter'. So John does not pretend that Bill is *uttering* the sentence, in this example (as opposed to (2)). It follows that Bill is not 'the speaker', i.e. the person who is presented as uttering the sentence. John, the actual utterer, is the speaker in this example. Still a form of pretence is at work, for John, qua speaker, does not express his own point of view but that of Bill.

A similar phenomenon occurs in irony. In irony the speaker says something without actually asserting what she says or 'makes as if to say' (Grice). The point of view expressed by the utterance is not that of the speaker, but that of another (actual or potential) agent whom the speaker attempts to ridicule by displaying his view in a context in which it is likely to seem dramatically inappropriate (Sperber and Wilson 1981, 308–10). For example, just after having shown great ingenuity in solving the difficult problem at hand, John can say to Bill: 'Remember, I am stupid and I don't understand the matter'. In saying this John attempts to ridicule Bill: he expresses his view (the view Bill is supposed to have voiced at an earlier point in the conversation) at a time when it is pretty clear that that view dramatically conflicts with the facts. By showing how inept the view is, given the circumstances, the speaker often manages to convey the opposite of that view – but that is not definitive of irony: it is merely a likely consequence of the basic mechanism, involving 'pretence' (Clark and Gerrig 1984) or 'echoic mention' (Sperber and Wilson 1981).

Let us use the label 'displayed assertion' for the type of case I have illustrated: the cases in which the utterer does not pretend that someone else is uttering the sentence but where, nevertheless, a form of pretence is at work because the speaker expresses the view of someone else rather than his own. In such cases, as we have seen, the reference of 'I' does not shift: in (7), 'I' refers to John, who utters the sentence, rather than to Bill, whose view is being expressed. Tenses also take their normal, unshifted values in such cases. So imagine John is reporting his exchange with Bill, several months later. He can say:

(8) He kept disparaging my contributions. I was stupid, I did not understand the matter. He would be better off if I stopped helping... – I wasn't discouraged, and I managed to solve the problem.

In (8) we find sentences which express John's point of view ('he kept disparaging my contributions', 'I wasn't discouraged, and I managed to solve the problem') and sentences in 'free indirect speech' which express Bill's point of view ('I was stupid, I did not understand the matter', 'he would be better off if I stopped helping'). Even in the latter, however, the pronouns and the tenses take features of the actual context of utterance as indices: the referent of 'I' (the speaker) is John, the referent of 'he' is Bill, and the time of the exchange between John and Bill is presented as past, that is, as anterior to the time of utterance of (8). All this suggests that the context of utterance does not shift in this type of case.

Still, we cannot straightforwardly conclude that no context-shift takes place, for there are plenty of indexicals (e.g. the demonstratives, 'today' and 'tomorrow', 'here' and 'now') whose value is likely to shift when they occur in free indirect speech. What follows is a made up example:

(9) The butler came back with the answer. Tomorrow, Lady B. would see me with pleasure; but she was too busy now.

Let us assume (9) is uttered in a context c, with John as speaker and t^* as time of utterance. The first person pronoun 'me' in (9) refers to John, and the past tense to a time anterior to t^*, as expected. But 'tomorrow' refers to the day following the day of the reported speech act, rather than to the day following the day on which (9) is uttered. Similarly, 'now' refers to the time of the reported speech act, not to the time of utterance.

Schlenker says that what shifts in such cases is not the context of utterance but the *context of thought* (Schlenker 2004). Even though John is the speaker (the agent of the context of utterance), the thinker (the agent of the context of thought) is Bill; and a similar distinction can be made with respect to the other features of the context: the time of thought is distinct from the time of utterance, etc. In our example, however, Bill need not really think, or have thought, the thought that is in question (to the effect that John is stupid and does not understand the matter). We can imagine that Bill was insincere, and perhaps overtly so, when he said, or implied, that John was stupid and incompetent. Still John can use (8) to describe the situation. So the notion of 'context of thought' is not quite appropriate. Of course, there are many cases in which a sentence in free indirect speech pictures a *thought act* rather than a speech act. But in all cases the act on display is an act of *assertion* or *judgement* or more broadly an expression of attitude[5] (whether sincere or insincere, public or private). The act of assertion is precisely what the speaker does *not* perform when she says that *p* ironically; rather, she plays someone else's part and *mimics* an act of assertion accomplished by that person. She does so not by pretending that that person is speaking – if that were the case, 'I' would refer to that person under the pretence – but by herself endorsing the function of speaker and saying that *p*, while (i) not taking responsibility for what is being said, and (ii) implicitly ascribing that responsibility to someone else, namely the person whose act of assertion is being mimicked.

I conclude that the distinction we need is a distinction between the *locutionary context* (the context of utterance, whose agent is John), and the *illocutionary context* (the context of assertion, whose agent is Bill).[6] In the traditional framework of speech act theory, there is no room for such a distinction. An illocutionary act is taken to be performed *in* performing a locutionary act (Austin 1975), in such a way that there is a single context, and two possibilities. Either the agent of the locutionary act (the speaker) performs the illocutionary act (e.g. seriously asserts the proposition he is expressing) or he does not. If he does, the speaker is the agent of the assertion, the time of speech is the time of the assertion, and so on. So there is a single context, and two acts (the locutionary act and the illocutionary act) performed in that context. If the speaker does not perform the illocutionary act, then, again, there is a single context, but this time there is a single act performed in that context: the locutionary act.

To account for displayed assertion, a revision of the standard framework has been suggested (Ducrot 1980, 33–56; Recanati 1981/1987, 233–5). Remember that the 'context of utterance' in the sense that is relevant to the analysis of indexicals is determined by the meaning of the utterance: the utterance, in virtue of its meaning, presents itself as uttered by *x*, at time *t*, etc. The speaker (i.e. the reference of 'I', distinguished from the actual utterer) is the person the utterance presents as uttering it. We can extend this idea and say that it is also part of the meaning of the utterance that a certain illocutionary act (e.g. the act of asserting that John is stupid) is performed: but instead of saying, as traditional speech act theory does, that an utterance presents a certain illocutionary act as being performed *by this very utterance* (hence in the context of utterance), we can say that the utterance presents a certain illocutionary act as performed by *y* at time *t'* and place *l'* in possible world *w'*. That is, we drop the assumption that the context of assertion can only be the context of utterance. Normally, of course, the two contexts will coincide; but, in view of utterances like (7)–(9), one should make room for the possibility of a divergence between them. When the two contexts coincide, the speaker who performs the locutionary act will be said to have performed also the corresponding illocutionary act. Not so when the two contexts do not coincide, as in irony or free indirect speech. In such cases the illocutionary act is not actually performed, but is merely displayed, represented.

The distinction between the two contexts enables us to account for the different behaviour of the pronouns and the tenses on the one hand, and the remaining indexicals on the other hand (Schlenker 2004). The latter can have their value determined by features of the illocutionary context, while tenses and pronouns strictly depend upon the (locutionary) context of utterance.

5. conclusion

In this chapter I have distinguished between three types of cases involving a shift of context affecting the semantic values of indexicals. Certain features of the context (the 'intentional' features) can be shifted at will. What can be shifted in this way includes – inter alia – the addressee feature of the context, the language feature of the context (including the standards of precision), or the *demonstrata*. Other features of the context can be shifted through pretence. Following a number of authors, I have distinguished two types of context-shifting pretence. The first type of context-shifting pretence is illustrated by direct speech reports, delayed communication, the historical present, and the presentifying uses of 'here' which are the spatial counterpart of the historical present. The second type of context-shifting pretence is illustrated by various sorts of displayed assertion (nonquotational echoes, irony, free indirect speech).

I have argued that the distinction between two types of context-shifting pretence corresponds to the distinction between the locutionary act and the illocutionary act. If I am right, speech act theory must be amended so as to make room for a correlative distinction between the locutionary context and the illocutionary context. This distinction makes sense once we realize that the context (whether locutionary or illocutionary) is not a brute reality but, rather, an aspect of the meaning of the utterance. As Ducrot often suggested, the meaning of an utterance is *a picture of the speech act it is used to perform*. In line with the complexity involved in the Austinian notion of speech act, that picture is best construed as twofold: it is both a picture of the locutionary act and a picture of the illocutionary act, each act being presented as taking place in a context that need not be the same in both cases.

notes

1. See Nunberg (1993) for the distinction between the *demonstratum* (qua index) and the actual referent. One may also equate the index with the demonstrated *place* (in such a way that 'this car' refers to the car at the indicated place) (Lyons 1975; Recanati 2004).
2. A context, in that sense, is not an abstract object – a sequence of features – as Kaplanian 'contexts' are. It is a concrete situation with a particular individual in it endowed with complex mental states (e.g. beliefs and intentions). 'Improper' contexts in Kaplan's sense – e.g. contexts in which the agent does not exist at the time of the context – are obviously ruled out, but so are 'proper' Kaplanian contexts in which no utterance is made or no language exists or the agent is unable to think or talk.
3. This example and the paragraph about it are borrowed from Recanati (2000, 171).
4. This approach to quotation and direct speech has been pursued by a number of authors, to whom I refer the interested reader (see in particular Clark and Gerrig 1990; Clark 1996; Recanati 2001).
5. Among the 'expressions of attitude' I include expressions of affective attitudes (as in exclamations, curses, etc.)
6. I use 'illocution' in an extended sense, to cover thought acts as well as speech acts.

references

Austin, J. (1975). *How to Do Things with Words*. 2nd edn, Oxford: Clarendon Press.
Barwise, J. and J. Perry (1983). *Situations and Attitudes*. Cambridge, Mass.: MIT Press/Bradford Books.
Clark, H. (1996). *Using Language*. Cambridge: Cambridge University Press.
Clark, H. and R. Gerrig (1984). 'On the Pretence Theory of Irony'. *Journal of Experimental Psychology: General* 113: 121–26.
— (1990). 'Quotations as Demonstrations'. *Language* 66: 764–805.
Ducrot, O. (1980). 'Analyse de texte et linguistique de l'énonciation'. In O. Ducrot et al (eds). *Les Mots du Discours*. Paris: Minuit. 7–56.
— (1984). 'Esquisse d'une théorie polyphonique de l'énonciation'. In O. Ducrot (ed.). *Le Dire et le Dit*. Paris: Minuit. 171–233.
Kaplan, D. (1989). 'Demonstratives'. In J. Almog, H. Wettstein and J. Perry (eds). *Themes from Kaplan*. New York: Oxford University Press. 481–563.
Lewis, D. (1998). 'Index, Context, and Content'. In his *Papers in Philosophical Logic*. Cambridge: Cambridge University Press. 21–44.
Lyons, J. (1975). 'Deixis as the Source of Reference'. In E. Keenan (ed.). *Formal Semantics of Natural Language*. Cambridge: Cambridge University Press. 61–83.

Nunberg, G. (1993). 'Indexicality and Deixis'. *Linguistics and Philosophy* 16: 1–43.

Predelli, S. (1998). 'Utterance, Interpretation, and the Logic of Indexicals'. *Mind and Language* 13: 400–14.

Recanati, F. (1981/1987). *Meaning and Force*. Cambridge: Cambridge University Press, 1987 (Eng. trans. of *Les Enoncés performatifs*. Paris: Editions du Seuil, 1981).

— (1995). 'Le présent épistolaire: une perspective cognitive'. *L'Information grammaticale* 66: 38–44.

— (2000). *Oratio Obliqua, Oratio Recta: An Essay on Metarepresentation*. Cambridge, Mass.: MIT Press/Bradford Books.

— (2001) 'Open Quotation'. *Mind* 110: 637–87.

— (2004). 'Deixis and Anaphora'. In S. Szabo (ed.). *Semantics vs Pragmatics*. New York: Oxford University Press. 286–316.

Schlenker, P. (2004). 'Context of Thought and Context of Utterance: A Note on Free Indirect Discourse and the Historical Present'. *Mind and Language* 19: 279–304.

Sperber, D. and D. Wilson (1981). 'Irony and the Use-Mention Distinction'. In P. Cole (ed.). *Radical Pragmatics*. New York: Academic Press. 295–318.

12

a unitary approach to lexical pragmatics: relevance, inference and ad hoc concepts[1]

deirdre wilson and robyn carston

1. introduction

The relatively new field of lexical pragmatics explores the application of the semantics-pragmatics distinction at the level of individual words or phrases rather than whole sentences. The advantages of distinguishing semantic and pragmatic aspects of word meaning have long been recognized in pragmatically-oriented approaches to the philosophy of language, and were the starting point for Grice's *William James Lectures* (Grice 1967/1989, 3–21). However, the development of a separate field of lexical pragmatics was accelerated in the 1990s by a series of publications by linguists, psychologists and philosophers proposing more or less substantial departures from Grice's account.[2]

The approaches discussed in this chapter share the view that lexical interpretation typically involves the construction of an *ad hoc concept* or occasion-specific sense, based on interaction among encoded concepts, contextual information and pragmatic expectations or principles. Use of the term 'ad hoc concept' in this connection is often traced to the psychologist Lawrence Barsalou (1987, 1993), whose work on categorization showed that *prototypical narrowing* (i.e. the interpretation of a general term as picking out a subset of prototypical or stereotypical category members) was much more flexible and context-dependent than was standardly assumed. In later work (e.g. by the psycholinguist Sam Glucksberg and his colleagues, and by pragmatists working within the relevance-theoretic framework), it was suggested that the outcome of the ad hoc concept construction process could be either a narrowing or a *broadening* of the linguistically-specified meaning: that is, the communicated concept may be either more specific or more general than the encoded concept. This opens up the possibility of a unified account on which lexical narrowing and broadening (or a combination of the two) are the outcomes of a single interpretive process which fine-tunes the interpretation of almost every word. We will follow the standard practice of representing ad hoc concepts as starred concepts (e.g. HAPPY*, SHARK*, BREAK*).

The most radical versions of this unified approach argue not only that narrowing and broadening involve the same interpretive mechanisms and may combine in the interpretation of a single word, but that there is a continuum of cases of broadening, ranging from strictly literal use through approximation and other forms of loosening to 'figurative' cases such as hyperbole and metaphor, with no clear cut-off points between them. Such fully unified accounts reject the traditional distinction between literal and figurative meaning and claim that approximation, hyperbole and metaphor are not distinct natural kinds, requiring different interpretive mechanisms, but involve exactly the same interpretive processes as are used for ordinary, literal utterances. This is a substantial departure from the standard Gricean account.[3]

Whether or not they aim to provide a unified account of the full range of cases, most current approaches to lexical pragmatics also share the view that narrowing and/or broadening contribute to the truth-conditional content of utterances (what is asserted or explicated) as well as to what is implicated. That is, the ad hoc concepts created by the pragmatic interpretation of individual words and phrases are seen as constituents of the proposition the speaker is taken to have expressed, rather than merely contributing to implicatures, as in the standard Gricean account. Following Recanati (1993), we will call such approaches *truth-conditional pragmatic* approaches.[4, 5]

Although there is a growing consensus that lexical interpretation involves the construction of ad hoc concepts which contribute to the truth-conditional content of utterances, there is much less agreement on the nature of the interpretive mechanisms involved.[6] In this chapter, we will propose a radical version of the unified truth-conditional pragmatic account, using the framework of relevance theory, and compare it with some alternative accounts. The focus will be not so much on justifying the relevance-theoretic approach as compared to alternative pragmatic approaches, but on raising a more general question about the nature of the cognitive processes involved. We will argue (in line with Sperber and Wilson forthcoming; Wilson and Carston 2006) that lexical narrowing and broadening are genuinely *inferential* processes, and that an inferential account of lexical pragmatics is preferable to non-inferential accounts.

The chapter is organized as follows. Section 2 introduces and illustrates the basic data that a theory of lexical pragmatics should explain. Section 3 argues that the data call for a radical version of the unified truth-conditional pragmatic account, and that ad hoc concept construction is the unitary process required. In that section, we contrast fully inferential with partly inferential and purely associative accounts of the cognitive mechanisms involved in lexical interpretation, and in section 4, we propose an inferential account of lexical narrowing and broadening using the framework of relevance theory. Section 5 raises some further issues and considers some possible objections to a unified inferential approach.

2. varieties of lexical adjustment

The aim of this section is to illustrate the processes of lexical narrowing and lexical broadening, using a variety of examples which suggest that there is a continuum of cases between literal use, approximation, metaphor and hyperbole, with no clear divisions between them. We will try to show that narrowing and broadening are flexible, highly context-dependent processes which cannot be adequately handled in terms of code-like rules, and end by introducing a further range of data that a unified account of lexical pragmatics might help to explain.

Lexical narrowing involves the use of a word to convey a more specific sense than the encoded one, with a more restricted denotation (picking out a subset of the items that fall under the encoded concept). Narrowing may take place to different degrees, and in different directions. Some illustrations are given in (1):

(1) a. I'm not *drinking* tonight.
     b. Buying a house is easy if you've got *money*.
     c. Churchill was a *man*.

In various different circumstances, the speaker of (1a) might be understood as conveying that she will not drink any liquid at all, that she will not drink any alcohol (or any of a certain type of alcohol, e.g. spirits), or that she will not drink significant amounts of alcohol. Each successive interpretation is narrower than the previous one, with a more restricted denotation.[7] (1b) suggests a pragmatic motive for narrowing. On a literal interpretation, the speaker would be understood as making the blatantly false claim that buying a house is easy for someone with any money at all;

the effect of narrowing is to yield a more plausible, informative or relevant interpretation on which the speaker is understood as claiming that buying a house is easy for someone with a suitable amount of money. (1c) shows that narrowing may take place not only to different degrees but also in different directions: in different situations of utterance, the speaker might be understood as conveying that Churchill was a typical man or that Churchill was an ideal man (where the notion of what constitutes a typical man or an ideal man, like the notion of what constitutes a significant amount of alcohol in (1a) or an appropriate amount of money in (1b), is itself heavily context-dependent) (cf. Barsalou 1987, 1993). An adequate pragmatic account of narrowing should shed some light on what triggers the narrowing process, what direction it takes, and when it stops.

One way of bringing out the flexibility and context dependence of narrowing is to consider the variety of interpretations that the same word would receive in different linguistic contexts. Standard examples discussed in the philosophical literature include the verbs 'open', 'cut' and 'leave', as illustrated in (2):

(2) a. *cut* the lawn/someone's hair/a cake/one's finger/a pack of cards/
         ...

     b. *open* curtains/one's mouth/a book/a bottle/a road/the mountain/
         ...

     c. *leave* the house/home/food on a plate/one's spouse/a note/ ...

There is no standard or stereotypical method for *cutting, opening* or *leaving* tout court, but there are standard methods for *cutting hair, cutting a lawn, opening curtains,* and so on, each of which involves a narrowing of the more general concepts CUT, OPEN and LEAVE (Searle 1980). A similar point is made in an experimental study of adjectives by the psychologist Gregory Murphy (1997). Taking as an example the adjective 'fresh', and using a variety of experimental techniques, he showed that it has innumerable slightly different interpretations across contexts. One method was to ask participants to provide *antonyms* for its occurrence in different adjective-noun combinations. Some of the most frequent responses are listed in (3) (Murphy 1997, 237–9):

(3) *fresh*   ANTONYMS
     shirt   dirty
     vegetables   rotten
     fish   frozen

sheets	recently slept in
water	dirty/salt
bread	stale
air	polluted
outlook	tired
assistant	experienced
idea	old

This clearly illustrates the point that what is arguably a single lexical item, encoding a general concept FRESH, gets specified/narrowed/fine-tuned in slightly different ways in different linguistic contexts, and supports the more general claim that discourse context and pragmatic expectations strongly influence the direction in which narrowing takes place.[8]

Lexical broadening involves the use of a word to convey a more general sense than the encoded one, with a consequent expansion of the linguistically-specified denotation. As noted above, radical versions of the unified approach to lexical pragmatics such as the one proposed in relevance theory treat approximation, hyperbole and metaphor as subvarieties of broadening which differ mainly in the degree to which the linguistically-specified denotation is expanded. *Approximation* is the case where a word with a relatively strict sense is marginally extended to include a penumbra of items (what Lasersohn 1999 calls a 'pragmatic halo') that strictly speaking fall outside its linguistically-specified denotation. Some illustrations are given in (4):

(4)   a.   That bottle is *empty*.
      b.   This policy will *bankrupt* the farmers.
      c.   The garden is *south-facing*.

In (4a), the word 'empty', which has a relatively strict sense, might be intended and understood as an approximation, so that the speaker would be interpreted as claiming that the bottle in question is EMPTY*: that is, close enough to being EMPTY for the differences to be inconsequential for the purpose at hand (for instance, collecting bottles for recycling). In (4b), the word 'bankrupt' may be intended and understood either literally (BANKRUPT) or as an approximation (BANKRUPT*), in which case the speaker would be interpreted as claiming that the policy will bring the farmers close enough to bankruptcy for the differences to be inconsequential. Similarly, in (4c), the term 'south-facing' may be used literally (to mean that the garden faces due south), or as an approximation (SOUTH-FACING*), meaning that the garden faces in a generally southerly direction.

On more radical versions of the unified approach, hyperbole is seen as involving a further degree of broadening, and hence a greater departure from the encoded meaning. For instance, a parent might say (4a) hyperbolically while pointing to a three-quarters-empty bottle, intending to convey that a teenager has drunk too much. Similarly, an opposition member might use (4b) to indicate hyperbolically that as a result of the government's policy, the farmers will be substantially poorer than might have been expected or desired; and a new house owner might say (4c) hyperbolically of a house described in the estate agent's brochure as facing east-south-east, intending to implicate that she has made the right choice. The fact that in each of these examples ('empty', 'bankrupt', 'south-facing') there seems to be a gradient or continuum of cases between literal use, approximation and hyperbole makes it worth looking for a unified account in which the same interpretive mechanisms apply throughout.

Within the fully unified account we are proposing, metaphor is seen as a still more radical variety of broadening than hyperbole, involving a greater departure from the encoded meaning. Consider (5a)–(5c):

(5) a. Sally is a *chameleon.*
     b. John's critics are *sharpening their claws.*
     c. The agenda isn't *written in stone.*

The encoded meaning of the word 'chameleon' is (let's say) the concept CHAMELEON, which denotes animals of a certain kind. In appropriate circumstances, however, (5a) might be metaphorically used to convey that Sally, who is not literally a CHAMELEON, has a capacity to change her appearance to fit in with her surroundings, remaining unnoticed by her enemies and escaping attack (etc.). On the type of approach we envisage, this metaphorical use would be seen as involving an expansion from the category CHAMELEON to the category CHAMELEON*, which includes both actual chameleons and people who share with chameleons the encyclopaedic property of having the capacity to change their appearance in order to blend in with their surroundings (etc.). Similarly, in (5b) the category of events that literally involve sharpening of claws may be extended to include other events which have the encyclopaedic property of being preparations for attack, and in (5c) the category WRITTEN IN STONE is broadened to include other items that are difficult to alter. These are relatively conventional metaphors, which are interpreted along fairly well-established lines (costing relatively little processing effort and yielding relatively limited and predictable effects). Novel metaphors allow more latitude in interpretation, and may call for a greater effort of memory or imagination, yielding richer rewards (see, for example, Pilkington 2000, Sperber and Wilson forthcoming).

Examples (4a)–(4c) above were designed to show that there is no clear dividing line between approximation and hyperbole. The examples in (6) below provide evidence of a gradient or continuum of cases between literal use, approximation, hyperbole and metaphor:

(6) a. That film *made me sick.*
     b. The water is *boiling.*
     c. That book *puts me to sleep.*

In (6a), for instance, the speaker may be understood as conveying that she actually vomited (a literal interpretation), that she came close enough to vomiting for the differences not to matter (an approximate interpretation), that the film made her physically queasy (a hyperbolic interpretation), or that the film induced some mental discomfort (etc.) (a metaphorical interpretation). Similar points apply to (6b) and (6c). In section 4, we will suggest how such cases might be handled on a unified inferential account.

A further variety of broadening, which we will call *category extension*, is typified by the use of salient brand names ('Hoover', 'Xerox', 'Sellotape') to denote a broader category (vacuum cleaners, photocopiers, sticky tape) including items from less salient brands. Personal names ('Chomsky', 'Shakespeare') and common nouns both lend themselves to category extension (cf. Glucksberg 2001, 38–52). Some more creative uses are illustrated in (7a)–(7d):

(7) a. Iraq is this generation's *Vietnam.*
     b. I don't believe it – they've appointed another *Chomsky.*
     c. Handguns are the new *flick-knives.*
     d. Ironing is the new *yoga.*

In (7a), 'Vietnam' may be understood as conveying an ad hoc concept VIETNAM*, which represents the category of disastrous military interventions. In (7b), 'Chomsky' might be understood as conveying an ad hoc concept CHOMSKY*, which represents a broader category of forceful exponents of a particular approach to linguistics. In (7c), FLICK-KNIVES* might represent the broader category of teenage weapons of choice, and in (7d) – a typical piece of lifestyle writer's discourse – YOGA* might be seen as representing the category of fashionable pastimes for relieving stress. These cases of category extension are not analyzable as approximations.

The claim in (7a) is not that Iraq is a borderline case, close enough to being Vietnam for it to be acceptable to call it 'Vietnam', but merely that it belongs to a broader category of which Vietnam is a salient member; and so on for the other examples. What approximation and category extension have in common is that they are both analyzable as outcomes of a single pragmatic process of lexical adjustment which results in an ad hoc category whose denotation is broader than that of the lexically encoded concept.

Neologisms and word coinages provide further data for a theory of lexical pragmatics and shed some light on the nature of the mental mechanisms involved. Experiments by Clark and Clark (1979) and Clark and Gerrig (1983) show that newly-coined verbs derived from nouns, as in (8a)–(8b), and the recruitment of proper names into compound verbs or adjectives, as in (8c)–(8d), are no harder to understand than regular uses:[9]

(8) a. The boy *porched* the newspaper.
     b. She *wristed* the ball over the net.
     c. He *did a Napoleon* for the camera.
     d. They have a lifestyle which is very *San Francisco*.

Understanding (8a) and (8b) depends on knowing the encoded meaning of the nouns 'porch' and 'wrist' and having appropriate background knowledge, in the one case, about newspaper deliveries in certain communities and, in the other, about the various arm movements of competent tennis players. Other cases are much more idiosyncratic and depend not so much on general knowledge but on a specific context; see, for instance, Clark's (1983) discussion of 'Max tried to *teapot* a policeman', where 'to teapot X' meant in the particular scenario 'to rub the back of the leg of X with a teapot'. This point is worth emphasizing, since it indicates that there is no principled limit on the possible interpretations of words in use (i.e. given that there are indefinitely many possible contexts, there are indefinitely many possible adjustments of the encoded sense(s)). The interpretations of (8c) and (8d) again depend on having certain kinds of fairly general encyclopaedic information: about Napoleon's typical bodily stance in public, and about the way in which people live, or are reputed to live, in San Francisco (laid-back, leisurely, well off). The speed and apparent ease with which experimental participants understand these neologisms suggests that lexical-pragmatic processes apply 'on-line' in a flexible, creative and context dependent way.

A further range of examples that a theory of lexical pragmatics might help to explain are pun-like cases involving an element of equivocation or word play. Consider (9):

(9) Not all *banks* are river banks.

Most English hearers intuitively understand this as both true and informative: that is, they intuitively interpret 'bank' as picking out *both* the set of river banks *and* the set of financial institutions. The question is how the interpretation is best explained. One possibility is to go meta-linguistic and treat 'bank' here as representing the set of things that are *called* 'banks'. An alternative possibility suggested by the ad hoc concept approach is to treat the interpretation as involving the on-line construction of an ad hoc concept BANK* whose denotation includes both the set of river banks and the set of financial institutions. This approach might shed some light on the common use of pun-like comparisons such as those in (10), in which adjectives such as 'cold' and 'hard' have to be simultaneously understood in both physical and psychological senses:[10]

(10) a.   His mind was as *cold* as the ice forming on the windscreen.
      b.   His eyes were as *cold* as polar ice.
      c.   His voice was low and as *cold* as steel.
      d.   Jane is as *hard* as nails.
      e.   Sue is as *tough* as old leather.
      f.   Jimmy is as *sharp* as a knife.

As the range of cases surveyed here indicate, lexical adjustment may be a one-off process, used once and then forgotten, creating an ad hoc concept tied to a particular context that may never occur again (a 'nonce' sense, as Clark 1983 puts it). However, some of these pragmatically constructed senses may catch on in the communicative interactions of a few people or a group, and so become regularly and frequently used. In such cases, the pragmatic process of concept construction becomes progressively more routinized, and may ultimately spread through a speech community and stabilize as an extra lexical sense. We would therefore expect a unified account of lexical pragmatic processes to shed light on the nature of polysemy (the fact that many words have a range of distinct, though related, senses) and on processes of lexical change more generally.[11] In fact, it is often pointed out that pragmatic processes of broadening, narrowing and metaphorical extension play a major role in semantic change (Lyons 1977; Traugott and Dasher 2001). If our unified account is correct, the resulting senses should all be seen as outcomes of the frequent and widespread application to a particular lexical item of a single pragmatic process of ad hoc concept construction.

3. approaches to lexical adjustment

Many pragmatic or philosophical accounts seem to take for granted that narrowing, approximation and metaphorical extension are distinct pragmatic processes, which lack common descriptions or explanations and need not be studied together. For instance, narrowing is often analyzed as a case of default inference to a stereotypical interpretation,[12] approximation has been seen as linked to variations in the standards of precision governing different types of discourse,[13] and metaphor is still quite widely treated on Gricean lines, as a blatant violation of a maxim of truthfulness, with resulting implicature.[14] These accounts do not generalize: metaphors are not analyzable as rough approximations, narrowings are not analyzable as blatant violations of a maxim of truthfulness, and so on. Separate analyses of approximations and figurative utterances could be justified by showing that there is a sharp boundary between them, but as examples (4a)–(4c) and (6a)–(6c) were designed to show, in many cases, no clear cut-off point exists. We have argued in some detail elsewhere that there are also internal descriptive and theoretical reasons for wanting to go beyond these existing accounts and develop a more unified approach (see Carston 1997, 2002; Wilson and Sperber 2002; Wilson 2003). We will not repeat those points here, but assume that the conclusion they point to is correct: that is, that narrowing and broadening (including metaphorical cases) are complementary processes, one restricting and the other extending the category denoted by the linguistically-encoded concept, so that a unitary account is well worth pursuing.

In the next section, we will outline the relevance-theoretic view that lexical comprehension involves a process of ad hoc concept construction, based on information readily accessible from the encyclopaedic entries of the encoded concepts and constrained by expectations of relevance.[15] In the rest of this section, we want to establish two preliminary points: first, that lexical pragmatic processes such as narrowing and broadening contribute to truth-conditional content (what is asserted or explicated) rather than merely affecting implicatures, as on standard Gricean accounts; second, that current approaches which agree on this point differ significantly on the nature of the cognitive mechanisms involved, and specifically, on the extent to which they are properly inferential.

First, some arguments supporting the truth-conditional view. Perhaps the clearest evidence comes from neologisms such as those exemplified in (8a)–(8d). Verbs such as 'porch', 'wrist' and 'teapot' were coined for experimental purposes and have no encoded meanings in English: thus, if the ad hoc concepts PORCH*, WRIST* and TEAPOT* do not contribute to the proposition expressed or asserted by these utterances, there is no proposition expressed or asserted at all. This runs counter to the clear and widespread intuition that these utterances can be used to make assertions in the regular way, and would make it very difficult to provide an adequate account of how particular implicatures are warranted in these cases. More generally, any analysis of how utterances are used in communication must take account of potential differences in the acquisition and organization of lexical meanings among members of a speech community. A word that is familiar to the speaker of an utterance and has a regular encoded meaning in English may nonetheless be unfamiliar to the hearer, who will be forced to interpret it inferentially along similar lines to neologisms. Conversely, a word that is unfamiliar to the speaker and produced as a neologism may be one the hearer has encountered before and assigned a regular encoded meaning. Given such differences, the idea that only encoded concepts can contribute to the truth-conditional content of utterances appears rather arbitrary and unworkable.

There is also evidence that it is the pragmatically adjusted meaning of a word or phrase, rather than the linguistically encoded meaning, that falls within the scope of sentence operators such as negation, conditionals, disjunction, 'because', imperative and interrogative moods, etc. Consider the examples in (11):

(11) a. No teenager is a *saint*.
      b. If the bottle is *empty*, leave it out for recycling.
      c. Be an *angel* and pick up the shopping for me on the way home.
      d. Either you become a *human being* or you leave the group.

In (11a), if the encoded meaning of 'saint' is interpreted as falling within the scope of negation, the speaker will be understood as making the trivial claim that no teenager has been canonized. In fact, the speaker of (11a) would generally be understood as making the more plausible, informative or relevant claim that no teenager falls in the category of SAINTS* (that is, roughly, people of outstanding virtue). But in that case, it is the adjusted meaning rather than the encoded meaning that falls within the scope of negation and contributes to the proposition expressed. Similar points apply to the other examples. In the case of (11d), for instance, given that the addressee is a human being already, it would be impossible for him to comply with the first disjunct, literally understood (and therefore pointless for the speaker to ask him to comply with it). Clearly, what the hearer is being encouraged to do as an alternative to leaving the group is to start behaving in a more reasonable or sensitive way (that is, to become a HUMAN BEING*). But in that case, it is the adjusted meaning rather than the encoded meaning that falls within the scope of the disjunction operator and contributes to the proposition expressed. (For discussion and illustration of these 'embedding tests' applied to cases of lexical adjustment, see Recanati 1995; Levinson 2000; Carston 2002; Wilson and Sperber 2002.)

A third piece of evidence comes from the fact that lexical pragmatic processes may lead to semantic change, so that what starts out as an ad hoc concept may end up (for at least some members of a speech community) as a new encoded sense. It may well be, for instance, that as a result of frequent metaphorical use, some speakers of English represent words such as 'saint' or 'angel' as having an extra encoded sense (SAINT*, ANGEL*).[16] For these people, 'saint' and 'angel' are genuine cases of polysemy, and the comprehension of (11a) and (11c) does not involve ad hoc concept construction but is a simple matter of disambiguation (choosing which of two or more encoded senses should figure in the proposition expressed). For others who have encountered these metaphors less frequently or not at all, 'saint' and 'angel' may have only a single encoded sense (SAINT, ANGEL) and the interpretation of (11a) and (11c) would involve constructing (or reconstructing) an appropriate ad hoc concept. In the first case, where 'saint' and 'angel' are genuinely polysemous and interpreted via disambiguation, there is no doubt that the encoded senses SAINT* and ANGEL* would contribute to the truth-conditional content of (11a) and (11c), and hence to what is asserted or explicated. But it is implausible to suppose that (11a) and (11c) would be understood as expressing or asserting entirely different propositions depending on whether the concepts SAINT* and ANGEL* are recovered by disambiguation or ad hoc concept construction. One of the most important functions of pragmatic inference is to compensate for grammatical and lexical differences among members of a speech community, so that addressees with different encoded senses can end up with the same interpretations, albeit via different routes.[17] Thus, all the available evidence points to the conclusion that ad hoc concepts contribute to the truth-conditional content of utterances, rather than merely to implicatures.

As noted above (section 1), current truth-conditional accounts of lexical pragmatics differ significantly as to the cognitive mechanisms involved in the lexical adjustment process. At one extreme are fully inferential accounts, which treat utterance interpretation in general, and lexical adjustment in particular, as properly inferential processes, taking a set of premises as input and yielding as output a set of conclusions logically derivable from, or at least warranted by, the premises. According to relevance theory, for instance, the interpretation of (5a) above ('Sally is a chameleon') would involve an overall non-demonstrative inference process which takes as input a premise such as (12a) (together with other contextual assumptions) and yields as output a conclusion such as (12b):

(12) a. The speaker has said 'Sally is a chameleon' (i.e. a sentence with a fragmentary decoded meaning requiring inferential completion and complementation).
      b. The speaker meant that Sally$_x$ is a CHAMELEON*, Sally$_x$ is changeable, Sally$_x$ has a capacity to adapt to her surroundings, it's hard to discern Sally$_x$'s true nature (etc.).

Since utterance interpretation takes place at a risk, the truth of the premise in (12a) cannot guarantee the truth of the conclusion in (12b), but, according to relevance theory, hearers have an automatic inferential heuristic for constructing the best interpretation given the evidence available to them. This interpretation itself has an internal logical structure: its construction involves the application of deductive inference processes which take as input premises such as 'Sally is a CHAMELEON*' (together with further contextual premises) and yield as output conclusions such as 'Sally is changeable', 'Sally has a capacity to adapt to her surroundings' (etc.) which follow logically from the set of premises chosen. Thus, the account is doubly inferential: on the one hand, the implicatures of an utterance must be deducible from its explicatures (together with appropriate contextual assumptions); on the other, the fact that the speaker has uttered this sentence on this particular occasion must (together with appropriate contextual assumptions) warrant the conclusion that she meant to convey this particular set of explicatures and implicatures. We will develop these ideas in more detail in section 4 (for further discussion, see Carston 1997, 2002, 2007; Sperber and Wilson 1998, forthcoming; Wilson and Carston 2006; Wilson and Sperber 2002).

At the other extreme from this account are predominantly non-inferential accounts. Examples include the computational account of predicate interpretation proposed by Kintsch (2000, 2001), connectionist accounts, and many treatments of metaphor within the cognitive linguistics framework (Lakoff 1987, 1994; Fauconnier and Turner 2002). Kintsch, for instance, uses a spreading activation model based on statistical associations among lexical items in a corpus to account for differences between the literal and metaphorical interpretations of the predicate 'is a shark'. According to his data, close associates of the word 'shark' include the words 'fins', 'dolphin', 'diver' and 'fish', and these associations provide the basis for his account. These are classic cases of non-inferential association, in which the associates of 'shark' are not logically related to it in any systematic way (for instance, 'x is a shark' entails 'x is a fish', but does not entail 'x is a dolphin' or 'x is a diver') and the associations provide no basis for drawing warranted conclusions. Kintsch sees this as a potential weakness in his model:

> For instance, [the model] fails to explain the relations among *shark* and its neighbours – that is, how we understand that a shark **has fins**, **looks like** *a dolphin,* **is a danger to** *divers,* and **is a** *fish.* (Kintsch 2000, 259; highlighting added)

By contrast, many cognitive linguistic models of lexical interpretation treat a non-inferential process of 'domain mapping' (i.e. the setting up of systematic correspondences between items from distinct cognitive domains) as the key to metaphor interpretation. On this approach, the interpretation of (5a) above ('Sally is a chameleon') might involve a mapping between the domain of animals and the domain of people. Here again the associations are of a non-inferential kind.

Between these two extremes lie mixed associative/inferential approaches: for instance, Recanati (1995, 2004) distinguishes 'primary', strictly associative, pragmatic processes from 'secondary', properly inferential, pragmatic processes, with the move from decoded meaning to explicature (e.g. from CHAMELEON to CHAMELEON*) being treated as a primary, hence non-inferential, process and the move from explicatures to implicatures (e.g. from the premise that the speaker said that Sally$_x$ is a CHAMELEON* to the conclusion that she meant that Sally$_x$ changes to fit her surroundings (etc.)) as secondary and properly inferential. (On inferential versus non-inferential approaches, see Carston 2007; Recanati 2002, 2004; Sperber and Wilson forthcoming; Wilson and Carston 2006.)

There is a general theoretical point to make about the relation between these approaches. From a cognitive point of view, all inferential relationships are also associations: an inferential mechanism establishes systematic correspondences between (constituents of) premises and (constituents of) conclusions. Thus, for many English speakers, the concept ANGEL is inferentially associated with the concept VERY GOOD AND KIND, the concept CHAMELEON is inferentially associated with the concept CHANGES TO FIT ITS SURROUNDINGS, and so on. However, as illustrated above, not all associations are inferential. In the minds of many speakers of English, for instance, 'shark' is non-inferentially associated with 'diver', 'salt' with 'pepper', 'love' with 'hate', and so on. In a purely associationist account, the fact that some associates happen to be inferentially related provides no basis for deriving warranted conclusions unless some additional machinery is introduced to set up appropriate inferential links. In a properly inferential account, the only associations that play a role in lexical adjustment are inferential ones. Thus, the claim that lexical adjustment is a properly inferential process is considerably more constrained than the claim that it is a general associative process, and an adequate properly inferential account would therefore be preferable on theoretical grounds. In the next section, we propose a fully inferential relevance-theoretic account of the fast, on-line pragmatic process of lexical adjustment. At the end of the chapter, we return to the issue of inferential versus non-inferential processes and consider some possible objections to a unified inferential account.

4. an inferential account of lexical adjustment

An adequate account of lexical narrowing and broadening must answer four questions:

i.   What triggers the lexical adjustment process (why not simply accept the encoded sense)?
ii.   What determines the direction that the adjustment process takes?
iii. How does the adjustment process work in detail?
iv.   What brings it to an end?

Relevance theory treats lexical narrowing and broadening, like utterance interpretation in general, as guided by expectations of relevance. Relevance is defined as a property of utterances and other inputs to cognitive processes (e.g. external stimuli such as sights and sounds, and internal representations such as thoughts, memories or conclusions of inferences). An input is *relevant* to an individual when it connects with available contextual assumptions to yield positive cognitive effects (e.g. true contextual implications, warranted strengthenings or revisions of existing assumptions). For present purposes, the most important type of cognitive effect is a *contextual implication*: an implication deducible from input and context together, but from neither input nor context alone. Other things being equal, the greater the cognitive effects, and the smaller the mental effort required to derive them (by representing the input, accessing a context and deriving any contextual implications), the greater the relevance of the input to the individual at that time.[18]

Relevance theory makes two general claims about the role of relevance in cognition and communication. According to the Cognitive Principle of Relevance, human cognition tends to be geared to the maximization of relevance. According to the Communicative Principle of Relevance, utterances (and other acts of ostensive communication) are special among cognitive inputs in that they raise presumptions or expectations of relevance in their addressees. Typically, an utterance creates both a general presumption of *optimal relevance* (that the utterance is at least relevant enough to be worth the addressee's processing effort, and is, moreover, the most relevant one compatible with the speaker's abilities and preferences) and more occasion-specific expectations about where the relevance of the utterance will lie (what sort of contextual implications it will have). The central claim of the relevance-based account of pragmatic processing is that addressees take the fact that the speaker has uttered a sentence with a certain linguistic meaning as a clue to the speaker's intentions, and use the following heuristic to derive a warranted conclusion about the speaker's meaning:

Relevance-theoretic comprehension heuristic:
(a) Follow a path of least effort in constructing an interpretation of the utterance (that is, test interpretive hypotheses in order of their accessibility);
(b) Stop when your expectation of relevance is satisfied (or abandoned).

According to this heuristic, at each point in the on-line processing of an utterance, the addressee tentatively chooses the most accessible interpretation, and reconsiders this choice only if it seems unlikely (on the basis of the available evidence) to lead to an overall interpretation that satisfies his expectation of relevance. The same procedure applies to the full range of pragmatic tasks: assigning referents to referential expressions, disambiguating ambiguous words or structures, supplying contextual assumptions, deriving implications, etc. Thus, the fact that an interpretation is highly accessible gives it an initial degree of plausibility. A hearer using this heuristic will stop at the first overall interpretation that satisfies his expectation of relevance: this is his best hypothesis about the speaker's meaning given the evidence available to him.

This procedure applies equally to the adjustment of lexical meaning, which (following the arguments of the last section) we will treat as contributing both to the proposition expressed by an utterance and to its contextual implications or implicatures (i.e. intended contextual implications). Consider how the verb 'rest' might be understood in the following exchange:

(13) Bill: I'm doing the 10km circuit run this afternoon. Wanna come
             with me?
      Sue: No thanks, I'm *resting* today.

The verb 'rest' has a rather general meaning, which covers any degree of inactivity (physical or mental), from sleeping to staying awake but not moving much to performing a range of not very strenuous tasks (with many more possibilities in between). Suppose now that Sue is quite an athletic person, who exercises regularly: then her use of 'rest' here is plausibly understood as expressing the ad hoc concept REST*, which indicates a much lower degree of physical activity than she undertakes on her training days but is still quite compatible with her pottering about the garden or walking to the shops. A hearer using the relevance-theoretic comprehension heuristic would narrow the encoded concept REST just so far as is required to satisfy his expectation of relevance (e.g. by explaining why Sue is refusing his invitation), and no further. This particular narrowing would cost Bill little effort, given his knowledge of Sue's exercise habits, and provide him with a range of contextual implications (e.g. she won't come with me today because she is RESTING*, she may come another day when she isn't RESTING*, etc.). In different circumstances – for instance, in response to the question 'Would you like to walk to the corner shop with me?' – REST would have to be narrowed much further.

    Given the commitment of relevance theory to a unitary account of lexical pragmatic processes, the same kind of analysis should carry over to cases of concept broadening (including metaphorical uses). Let's look at an example, going into a little more detail about how the adjustment process works. Consider the following exchange, focusing on Mary's use of the word 'angel':[19]

(14) Peter: Will Sally look after the children if we get ill?
      Mary: Sally is an *angel*.

The decoded meaning of the sentence Mary uttered contains the concept ANGEL, which activates a range of logical properties (e.g. an angel is a SUPERNATURAL BEING OF A CERTAIN KIND), enabling deductive inferences to be drawn (e.g. from the proposition that Sally is an ANGEL, it is deducible that Sally is a SUPERNATURAL BEING OF A CERTAIN KIND). The decoded concept ANGEL also activates a variety of more or less strongly evidenced encyclopaedic properties of different subsets of angels (good angels, guardian angels, avenging angels, dark angels, fallen angels, and so on) enabling further conclusions to be drawn (e.g. the proposition that Sally is a (good) angel, if processed in a context containing the assumption that (good) angels are exceptionally kind, contextually implies that Sally is exceptionally kind). Some plausible encyclopaedic properties of (good) angels are given in (15):

(15) Encyclopaedic properties of (GOOD) ANGEL:
      EXCEPTIONALLY GOOD AND KIND
      WATCHES OVER HUMANS AND HELPS THEM WHEN NEEDED
      VIRTUOUS IN THOUGHT AND DEED
      MESSENGER OF GOD, etc.

Since the stereotypical angel is a good angel, and the encyclopaedic properties of stereotypical category members are likely to be highly accessible as a result of frequent use, some of the properties in (15) are likely to be strongly activated by use of the word 'angel'. In the discourse context in (14), where Peter is expecting an answer about Sally's readiness to look after children, encyclopaedic properties having to do with kindness, helpfulness and watchfulness are likely to receive additional activation from other items in the context, and would therefore be most accessible for use in deriving contextual implications. Using the relevance-theoretic comprehension heuristic, Peter therefore tentatively assumes that among the implicatures of Mary's utterance are contextual implications such as those in (16):

(16) SALLY IS EXCEPTIONALLY GOOD AND KIND.
      SALLY IS WATCHFUL AND WILL HELP WHEN NEEDED.
      SALLY WILL LOOK AFTER THE CHILDREN IF PETER AND MARY GET ILL.

Of course, Sally is not a supernatural being, and therefore not an ANGEL, so the contextual implications in (16) are not yet properly warranted. However, by narrowing the denotation of ANGEL to include only good angels and broadening it to include people who share with good angels some of the encyclopaedic properties in (15), Peter can interpret Mary as asserting that $Sally_x$ is an ANGEL* and implicating that she is helpful, kind, watchful (etc.), and will look after the children if Peter and Mary are ill. Having found an interpretation which satisfies his expectations of relevance, at this point he should stop.

According to this account, lexical adjustment is a special case of a more general process of *mutual parallel adjustment* in which tentative hypotheses about contextual assumptions, explicatures and contextual implications are incrementally modified so as to yield an overall interpretation which satisfies the hearer's expectations of relevance.[20] In (14), the decoded concept ANGEL suggests a range of potential implications which would satisfy Peter's expectations of relevance provided that they were properly warranted. Using the relevance-theoretic comprehension heuristic, he tentatively accepts these implications and looks for an interpretation of 'angel' which would justify their derivation. In the discourse context in (14), the most accessible adjustment of the encoded concept ANGEL (and hence the one favoured by the heuristic) is the ad hoc concept ANGEL*, which is narrower than ANGEL in some respects, and broader in others. On this account, the implications in (16) are derived by regular forward inference from the premise that Sally is a (GOOD) ANGEL (together with additional contextual assumptions), and they in turn provide the basis for a 'backward' inference to the adjusted propositions ($Sally_x$ is an ANGEL*, ANGELS* are exceptionally kind (etc.)) which justify their acceptance as part of an overall interpretation that satisfies the hearer's expectations of relevance.[21] Both narrowing and broadening emerge as by-products of the search for relevance, and the same encoded concept may be narrowed or broadened (or both) to different degrees and in different ways across different occasions of use.

We suggested above (section 2) that 'approximation', 'hyperbole', 'metaphor' are not distinct theoretical kinds, requiring different interpretive mechanisms, but merely occupy different points on a continuum of degrees of broadening. To illustrate this point in more detail, consider (17):

(17)   The water is boiling.

This utterance might be intended and understood literally, or as an approximation, a hyperbole or a metaphor, with no clear cut-off points between these various possibilities. On the relevance-theoretic account outlined above, all these interpretations are arrived at in the same way, by adding to the context encyclopaedic information made accessible by the encoded concept BOILING (and by other concepts activated by the utterance or the discourse) and deriving enough implications to satisfy the hearer's expectations of relevance. What makes the resulting interpretation intuitively 'literal', 'approximate', 'hyperbolical' or 'metaphorical' is simply the particular set of encyclopaedic assumptions actually deployed in making the utterance relevant in the expected way.

Let's suppose that the encyclopaedic properties simultaneously activated by both 'water' and 'boiling' (and therefore potentially highly accessible for the interpretation of (17)) include those in (18a)–(18d):

(18) BOILING WATER: Encyclopaedic properties[22]
    a. SEETHES AND BUBBLES, HIDDEN UNDERCURRENTS, EMITS VAPOUR, etc.
    b. TOO HOT TO WASH ONE'S HANDS IN, TOO HOT TO BATHE IN, etc.
    c. SUITABLE FOR MAKING TEA, DANGEROUS TO TOUCH, etc.
    d. SAFE TO USE IN STERILIZING INSTRUMENTS, etc.[23]

Then (17) would be intuitively 'metaphorical' if the implications that make the utterance relevant in the expected way depend on (18a), but not on (18b)–(18d) (so that the speaker is not understood as committed to the claim that the water is hot); it would be intuitively a 'hyperbole' if these implications depend on (18b), but not on (18c)–(18d); it would be an 'approximation' if these implications depend on (18c), but not on (18d), and it would be 'literal' if the deployment of (18d) is crucial to making the utterance relevant in the expected way (so that the denotation of the concept expressed includes only items that are actually BOILING). In each case, the comprehension process works in the same way, by selection of an appropriate set of encyclopaedic assumptions to act as premises for the derivation of the expected contextual implications. The appropriateness of different sets of encyclopaedic assumptions depends, on the one hand, on their degree of accessibility in the particular discourse context, and, on the other, on the potential contextual implications they yield. As always, the hearer's goal is to derive enough implications, at a low enough cost, to satisfy the particular expectations of relevance raised by the utterance in that discourse context.

In this section, we have proposed a fully inferential account of lexical narrowing and broadening which answers the four basic questions of lexical pragmatics as follows:

i.   Narrowing and broadening are triggered by the search for relevance.
ii. They follow a path of least effort in whatever direction it leads.
iii. They come about through *mutual adjustment* of explicatures, contextual assumptions and implications (or implicatures) so as to satisfy the expectations of relevance raised by the utterance.
iv. They stop when these expectations are satisfied.

As suggested above (section 3), this account treats utterance comprehension as doubly inferential: it consists of an overall non-demonstrative inference process in which the deductive inference processes required to derive the contextual implications that satisfy the hearer's expectations of relevance play an essential role. Overall, comprehension starts from the premise that the speaker has uttered a sentence S (e.g. 'Sally is an angel') with a certain encoded meaning, and arrives at the warranted conclusion that the speaker meant that $P_1...P_n$ (e.g. that Sally$_x$ is an ANGEL*, that she is good, kind, watchful and will help look after the children). This overall non-demonstrative process is carried out by the relevance-theoretic comprehension heuristic, a domain-specific form of inference justified only for overt communication (Sperber and Wilson 2002). In order to arrive at a warranted conclusion about the speaker's meaning, the hearer must perform a range of deductive inferences (e.g. from ANGEL/ ANGEL* to VERY GOOD AND KIND, WATCHFUL, HELPFUL (etc.)) in order to derive enough contextual implications to satisfy his expectations of relevance. According to relevance theory, these two types of inference are intimately connected. It is only by deriving (deductive) contextual implications, as in (16) above, that the hearer can justify a particular hypothesis about the speaker's meaning as the best explanation of the fact that she uttered sentence S. By contrast, non-inferential accounts of lexical adjustment involve neither type of inference, while mixed associative/inferential approaches such as Recanati's (1995, 2004) involve a combination of deductive inference and inference to the best explanation which takes as input the associatively constructed explicit content (or the fact that the speaker has expressed it)[24] and arrives at a warranted conclusion about the intended implicit content. As noted in section 3, an adequate properly inferential account is more constrained than non-inferential and mixed inferential-associative accounts, and is therefore preferable on theoretical grounds. We believe the account of lexical adjustment we have proposed in this section is descriptively adequate. In the next section, we will consider some further data which might be seen as raising problems for this account.

5. questions and implications

In this final section, we will briefly consider some broader questions about inferential accounts of lexical adjustment. While some (in our view) can be straightforwardly answered, others raise genuine issues for future research.

An objection sometimes raised to inferential accounts of metaphor interpretation is that they cannot handle the so-called *emergent property* issue. To illustrate, consider the utterance in (19):

(19)   That surgeon should be dismissed. He is a *butcher*.

The speaker of (19) is plausibly understood as conveying that the surgeon in question is extremely incompetent, dangerous, not to be trusted with the lives of patients, and so on. These properties are not standardly associated with either SURGEON or BUTCHER in isolation, but 'emerge' in the course of the interpretation. Emergent properties raise a problem for all accounts of metaphor interpretation. The challenge for inferential accounts is to show how they can be inferentially derived (see Carston 2002, ch. 5, for a fuller discussion of the dimensions of the problem).

On the relevance-theoretic approach outlined in section 4, the interpretation of (19) would involve adding to the context encyclopaedic information made accessible by the encoded concept BUTCHER (or by other concepts activated by the utterance or the discourse) and deriving the contextual implications that the surgeon is incompetent, dangerous, not to be trusted with the lives of patients, etc. But, as Vega Moreno (2004, 298) points out:

> The properties that the hearer takes the speaker to be attributing to the surgeon are not stored as part of his representation of 'butcher', so must be derived by some other means than simply searching through his knowledge about butchers.

In recent relevance-theoretic accounts, it has been argued that emergent properties are analyzable as genuine contextual implications which emerge in the course of the mutual adjustment process based on contextual premises derived from several sources.[25] In (19), for instance, the speaker may be understood as asserting that the surgeon in question is a BUTCHER*, where BUTCHER* is a regular adjusted concept based on encyclopaedic information associated with the encoded concept BUTCHER, denoting people who share with butchers the encyclopaedic property of cutting flesh in a certain way (using the same techniques as butchers, with the same intentions, concern for welfare, degree of skill, and so on). From the proposition that the surgeon is a BUTCHER*, together with encyclopaedic information associated with the encoded concept SURGEON, it follows straightforwardly that the surgeon in question is grossly incompetent, dangerous, not to be trusted with the lives of patients, and deserves to be dismissed. Contextual implications of this type are highly accessible in the discourse context in (19), and would help to satisfy the hearer's expectations of relevance; they are therefore likely to be accepted as implicatures by a hearer using the relevance-theoretic comprehension heuristic. This account is genuinely inferential, and the 'emergent properties' are straightforwardly analyzable as both contextual implications and implicatures.[26]

There are more general questions about the relation between fully inferential accounts and non-inferential or partly inferential accounts, which deserve greater consideration than we have space for here. We will just mention two of them. First, how far is our inferential account of narrowing and broadening theoretically and empirically distinguishable from purely or partly associative accounts? This question (in our view) has a straightforward answer. Throughout this chapter, we have argued that the relevance-theoretic account of lexical narrowing and broadening is much more constrained than associative accounts, and if empirically adequate, would be theoretically preferable for that reason. If the only associations exploited in lexical adjustment are inferential ones which narrow or broaden the denotation of the encoded concept, purely or partly associative accounts will vastly overgenerate, and some method for filtering out unwanted associations will be required. A typical method of filtering is to distinguish a designated set of permissible mapping relations (e.g. metaphorical mapping is seen as based on resemblance relations between source and target domains, metonymic mapping as based on contiguity relations, synecdoche on part-whole relations, etc.), with an additional pragmatic constraint that the output of the mapping must be 'noteworthy', 'salient', or 'fit the context' in some way (cf. Nunberg 1995; Recanati 2004). Quite apart from their reliance on such theoretically unelaborated pragmatic notions, these treatments do not generalize in any obvious way. In mapping accounts, for instance, metaphor and narrowing are normally seen as involving distinct types of mapping relation,[27] while hyperbole, approximation and category extension are usually not treated in terms of mapping at all. In clear contrast with this, we have argued that lexical narrowing and broadening involve a single interpretive mechanism, and that metaphor, hyperbole, approximation and category extension are all varieties of broadening, with no clear cut-off points between them. In fact, many of the associations/ mappings repeatedly mentioned in the cognitive linguistics literature (e.g. between properties of particular animals and human psychological traits, or between machines and humans; cf. Lakoff 1987, 1994; Gibbs and Tendahl 2006) may well have come about as by-products of inferential communication and comprehension (for discussion, see Sperber and Wilson forthcoming). Of course, these considerations do not show that inferential accounts of narrowing and broadening are right and associative or 'mapping' accounts are wrong, but they do underline the clear theoretical and empirical differences between them.

A question which is much less straightforwardly answerable has to do with a range of lexical-pragmatic processes not explicitly discussed in section 4 – metonymy, synecdoche, neologisms, blends, puns, 'transfers of meaning', and so on. Many such examples have been insightfully analyzed in purely or partly non-inferential terms, often from a cognitive linguistics perspective. To take just one illustration, consider the cases of 'metonymy' or 'transfer of meaning' in (20):[28]

(20) a. *The saxophone* walked out.
      b. *Downing Street* refused to give an interview.
      c. Which *wide body jets* serve dinner?
      d. *Nixon* bombed Hanoi.

In each of these utterances, the speaker is plausibly understood as referring to someone or something that is not explicitly mentioned, but that stands in some designated relation to the item which is denoted by the italicized expression. Examples of this type are standardly analyzed as involving domain mappings or correspondences between source and target domains (e.g. between musical instruments and their players, locations and the people who work there, those who give orders and those who carry them out). While relevance theorists have devoted a lot of attention to reanalyzing metaphorical 'mappings' in inferential terms, they have so far been much less concerned with 'metonymic mappings' such as those in (20),[29] and it is a genuine question how far such examples can be reanalyzed in purely inferential terms. We will not attempt a reanalysis here, but simply make a few brief observations suggesting lines on which this issue might be approached.

Notice, first, that the notion of metonymy is harder to grasp intuitively than the notion of metaphor. While theorists and ordinary speakers of a language tend to agree on which utterances are metaphorical, there is much less agreement on which are cases of metonymy. In the cognitive linguistics literature, for instance, all the examples in (20) are standardly described as involving a metonymic use of the italicized noun phrases. However, anaphora-based tests proposed by Nunberg (1995, 2004) suggest that in (20c) and (20d) it is not the italicized noun-phrases but the predicates 'serve dinner' and 'bombed Hanoi' that are used in an extended sense. If so, these examples should be straightforwardly reanalyzable in inferential terms, as cases of lexical broadening based on ad hoc concept construction. What remains then is a small residue of cases, including (20a) and (20b), which seem to involve genuine reference substitution and which are not straightforwardly reducible to lexical narrowing or broadening. We hope to return in future work to the question of whether these cases can be handled in inferential terms.

notes

1. This work is part of an AHRC-funded project 'A Unified Theory of Lexical Pragmatics' (AR16356). We are grateful to our research assistants, Patricia Kolaiti, Tim Wharton and, in particular, Rosa Vega Moreno, whose PhD work on metaphor we draw on in this chapter, and to Paula Rubio Fernandez, Vladimir Žegarac, Nausicaa Pouscoulous, Hanna Stoever and François Recanati, for helpful discussions. We would also like to thank Dan Sperber for sharing with us many valuable insights on metaphor and on lexical pragmatics more generally, and Noel Burton-Roberts for insightful comments and editorial patience.
2. See, for instance, Blutner (1998) and Lascarides and Copestake (1998) in formal linguistics, Barsalou (1987, 1993) and Glucksberg, Manfredi and McGlone (1997) in psychology, and Recanati (1995), Carston (1997) and Sperber and Wilson (1998) in pragmatics and philosophy of language.
3. Among those who explicitly reject the traditional literal-figurative distinction are Atlas (2005), Carston (1997, 2002), Kintsch (2000), Sperber and Wilson (1998, forthcoming) and Wilson (2003); however, not all of them explicitly advocate a fully unified approach to lexical pragmatics.
4. For many philosophers of language, the term 'truth-conditional pragmatics' is closely associated with the position known as 'contextualist semantics', aspects of which we do not necessarily endorse. However, for ease of exposition, we continue to use the label in this chapter, since it provides a clear way of distinguishing the kind of account we advocate from those that relegate all but the bare minimum of pragmatically contributed meaning to the secondary level of conversational implicature.
5. A fully unified truth-conditional account in which metaphor and hyperbole are seen as contributing to the proposition asserted or explicated has to allow for a much greater degree of indeterminacy at the level of truth-conditional content than is envisaged on standard Gricean accounts.
6. There are also widely differing views on the nature of lexical meaning, concepts and ad hoc concepts. We hold the broadly Fodorian view that the mentally-

represented concepts encoded by lexical items are atomic (unstructured), coupled with the assumption that atomic concepts provide access to various kinds of mentally represented information, in particular encyclopaedic information about the entities that fall in their denotation. For discussion, see Sperber (1996), Sperber and Wilson (1998), Carston (2002, ch. 5), Wilson and Sperber (2002) and Horsey (2006).

7. Arguably, the verb 'drink' has now acquired an additional lexical sense as a result of frequent narrowing to the more specific sense 'drink alcohol'. However, the further narrowings to 'drink substantial amounts of/certain types of alcohol' do not seem to have become lexicalized (and in any case, the notion of what constitutes a substantial amount or an appropriate type of alcohol is itself highly context-dependent).

8. It is worth noting that the narrowings induced by linguistic context are not invariably accepted, but may be overridden or pre-empted by salient features of extralinguistic context. For example, in a shop that sells ready-made lawn turf, cutting it will not involve the usual mowing but rather the action of slicing it into transportable strips (see Searle 1980) or, when we're out on a picnic, the bread may cease to be fresh, not because it is stale but because it has fallen on the ground and is covered with dirt. So, as Blutner (1998) points out, even in those cases where a particular pragmatic narrowing is regularly derived on the basis of a particular linguistic collocation, the process is too flexible and context-dependent to be treated in code-like terms.

9. For discussion of more complex cases such as blends (e.g. 'swingle', 'fruitopia', 'cattitude'), which require a greater amount of processing effort, see Lehrer (2003).

10. For a discussion of the processes that account for the 'double function' (physical and psychological) of these and a wide range of other adjectives, see Wilson and Carston (2006), and for an interesting hypothesis about the unitary conceptual basis underlying the dual uses, see Asch (1958).

11. Of course, a full explanation of lexical semantic change would require, in addition to the account of lexical pragmatic processes, an account of how and why certain representations spread (catch on) in a community or culture while others do not. For a naturalistic approach to the 'epidemiology' of representations (including semantic representations), which takes account of a variety of contributing mental and environmental phenomena, see Sperber (1996).

12. See, for example, Levinson (2000) and Blutner (1998, 2004). For discussion, see Horn (1984, this volume) and Lakoff (1987).

13. See, for example, Lewis (1979) and Lasersohn (1999). For discussion, see Gross (2001).

14. See, for example, Grice (1975), Levinson (1983), and, for a recent defence, Camp (2006).

15. The accounts of Barsalou (1987) and Glucksberg (2001, 2003) share the assumption that encyclopaedic information associated with a mentally-represented category or concept may be used to restrict or extend its denotation in an ad hoc, occasion-specific way and they both mention the role of considerations of relevance in selecting an appropriate set of attributes. However, neither is aiming to develop a unified pragmatic account: Barsalou is mainly concerned with narrowing, while Glucksberg is mainly concerned

with broadening (and specifically, with metaphor and category extension), and neither offers detailed suggestions about what factors trigger lexical-pragmatic processes, what direction they take, and what makes them stop.

16. The fact that metaphorical senses may become lexicalized suggests that not all encoded meanings are 'literal' as this term is generally understood. For ease of exposition, we will continue to describe the interpretation of an utterance as 'literal' if the encoded concept and the communicated concept coincide.

17. See Rubio Fernandez (2005, submitted) on interesting differences in the nature of the psychopragmatic processes (specifically, the role of 'suppression') involved in meaning selection and meaning construction. For more general discussion of the processes of meaning construction, from the relatively conventional to the more creative, see Vega Moreno (2005, forthcoming).

18. For much fuller exposition of relevance theory, and comparison with alternative approaches, see Sperber and Wilson (1986/1995), Carston (2002), Wilson and Sperber (2004).

19. As noted above, for quite a few people, 'angel' may have acquired a further encoded sense (ANGEL*), and so be a case of polysemy. This is not a problem, since our approach can be taken in three ways: (a) as providing an account of the on-line process of concept construction for anyone for whom this is not a conventionalized usage; (b) as providing an account of the origin of the extra sense of the word for those for whom it is a case of polysemy; (c) as providing an account of how children acquire figurative senses of words, which is usually later than their acquisition of non-figurative meanings (see, for example, Levorato 1993). Anyone who wants to check out how the account here works for more novel examples could try the following from Rubio Fernandez (2005): 'John is a cactus', 'Today you are a Dalmatian', 'Every lecture from Professor Plum was a lullaby'.

20. The process is parallel rather than sequential, with hypotheses being constructed and adjusted by following a path of least effort, which may differ across individuals and discourse contexts. See Wilson and Sperber (2002, 2004).

21. On the role of 'backward' inference in the mutual adjustment process, see Sperber and Wilson (1998), Wilson and Sperber (2002), Carston (2002), Wilson and Carston (2006).

22. To save space, we present these simply as properties rather than as complete propositions. However, since the function of encyclopaedic information is to provide premises for the derivation of contextual implications, each property should be seen as a constituent of a complete proposition.

23. Here, the 'etc.' is intended to cover encyclopaedic properties of strictly BOILING water that do not hold for broader interpretations; in (18c), it covers encyclopaedic properties that hold both for strictly BOILING water and for water that is almost BOILING (i.e. BOILING*), but not for water that is BOILING** or BOILING***; and so on for (18b) and (18a). We are not claiming, of course, that encyclopaedic information is neatly organized in this way: merely that the choice of a particular set of assumptions in the course of the mutual adjustment process will determine whether the utterance is intuitively 'literal', 'approximate', 'metaphorical', and so on.

24. For further discussion of Recanati's (2004, 32) view that for explicature 'the dynamics of accessibility does everything and no "inference" is required', see Carston (2007) and the response in Recanati (2007).

25. For discussion and relevance-theoretic treatments of the emergent property issue, see Vega Moreno (2004, 2005, forthcoming), Wilson and Carston (2006) and Sperber and Wilson (forthcoming).
26. For fuller discussion of the relation between contextual implications and implicatures, see Sperber and Wilson (forthcoming).
27. For instance, Lakoff (1987, ch. 5) treats stereotypical narrowing and category extension as involving metonymic mappings.
28. See Lakoff (1987), Nunberg (1995, 2004), Recanati (1995, 2004), Panther and Radden (1999).
29. For an interesting preliminary relevance-theoretic account of metonymy, see Papafragou (1996).

references

Asch, S. (1958). 'The metaphor: a psychological inquiry'. In R. Tagiuri and L. Petrullo (eds). *Person Perception and Interpersonal Behavior*. Stanford, CA: Stanford University Press. 86–94.

Atlas, J.D. (2005). *Logic, Meaning, and Conversation*. Oxford: Oxford University Press.

Barsalou, L. (1987). 'The instability of graded structure in concepts'. In U. Neisser (ed.). *Concepts and Conceptual Development*. New York: Cambridge University Press. 101–40.

— (1993). 'Flexibility, structure, and linguistic vagary in concepts: Manifestations of a compositional system of perceptual symbols'. In A. Collins, S. Gathercole, A. Conway and P. Morris (eds). *Theories of Memory*. Hove: Lawrence Erlbaum Associates. 29–101.

Blutner, R. (1998). 'Lexical pragmatics'. *Journal of Semantics* 15: 115–62.

— (2004). 'Pragmatics and the lexicon'. In L. Horn and G. Ward (eds). *The Handbook of Pragmatics*. Oxford: Blackwell. 488–514.

Camp, E. (2006). 'Contextualism, metaphor, and what is said'. *Mind and Language* 21: 280–309.

Carston, R. (1997). 'Enrichment and loosening: Complementary processes in deriving the proposition expressed?' *Linguistische Berichte* 8: 103–27.

— (2002). *Thoughts and Utterances: The Pragmatics of Explicit Communication*. Oxford: Blackwell.

— (2007). 'How many pragmatic systems are there?' In M.-J. Frapolli (ed.). *Saying, Meaning, Referring: Essays on the Philosophy of François Recanati*. London: Palgrave Macmillan. 18–48.

Clark, E. and H. Clark (1979). 'When nouns surface as verbs'. *Language* 55: 767–811.

Clark, H. (1983). 'Making sense of nonce sense'. In G. Flores d'Arcais and R. Jarvella (eds). *The Process of Language Understanding*. New York: Wiley. 297–331.

Clark, H. and R. Gerrig (1983). 'Understanding old words with new meanings'. *Journal of Verbal Learning and Verbal Behavior* 22: 591–608.

Fauconnier, G. and M. Turner (2002). *The Way We Think: Conceptual Blending and the Mind's Hidden Complexities*. New York: Basic Books.

Gibbs, R. and M. Tendahl (2006). 'Cognitive effort and effects in metaphor comprehension: Relevance theory and psycholinguistics'. *Mind and Language* 21: 379–403.

Glucksberg, S. (2001). *Understanding Figurative Language: From Metaphors to Idioms*. Oxford: Oxford University Press.

— (2003). 'The psycholinguistics of metaphor'. *Trends in Cognitive Science* 7: 92–6.

Glucksberg, S., D. Manfredi and M. McGlone (1997). 'Metaphor comprehension: How metaphors create new categories'. In T. Ward, S. Smith and J. Vaid. (eds). *Creative Thought: An Investigation of Conceptual Structures and Processes.* Washington, DC: American Psychological Association. 327–350.

Grice, H.P. (1967/1989). 'Logic and Conversation'. William James lectures. Repr. in H.P. Grice, 1989. *Studies in the Way of Words*. Cambridge, Mass.: Harvard University Press. 1–143.

— (1975). 'Logic and conversation'. In P. Cole and J. Morgan (eds). *Syntax and Semantics 3: Speech Acts*. New York: Academic Press. 41–58.

Gross, S. (2001). *Essays on Linguistic Context-Sensitivity and its Philosophical Significance*. London: Routledge.

Horn, L. (1984). 'Toward a new taxonomy for pragmatic inference: Q-based and R-based implicature'. In D. Schiffrin (ed.). *Meaning, Form and Use in Context (GURT '84)*. Washington: Georgetown University Press. 11–42.

— (this volume). 'Neo-Gricean pragmatics: A Manichaean manifesto'.

Horsey, R. (2006). 'The Content and Acquisition of Lexical Concepts'. PhD thesis, University College London.

Kintsch, W. (2000). 'Metaphor comprehension: A computational theory'. *Psychonomic Bulletin & Review* 7: 257–66.

— (2001). 'Predication'. *Cognitive Science* 25: 173–202.

Lakoff, G. (1987). *Women, Fire and Dangerous Things*. Chicago, IL: Chicago University Press.

— (1994). Conceptual metaphor home page. Available at <http://cogsci.berkeley. edu/lakoff/MetaphorHome.html>.

Lascarides, A. and A. Copestake (1998). 'Pragmatics and word meaning'. *Journal of Linguistics* 34: 55–105.

Lasersohn, P. (1999). 'Pragmatic halos'. *Language* 75: 522–51.

Lehrer, A. (2003). 'Understanding trendy neologisms'. *Italian Journal of Linguistics/ Rivista di Linguistica* 15: 284–300.

Levinson, S. (1983). *Pragmatics*. Cambridge: Cambridge University Press.

— (2000). *Presumptive Meanings*. Cambridge, Mass.: MIT Press.

Levorato, M.C. (1993). 'The acquisition of idioms and the development of figurative competence'. In C. Cacciari and P. Tabossi (eds). *Idioms: Processing, Structure, and Interpretation*. New Jersey: Lawrence Erlbaum. 101–23.

Lewis, D. (1979). 'Scorekeeping in a language game'. *Journal of Philosophical Logic* 8: 339–59. Repr. in D. Lewis 1983. *Philosophical Papers*. Vol. 1. Oxford: Oxford University Press. 233–49.

Lyons, J. (1977). *Semantics*. Volume 2. Cambridge: Cambridge University Press.

Murphy, G. (1997). 'Polysemy and the creation of novel word meanings'. In T. Ward, S. Smith and J. Vaid (eds). *Creative Thought: An Investigation of Conceptual Structures and Processes*. Washington, DC: American Psychological Association. 235–65.

Nunberg, G. (1995). 'Transfers of meaning'. *Journal of Semantics* 12: 109–32.

— (2004). 'The pragmatics of deferred interpretation'. In L. Horn and G. Ward (eds). *The Handbook of Pragmatics*. Oxford: Blackwell. 344–64.

Panther, K.U. and G. Radden (eds). (1999). *Metonymy in Language and Thought.* Amsterdam: John Benjamins.

Papafragou, A. (1996). 'On metonymy'. *Lingua* 99: 169–95.

Pilkington, A. (2000). *Poetic Effects: A Relevance Theory Perspective.* Amsterdam: John Benjamins.

Recanati, F. (1993). *Direct Reference: From Language to Thought.* Oxford: Blackwell.

— (1995). 'The alleged priority of literal interpretation'. *Cognitive Science* 19: 207–32.

— (2002). 'Does linguistic communication rest on inference?' *Mind and Language* 17: 105–26.

— (2004). *Literal Meaning.* Cambridge: Cambridge University Press.

— (2007). 'Reply to Carston'. In M-J. Frapolli (ed.). *Saying, Meaning, Referring: Essays on the Philosophy of François Recanati.* London: Palgrave Macmillan. 49–54.

Rubio Fernandez, P. (2005). 'Pragmatic Processes and Cognitive Mechanisms in Lexical Interpretation'. PhD dissertation, University of Cambridge.

— (submitted). 'Suppression in metaphor interpretation: Differences between meaning selection and meaning construction'. Ms, Department of Phonetics and Linguistics, University College London.

Searle, J. (1980). 'The background of meaning'. In J. Searle, F. Keifer and M. Bierwisch (eds). *Speech Act Theory and Pragmatics.* Dordrecht: Reidel. 221–32.

Sperber, D. (1996). *Explaining Culture: A Naturalistic Approach.* Oxford: Blackwell.

Sperber, D. and D. Wilson (1986/1995). *Relevance: Communication and Cognition.* 2nd edn. (with postface), 1995. Oxford: Blackwell.

— (1998). 'The mapping between the mental and the public lexicon'. In P. Carruthers and J. Boucher (eds). *Language and Thought: Interdisciplinary Themes.* Cambridge: Cambridge University Press. 184–200.

— (2002). 'Pragmatics, modularity and mind-reading'. *Mind and Language* 17: 3–23.

— (forthcoming). 'A deflationary account of metaphors'. In R. Gibbs (ed.). *Handbook of Metaphor.* 3rd edn. Cambridge: Cambridge University Press.

Traugott, E. and R. Dasher (2001). *Regularity in Semantic Change.* Cambridge: Cambridge University Press.

Vega Moreno, R. (2004). 'Metaphor interpretation and emergence'. *UCL Working Papers in Linguistics* 16: 297–322.

— (2005). 'Creativity and Convention: The Pragmatics of Everyday Figurative Speech'. PhD dissertation, University of London.

— (forthcoming). *Creativity and Convention: The Pragmatics of Everyday Figurative Speech.* Amsterdam: John Benjamins.

Wilson, D. (2003). 'Relevance Theory and lexical pragmatics'. *Italian Journal of Linguistics/Rivista di Linguistica* 15: 273–91.

Wilson, D. and R. Carston (2006). 'Metaphor, relevance and the "emergent property" issue'. *Mind and Language* 21: 404–33.

Wilson, D. and D. Sperber (2002). 'Truthfulness and relevance'. *Mind* 111: 583–632.

— (2004). 'Relevance theory'. In L. Horn and G. Ward (eds). *The Handbook of Pragmatics.* Oxford: Blackwell. 607–32.

index